A VANISHED PRESENT

A Vanished Present

THE MEMOIRS OF
ALEXANDER PASTERNAK

Edited and translated by
ANN PASTERNAK SLATER

A Helen and Kurt Wolff Book
Harcourt Brace Jovanovich, Publishers
San Diego   New York   London

Requests for permission to make copies of any
part of the work should be mailed to: Permissions,
Harcourt Brace Jovanovich, Publishers, Orlando,
Florida 32887.

Library of Congress Cataloging in Publication Data

Pasternak, Alexander, 1893–1982.
    A vanished present.

    "A Helen and Kurt Wolff book."
    Includes index.
    1. Pasternak, Alexander, 1893–1982. 2. Architects —
Russian S.F.S.R. — Biography.   I. Slater, Ann.   II. Title.
NA1199.P37A2   1984b   720'.92'4 [B]   84-6532
ISBN 0-15-193364-2

Printed in Great Britain

First American edition 1985

A   B   C   D   E

Ирине Николаевне Вильям
Жене и Другу

For Irina Nikolayevna William
Wife and Friend

TRANSLATOR'S ACKNOWLEDGEMENTS

ALL but two of my debts of gratitude are due to my family. The author, my uncle, and his nephew, Evgeny Borisovich Pasternak, helped me collect illustrations. My aunt, Irina Nikolayevna William, to whom the author dedicated his book, provided me with biographical information on her husband. My mother gave me constant, unstinting, and critical help with everything. Christopher Barnes was a generously encyclopaedic adviser, Judith Luna a meticulous and patient editor. To all of these I am grateful.

I would like to thank Harvill Press for permission to print extracts from Boris Pasternak's *An Essay in Autobiography* (1959), trans. Manya Harari, and Granada Publishing Ltd. for a passage from Boris Pasternak, *Safe Conduct* (1959), trans. Alec Brown.

CONTENTS

ILLUSTRATIONS

Between pages 8 *and* 9

Leonid Pasternak and Rosa Koffmann during their courtship. Odessa, *c.*1886.

The young Rosa Koffmann at the time of her first concerts. Odessa, *c.*1875.

Anton Rubinstein. Odessa, 1882.

Alexander and Boris, aged two and five, with their nanny, Akulina Gavrilovna. Moscow, 1895.

Between pages 40 *and* 41

Boris and Alexander with their mother. Sketch by Leonid Pasternak. Odessa, 1899.

Leonid, Alexander, Rosa and Boris Pasternak. Odessa, 1897.

Boris, his cousin Zhneya Freidenberg, Alexander and Rosa Pasternak. Odessa, *c.*1898.

The School of Art, Sculpture and Architecture, Myasnitskaya, No. 21. Moscow, *c.*1900.

Ice-cutting on the Moscow River, with the chimneys of the tram station in the background.

Boris and Alexander playing chess. Sketch by Leonid Pasternak. Moscow, *c.*1903.

Lydia and Josephine. Drawing by Leonid Pasternak. Moscow, 1908. *By courtesy of the Courtauld Institute, London.*

Between pages 72 *and* 73

Musicians at the piano. Drawings by Leonid Pasternak.
Scriabin. Moscow, 1909.
Rachmaninov. Moscow, 1916. *By courtesy of the Courtauld Institute, London.*
Busoni. Moscow, 1912.

Rosa, Boris, Leonid and Alexander in the dining-room of the Myasnits-kaya flat. Moscow, 1905.

Between pages 104 *and* 105

Giant's Strides. Raiki, 1908.

Family group on the dacha veranda. Raiki, 1907.

Akulina Gavrilovna, the children's nanny, knitting. Undated sketch by Leonid Pasternak. *By courtesy of the Courtauld Institute, London.*

Rosa at the piano, accompanied by Jacob Romm, Boris listening. Drawing by Leonid Pasternak. Moscow, 1905.

Lydia and Josephine with their father on the dacha steps. Raiki, 1908.

Moscow barricades. Postcard, 1905.

The Pasternaks' first hotel in Berlin. Postcard, 1906.

Between pages 136 *and* 137

Leonid and Alexander preparing for the Union of Russian Artists' spring exhibition. Moscow, 1911.

Details taken from an undated group photograph. Moscow, c.1910.
Scriabin and his second wife, Tatyana Feodorovna.
The conductor Nikisch, and Chaliapin behind him.
Koussevitsky and his wife.

Nikisch conducting. Sketch by Leonid Pasternak. Moscow, c.1910.

Josef Hofmann at the piano. Drawing by Leonid Pasternak. Bad Kissingen, 1912. *By courtesy of the Courtauld Institute, London.*

Vladimir Mayakovsky after he left school, c.1910.

Between pages 168 *and* 169

Isadora Duncan at the time of her first visit to Russia. Moscow, 1908.

Family group on the dacha veranda. Molodi, 1914.

Rosa at the piano, Lydia and Josephine listening. Drawing by Leonid Pasternak. Moscow, 1917. *By courtesy of the Courtauld Institute, London.*

Boris at the piano. Vsevolodo-Vilva, in the Urals, 1916.

Alexander. Moscow, c.1917.

Lydia. Sketch by Alexander. Moscow, 1916.

The opening of the Museum of Fine Art (now known as the Pushkin

Museum), with the arrival of the imperial party. Photograph by
Alexander. Moscow, 1913.

Between pages 184 *and* 185

Sailors draping the monument of Tsar Alexander III, before its ceremonial unveiling. Sketch by Leonid Pasternak. Moscow, 1913.

Cathedral Square, with plinth minus imperial statue, after the Revolution, *c.*1919.

The Cathedral of Christ the Saviour, with the Church of the Blessed
Virgin and the Golovteyev mansion to the right.

Alexander and colleagues, by the door of the Karpov Institute. Moscow,
*c.*1924.

'My son Boris'. Drawing by Leonid Pasternak. Berlin, 1923. *By courtesy
of the Courtauld Institute, London.*

Alexander. Drawing by Leonid Pasternak. Berlin, 1924. *By courtesy of the
Courtauld Institute, London.*

INTRODUCTION

ALEXANDER PASTERNAK was born in Moscow in 1893, three years after his brother Boris, the poet and author of *Doctor Zhivago*. The English reader may well be drawn to these memoirs, initially at least, for the light they shed on Boris Pasternak.

The light is generous and intense, but falls obliquely. There is a scrupulous evocation of the sights, smells, and sounds of the childhood shared by the two brothers—a childhood pungent with the smells of their father's oils and turpentine, and resonant with their mother's piano playing. For their father was the Russian Impressionist painter, Leonid Pasternak, and their mother, Rosa Koffmann, a concert pianist. In the cultured atmosphere of their home, artists and musicians like Serov and Scriabin were frequent guests; at school Alexander was a classmate of Mayakovsky, who later became his brother's associate. In this book the ordinary, day-to-day world where the brothers grew up is also described in detail. Starting with their earliest years, we are shown the gardens where their nanny let them play, the yards and churches seen from their flat windows, the games of 'doctors' and 'exhibitions' they invented together. We see the boys and their friends on the floor together, arguing over a board-game of the Russo-Japanese war or playing Red Indians on their summer holidays; Boris practising musical composition on the beach with his tutor; Boris practising his German and unsuccessfully affecting the mannerisms of a Berliner.

Yet Alexander Pasternak does not restrict himself to the childhood specifically shared with his brother. He writes, too, as the professional architect he was later to become, and this book is primarily the loving portrait of a world that has passed beyond recall. It is a lament for lost things—the bulldozed boulevards and houses; the superseded street-fairs and seasonal markets; the cabs, the cobbles, and the church bells. Such things are also the essence of his brother's poetry. As Alexander points out, quoting from Pasternak's *Safe Conduct*, it was Boris's belief that 'art did not invent the metaphor of its own accord, but found it in nature and reverently reproduced it'. The world Alexander describes in precise, even pedantically vivid detail, is the world his brother's poetic imagery transformed. Consequently, these reminiscences provide an unusual background commentary to Boris Pasternak's poetic work. And if Alexander's memoirs are set side by side with the early parts of Boris's autobiographical writings, a prose dialogue emerges in which the brothers complement each other's memories. The impressionistic glimpses of *Safe Conduct* and the suggestive terseness of *An Essay in Autobiography* are spelt out in the ruminative expansiveness and meticulous precision of the present work. For this reason, some relevant extracts from Boris Pasternak's prose have been included in footnotes to this translation. Together, they give us a rich picture of Moscow before the Revolution, and of a culture in its final years.

The potency of this portrait of a lost world is intensified by its unspoken contrast to the modern state. Much of what Alexander remembers from pre-Revolutionary Moscow is characterized by its cleanness and orderliness, its attractive appearance, its efficiency. Today's Russian would instinctively make the self-evident comparison with the squalor, ill-temper and inefficiency in much of the modern Soviet world, which the author never mentions. This is the unspoken half of the equation. *Then* the Post Office smelt of finely-waxed floors, of sealing wax and string. Then its officials were neatly turned out in blue-piped uniforms. Then they worked quickly and seriously. . . . There is a particular charge to much of what the author describes with such regretful nostalgia. It will be easily apparent to the English reader who is willing to forget the conveniences and accessible minor luxuries of his own society.

Such implicit comparisons intensify when Alexander Pasternak reaches the years of the Revolution. In his parenthetic remark, '(medals were not so commonplace in those days)', the reader will catch the ironic contrast with the present day. Nor will he need to have the grim implications of the book's last words spelt out to him. There is an obliqueness here which is quite different from the indirect light Alexander's memoirs shed on his brother's work. It is an obliqueness to which every Russian has become inured, an unwelcome habit of mind like the 'anxiety of waiting' with which the book ends. It is natural for Russians to use metaphors for taboo topics. Take the word 'cockroach' in the Thirties, for instance. It all began with Korney Chukovsky's poem, *Tarakanische*, 'the giant cockroach'. Innocently written for children in 1923, this comic poem described a cockroach that terrorized and slaughtered the animal world, till a sparrow realized it was no bigger than the rest of them, hopped up, and nipped off its head. It was a topical

subject! Russia was infested with cockroaches then; they are still a pest
in the city flats. But Chukovsky's tyrannical, baby-guzzling monster
happened to have flamboyant ginger moustaches, and later, in the years
of Stalin's Terror, the innocuous poem acquired a politically subversive
appeal. Many parents must have read it to their children with treasonable gusto.

Not all the unspoken undertones of this book are of this kind. Nor is
the lost world Alexander laments unequivocally ideal. Its antiquatedness
is freely admitted. There are also many touches which are particular to
Russia for simple, physical reasons. Station partings, for instance, recur
several times in the narrative. They carry a melancholy poignancy which
may seem overstated to us. But Russians still take railway goodbyes
seriously. The entire family, even the most distant relatives, turns out to
see you off. Your compartment is filled with flowers and fruit. All the
way down the corridor Russians are changing into 'railway clothes'—
sloppy smocks, slippers, pyjamas. In England we are used to reaching
our destination in a couple of hours, ten at most. In Russia, distances are
vast, journeys long, meetings rare, and partings are real partings.

Real partings. No wonder the author was filled with a horror of them.
He said goodbye to his parents one drizzling day in Berlin, and never
saw them again. . . .

Alexander's parents and two younger sisters had left Russia for Germany in 1921. His mother needed treatment for heart trouble, and the
visit was always intended to be a temporary one. Boris and Alexander,
already embarked on their separate careers, stayed in Moscow. Both
brothers visited their parents in Germany in the early Twenties, and
throughout the extensive family correspondence plans are frequently
made for the parents' return. It never happened. In 1924 the elder of the
two daughters, Josephine, married a distant cousin in Munich, and
settled there. The younger, Lydia, left for England in 1935 to marry an
Englishman. With Hitler's rise to power the rest of the family followed
her. Alexander Pasternak's mother died in London in 1939, a few weeks
before the war began. His father survived it to die in Oxford in 1945.
This translation has been written by the author's niece, a daughter of his
younger sister Lydia.

At the time when his parents left Moscow, Alexander was engrossed
in his first architectural work, designing and supervising the construction of the new Karpov Biochemical Institute. In the early years after the

Revolution such large-scale operations were rare and difficult to complete successfully—not least because materials were hard to come by, and in the severe winter frosts the entire workforce used to abscond without warning. Fresh replacements constantly had to be found. The Institute was finished in 1924, the year that Lenin died. Pasternak was seconded to help a certain Melnikov with the sarcophagus, and eventually he was asked to design the interior of the first, wooden Mausoleum, which no longer exists. A friend of his, the scientist Boris Zbarsky, was responsible for embalming the body. In this memoir, references to work on the Mausoleum are enigmatically laconic. One has to assume that a task of such state importance must have been fraught with complications. Apparently Melnikov was also a hot-tempered man and a difficult colleague.

In recognition of this service Pasternak was granted a year abroad. His wife Irina, who was also an architect, joined him in Berlin, where they stayed with his parents until the autumn of 1925. On their return to Russia Alexander was quickly absorbed by work on urban development, a subject on which he published a number of articles in *Soviet Architecture*, *Architécture d'aujourd'hui* and *Moskauer Rundschau*. From 1929 to 1933 he and his wife were among a team of architects invited to work under Le Corbusier during his visits to Moscow, where he built the Centrosoyuz Building. Like many other structures of the time, it was altered later and its rationale lost. The pillars on which it stood and the ornamental garden beneath them (which was projected by Pasternak's wife) were walled in to create a standard ground floor. The building now looks little different from any other apartment block, except that it is built of considerably nicer stone.

Pasternak's subsequent career shows him to have been a distinguished academic and practising architect. From 1932 until his retirement in 1956 he taught in the Architectural Institute, progressing from Senior Lecturer to Reader. According to his wife, one of his most interesting projects was a set of workers' cottages for a textile factory in Kaisarieh, Turkey. From 1935 to 1937 he was employed on the Moskva-Volga Canal, for which he designed the fourth lock—a task which won him, and the architects of the other locks, the 'Order of the Red Banner of Labour'. My uncle was proud of his lock—an elegant, classical structure—and wanted to show it to me on one of my visits to Moscow, but permission was refused. The lock itself may have been a source of pride; the decoration was not. My uncle never wore it, referred to it, or used it to acquire the minor advantages such honours were intended to bring.

In 1942 he became Senior Research Fellow in the Academy of Architecture, where he wrote an extensive learned work, *Methods of Investigating the Architectural Composition of Town Centres in Classic and Western Europe before the Eighteenth Century*, and another entitled *Towards the Problems of Architectural Composition in Soviet Town Centres*. He was also responsible for the publication of an illustrated volume on town centres and their amenities. His critical attitude to modern Russian urban development is very evident in this memoir, as is his love of the ancient world. His classic taste is also clear from his academic writings and his designs. His approach was imaginative and re-creative. I remember him once giving me an article he had written on Delphi as it would have appeared to the ancient Greek visitor. In it he reconstructed the original entry to the site, describing how each turn of the road would have brought such and such a temple into view, and speculating on the reasons for their order.

After the war, he combined his teaching duties with architectural work in Sebastopol, which had been severely blitzed. In 1956 he retired and transferred his interests to literature. His brother Boris admired Thornton Wilder's *The Ides of March*, and asked him to translate it for his second wife Zinaida. The translation was well received, although another version by E. Golsheva was ultimately chosen for publication by the journal *Novy Mir*, in 1976. (I think it is reasonable to infer that this choice was prompted by political motives.) Soon after finishing *The Ides of March* Pasternak began his memoirs, which were written between 1969 and 1975, Chapters 21 and 24 (in the arrangement of this translation) being added later, between 1975 and 1977. The book originally ended with the author's last memories of his mother's piano-playing.

In the last years of his life Pasternak began an ambitious project on 'The Rationale of the New in Architecture'. In the words of his widow, his death in January 1982, at the age of nearly eight-nine, broke off an undertaking 'which he had begun with all the passionate enthusiasm of his young and talented spirit'.

I first met my uncle in the summer of 1960. In the course of the previous decade, my mother and her sister had started receiving letters from their two brothers in Moscow. This was a great occurrence: there had been a total silence in the years after the war ended until the early Fifties, a period when it would have been extremely dangerous for a Russian to write abroad. Postcards, and then letters, began dribbling through at the time of Khrushchev's Thaw. Our whole family had been brought up to speak Russian at home, but our Russian relatives only became a reality when I was about eight years old. I can still remember my mother standing in the nursery, engrossed by a letter on big, shiny sheets of white paper covered in Boris's fluent purple script. Who was it from? I asked. Her brother, she said. I never realized she had a brother before—a brother, like I had a brother? Living in a far-away country where they spoke the language we used at home? It was a new world to imagine.

Then came the Nobel Prize and the fuss over *Doctor Zhivago*. Two years later Boris fell ill and we learned that he was dying. One evening my mother came upstairs, shaken by a telephone message that Boris was asking for her. The request was extraordinary—it was still very rare for anyone, especially a Russian living abroad, to travel to the USSR. For my mother, the hazards of a return after nearly forty years were nothing to her anxiety for her brother. She spent the next week trying to get a visa, in vain. Two days after Boris's death, it was granted. As a minor, I was still on my mother's passport and was able to go with her, briefly playing truant from school. As we crossed the Channel, we heard news of Boris's funeral broadcast on the ship's radio. The direct train from the Hook of Holland to Moscow had just been set up; we were the only passengers on its second run. After three days' journey we arrived in Moscow, to be met by a host of relatives, including my uncle Alexander, silver-haired and looking so much like my aunt at home. He was smiling broadly: he had most of his teeth then. (Later, they dwindled to three or four.) We were driven through the darkness to Boris's dacha in the pine forest of Peredelkino. They gave us a bare upstairs room with large windows, two bookshelves, a big desk, a divan, and an old iron single bed with a lumpy horsehair mattress. Boris's study, and Boris's bed, where I slept in awed discomfort.

From that first visit I vividly remember the family meals at Peredelkino, with Boris's first and second wives, the second wife's first husband, and the children by all three marriages, amicably seated at the same table; the great iron pans of some twenty eggs at once, fried into concrete and served up by Zinaida for breakfast; Boris's pencilled notice in the bathroom, warning you not to drop cigarette ends into the lavatory bowl

(Zinaida was a heavy smoker). We spent a weekend together in the village of Arkhanovo, staying in a traditional wooden house with elaborately carved window-frames. I remember my mother and my aunt Irina, helpless with laughter, like hippos half aground in the tiny Arkhanovo stream at dawn; and my uncle Alexander in a white shirt at the supper table, with a chain of garnets that someone had hung about his neck. I remember the path the mourners had trodden across the wide strawberry field which lay between Boris's dacha and the village cemetery on the opposite hill where his grave was freshly dug beneath three tall pines. My mother cried for the first time in the train back home, as the radio we couldn't turn off played 'Kalinka', that folk-song which begins 'Under a pine tree, under a green pine, lay me to sleep. . . .'

Boris had been laid to rest, but in Alexander and his wife Irina I discovered a favourite uncle and aunt, whose generous love for me I will never forget. After that first visit I returned many times.

Alexander Pasternak was an enchanting man, with a mischievous slant to his sly greenish-blue eyes and wicked smile. He did everything with a neatness he must have inherited from his mother, quietly dapper at breakfast-time in his threadbare Muscovite clothes, cutting meat and cheese in fine, regular slices, or tying up our unreliable suitcase with two economic, strategically-placed knots. The big board by the window which served as his desk was always kept clear, but for a few precious objects—an old majolica tile, picked up from the rubble of one of Moscow's many demolished churches; a plaster cast of a classic head; a little bronze statuette of a boy shouldering a goat; an old, nineteenth-century fob-watch with a silver chain of intertwining ivy-leaves. All objects rescued from the old world; relics, I now see, reflecting the tastes of this memoir.

But it would be wrong to think of him as a nostalgic sentimentalist. By nature he was ironic, wryly humorous, with a lucid detachment uncharacteristic of most Russians. He also had a delighted curiosity about our Western gadgets and conveniences. One sunny morning, his wife secretively beckoned me into their Moscow flat's single main room (which tripled as a dining-room, study, and bedroom accommodating anything from two to six people). My uncle tactfully slipped out. 'What's this?', my aunt asked, producing a box of Tampax I'd left in the bathroom. 'Is it what I think it is? And why on earth can't we have anything like that here!' (At that time, Russian women used cotton wool in handfuls as sanitary protection.) With much laughter, she called my uncle back into the room, and explained the curious object. In this memoir, his own delight is evident in descriptions of the inventive popular toys of his youth, or the lifts and street-vending machines Boris and he discovered as boys in Germany. Typically, it was Alexander and Irina, both in their eighties, who played with the miniature hurdy-gurdies and tiny, Japanese wind-up toys I sent for their great-grandson. On every visit we brought several years' store of Pears' Soap and Cherry Blossom Shoe Polish. There was something of the connoisseur in this—an exact appreciation of the ordinary trimmings of civilized life, which emerges in my uncle's recollections of the pre-Revolutionary Lenten candied fruits made by Prokhorov and by Balabukha of Kiev.

Many tastes familiar to me from our meetings over the next twenty years recur in this book. I was sent on architectural forays to hunt out the Menshikov Tower and the house of his childhood with its curving, colonnaded rotunda, just as I was dispatched to see the Centrosoyuz Building he had worked on under Le Corbusier. He sent me and my husband to Leningrad, armed with elaborate, hand-drawn maps and itineraries filling the four days of our visit with a stiff course of architectural sights and some good restaurants—itineraries which took him several days' meticulous work to compile. His reminiscences also contain many distinct memories which I can corroborate. For instance, both Boris and Alexander refer to the caricature their father made of the Grand-Duke Sergey Alexandrovich, a patron of the Art School and early victim of the Revolution. At supper one evening my uncle brought out a match-box, opened it, and carefully unfolded the scrap of paper hidden inside. There was the lean aristocrat in his rigid regimentals. The paper had been torn tidily into four, then mended with Sellotape. When I asked why, my uncle explained that in the turbulent years he had kept the fragments separate, as a political precaution. For similar reasons, I have also seen two prints of the same pre-Revolutionary group photograph of eleven men and women on a dacha veranda. On one print a black snail's-trail of spilt ink has neatly obliterated a single face. On the other (reproduced opposite page 104), he can still be seen. He was the Pasternaks' family doctor, Levin, who was shot during the Terror. It was safer not to be found in possession of his photograph. And yet he was much loved. Surreptitiously, both versions were saved.

This hoarding instinct is another characteristic my uncle betrays in his memoir. He lived in a small, crowded, impeccable flat. Its atmosphere of impoverished culture is exactly paralleled by that of Anton Rubinstein's sister, whose flat he describes visiting as a child. In the ingenious shelves and cupboards of their cramped surroundings, my aunt and uncle harboured precious curiosities, generally despised and destroyed in the years after the Revolution. They had, for instance, a box of old glass stereoscopic plates, with photographic views of the Swiss Alps, the Eiffel Tower, and some more risqué scenes—card-sharpers, can-can dancers (but my uncle destroyed the naughtiest of these before they could corrupt his son). There was a box of early children's pop-up books, survivors from his son's childhood, unlike the Marshak whose loss he laments in Chapter 6 of this memoir. There was a tin trunk full of his father's sketch-books, from which several illustrations have been taken. The same hoarding instinct continued to operate. One summer I left a plastic container half-full of Western soap-powder in my aunt and uncle's flat. The next year I returned, to catch my aunt powdering her nose with it. She had treasured it as a very special talcum powder, only to be used on the most important occasions. Most of my memories are filled with their laughter, just as they laughed then.

I think my uncle's life ended sadly. For many years he had lived in a block of flats he had designed with, and for, an architects' co-operative. There was still an architects' studio on its ground floor. Over the years, many of its clever features had been destroyed, like the pillars of the Centrosoyuz Building. But the parquet floors were still carefully waxed (and it was nearly impossible to find good beeswax in Moscow). The windows could still be folded back, leaf on leaf, to give an open wall with nothing between you and the trees outside. Then the block was requisitioned. At the age of seventy-nine, my uncle and aunt were moved into one of those mammoth housing developments on the city's furthest fringe. Visits to the centre became an impossibility, since the two-hour journey involved long waiting by waste-land bus stops and several changes in crowded trams and tubes. Yet my uncle stoically found pleasure in the forests and sweep of blocks around him, surveying them from his fourteenth floor, and hardly ever going outside.

There we talked about this translation. He told me to write freely, taking as my example Boris's unfettered and often inaccurate versions of Shakespeare, where the letter is boldly sacrificed to the spirit. I was to cut, prune, and rearrange as I saw fit. The style was to be colloquial, the spoken voice of a man mulling over his past. At the same time I found that he wrote with an old-world, *belle-lettriste* expansiveness, and I have tried to preserve something of this quality. My mother patiently oversaw my attempts, and saved me from many howlers.

I have transliterated the great majority of Russian names, translating only a small minority of street names whose meaning seemed worth conveying. All the footnotes are mine, not the author's. The book has been abbreviated by about a third, mainly by thinning the prose texture, rather than by omitting incidents. However, two portions have been cut. The shorter dwells on a classic text my uncle admired at school. It was Livy's description of the Roman defeat by Lake Trasimene, of which his own, free Russian version was given. There seemed little point in re-translating this. The longer portion (which I read in manuscript) was intended to be the final chapter, in which my uncle described the demolition of the Cathedral of Christ the Saviour. This enormous building used to stand before the family's flat windows, dominating the view, until it was destroyed in order to make room for the projected Hall of Soviets. Then practical problems intervened. Every time foundations for the Hall were laid, they flooded. The location, by the river Moskva, was blamed, and yet the nineteenth-century architects had successfully built their Cathedral on the same spot. Eventually the plan was abandoned and a mundane open-air swimming-pool took its place. In my uncle's account, there is a symbolic reverberance to the final pages on the Cathedral's destruction. With impeccable literary judgement, the Russian censors cut the passage. The book ends better where it does now.

A.P.S.

CHAPTER I

EARLY CHILDHOOD

THEY say that from the moment of birth a child is like a sponge: but a sponge absorbs any moisture without discrimination, good or bad, vinegar or water. After all, a sponge is only a sponge! Nor does the liquid it absorbs have any shape of its own: it adopts the form of the vessel into which it is poured.

Perhaps a new-born baby understands as little as a blind kitten or a puppy. Like them, it knows its scanty world by smell, sound, and taste. With familiarity it can begin to distinguish its small surroundings and its own restricted life from the unknown. At least, it was so with my older brother, myself, and, when their turn came, with my younger sisters. From sounds and smells we began our lessons in recognizing life.

My first memories were evoked and coloured by certain persistent, almost delicious sounds—sometimes cheerful, sometimes indulgent, sometimes terrifying me to tears by their loud ferocity, yet never, even at such moments, repelling me. Much later, when we grew so used to the smells and sounds that without them there was a sense of emptiness, we began to distinguish them by name: 'turpentine', or 'oils', 'music', or 'Mamma's playing'. But by then we were old enough to know the difference between Mamma's playing and our own games. These smells and sounds so saturated my childhood, that they were for me the commonplace, natural phenomena of our particular life. They were inevitable.

I do not intend to write the biographies of my father (the artist), my mother (the pianist), or my brother (the poet). Yet, since I have touched on my parents' professions, I should sketch in their childhood and their early married life.

In 1885, a certain Bachman wrote an account of my mother's childhood, based on carefully collected documents and contemporary press cuttings. From this I learned that by the age of five, Rosa

Koffmann showed exceptional musical gifts. Music was her childhood: it took for her the place of childish games. When she was eight she began to give concerts to great acclaim, as the reviews of those days show. Everything seemed propitious—the encouragement of her family, her temperament, her youth, her talent. Until the time of her marriage, the child, and then the young woman worked to become a professional. Nor did her ambitions end with marriage, which normally changes a girl's life, turning the last page of her adolescence.

No, her life was unique. She had no childhood at all. She spent her youth like an adult, training to be a professional performer. Three important musicians dominated her career: Ignatius Tedesco, her first teacher; Anton Rubinstein; and Theodor Leschetizky, with whom, at the suggestion of Rubinstein, she completed her training in Vienna. Three great masters (risking accusations of filial exaggeration, let me say it)—three great masters, who cultivated a student worthy of themselves. Yet when I think of that young concert pianist's fate, an apparently unrelated image forms in my mind.

It must have been 1907, or 1908. About that time, we spent several summers on an estate not far from Moscow. It belonged to a keen racehorse owner, whose horses were famous for the prizes they had won in trotting races. Suddenly I find myself in the crepuscular stable, its wide doors still closed, in the last expectant minutes. The glossy young filly is harnessed and ready to start. Nervously one tipped hoof rakes the floorboards; her full, bloodshot eye strains backwards unnaturally far, to follow the thick white suede glove of the groom patting her neck. I can almost hear her urging him—Come on! Hurry up! What are you dawdling for? She flares her nostrils, catching the rank stable smells, and, beyond them, the tantalizing, familiar whiff of the race-track's damp sand, the other horses, a distant breeze. In this dim waiting the doors suddenly open. Still in the gloom of the stable, with her inner eye she senses the hot sunlight, the glorious instant before the race, the dark crowd receding behind her . . . But beyond the doors there lies only the park, and a dusty avenue through the trees.

Maybe that young girl waited for her entrance into the brightly-lit concert hall with the same anxious haste. Maybe she, too, impatiently tasted the joys of coming performance—Come on! Hurry up! Why wait?

. . . Who knows? The biography tells us that Leschetizky arranged a major concert tour for her in Germany, France, and Belgium. But my mother fell ill, she nearly died, she survived. A series of other blows convinced her that the fates were against her.* With that blink of catastrophe, inexplicable and irreversible, her life changed. After her marriage and move to Moscow, a new woman was born, with a new life and a new understanding of her destiny. Impelled by the same vitality and the same artistic largesse with which she had pursued her musical career, she now took up her duties to her painter husband and her family. She entered her new home.

The other artist, her husband, had a much harder path to follow. His parents were simple people, his mother an illiterate. As the youngest of their six children he seems to have been their favourite, and, naturally, he returned their love. But his parents, like everyone else of their class, had no idea of this thing called 'Art'. They knew all about sign-writers —top-rank painters, whose artistry was displayed above every wine shop. People of my generation may remember those yellow-green signs, whose characteristic background passed imperceptibly from a wash of bright golden-yellow to clear green. I have no notion what the origin or the significance of that fine spectral gradation was, but the evenness of its transition was the accepted sign of mastery. The unlucky ones who failed this test stayed mere decorators, painting roofs, walls, and fences.

And now their youngest and dearest wanted to be a painter like that? It was unthinkable! They had their own ambitions for him: he was to be educated; he would become a chemist, a doctor, or a solicitor, at least.

* In this impressionistic account the author conflates the events of several years. His mother was born in 1867. She gave her first public concert in Odessa, at the age of eight. A year later, her second concert in the Odessa Town Hall brought her to the attention of a distinguished composer, pianist, and teacher, Ignatius Tedesco, who took her musical training in hand. Tedesco had a formative influence on her life, as her teacher and intimate friend, almost her second father. Under his tutelage she continued to give concerts in Odessa annually till the age of thirteen, when she met Anton Rubinstein. At his suggestion a tour was arranged for her through the major southern Russian cities—Kiev, Kharkov, and Poltava—to Moscow, and St Petersburg, where Rubinstein presented her to the public. Here she gave a number of concerts, including one with the Spanish violin virtuoso, Pablo Sarasate, to an audience of six thousand. Just before her culminating, solo concert in St Petersburg, she contracted severe typhoid, and the rest of the tour had to be cancelled. On her recovery a year later, a new tour was arranged to take her through Germany, France, and Belgium. The second day after her departure, the news of Tedesco's unexpected death was broken to her, and she fell seriously ill again. The tour was cancelled, and although it was later taken up in Russia, Poland, and Austria, it seems that the fifteen-year-old girl took the two consecutive blows as warnings. On Rubinstein's advice, however, she continued her studies with Leschetizky in Vienna from 1883 to 1889. During this period she met her future husband.

Meanwhile, the bewildered child was roughly scolded every time he began scribbling on his mother's scrubbed deal floors and clean furniture with burnt sticks stolen from the hearth. (After all, the poor boy had no paper!) With sudden slaps and cuffs the offending charcoal, which drew so smoothly, was flung in a wide parabola through the open window, to vanish in the grass of the yard. And so, till next time, his artistic activities were broken off.

Time passed. The child with the irresistible urge to dirty everything grew into a schoolboy, a student. But he led a double life. Outwardly, in acquiescence to his parents, he dutifully went through school with his contemporaries. In secret, he continued to draw—first teaching himself, then surreptitiously enrolling in the Odessa Art School. It was a difficult period in which he struggled in isolation to defend the art he loved. Finally everything that had to be done, was done: he finished his national service, he became independent, and began to study art seriously for the first time. He chose to leave Odessa for the Moscow School of Art. Contesting the single vacancy was the Countess Tatiana Tolstoy—and, of course, the place was given to her. On advice he travelled instead to Munich, where he won first place in the Academy of Fine Art. Drawing was taught well here, but painting neglected. Dissatisfied, he decided to move on to Paris. This move, though, was postponed. He returned to Odessa, where he became engaged. Paris was still his goal when he went to Moscow—again temporarily—and painted there his first serious picture, *Letter from Home*. This painting, the work of an utterly unknown artist, was seen and bought in its unfinished state by the eminent collector, Pavel Tretyakov. After its completion and successful exhibition with the leading artistic group, the Wanderers, it found its permanent home in Tretyakov's gallery.

All this coincided with the date of my parents' wedding, which took place in Moscow in 1889. The couple first settled in a small flat in the Lyzhin household. There, in Oruzheiny Lane, not far from the Theological Seminary, their first child, my brother Boris, was born in 1890. Three years later they moved to a larger, four-bedroomed flat in the same street, in the house of the Svechins, where I was born. I have in my hand envelopes directed to my father in this way, since street numbers used to be a less certain form of address than the householders' names. The dates are confirmed by the postmarks on their local, blue, St Petersburg stamps. The envelopes bear the sender's name

—the journal *North*, for which my father was illustrating an edition of Tolstoy's *War and Peace* from 1891 to 1893, as it went to the press.

The sounds of my childhood started up the minute my mother smoothed her skirts and sat down on her special chair, which was upholstered in red velvet and stood in front of a thing like a cupboard, black, and shiny as a mirror. When she had thrown back a sort of door, she began waving her head from side to side and bending forwards and back, doing something with her hands—parting them to either side, then quickly quickly collecting them together again. If anyone else, though, say Papa or my nanny, should sit with me on their knees, even on the same red chair, in front of that shiny black cupboard, there was no noise at all. No, then it was dumb! I could stretch as far as the candle stuck on some kind of yellow foot—I could even push it about, but still the cupboard was stubbornly silent. Yet if I crawled up to it, and caught hold of the other golden things (the little ledges where Mamma put her feet), they sank under my hands, and someone in the cupboard roused himself. Sighing heavily and in great dissatisfaction, he shifted and groaned, setting little bells ringing in a fine, transparent tone, while I, frightened out of my wits, scuttled away on all fours as fast as I could. Quickly appeased, the cupboard's mysterious prisoner fell silent again. Yet Mamma was obviously not frightened of him: if anything, he was afraid of her.

My early life did not pass by me unnoticed. Most probably I remembered this and that, without understanding what belonged where. No doubt my parents later added explanations and stories of their own, tidying my memories and lightening a burden of which I was not even aware. I am reminded of the transfers we adored as children, covered by that levelling grey film, through which the real colours could hardly be guessed. As soon as you moistened them and rubbed off the white-paper backing in little grey worms, a delightfully tinted picture emerged, dazzling in the unforgettable clarity of its colours. So, as a grown boy, I once stood in wonder, watching for the first time as a dusty, dried-up old chrysalis disgorged its butterfly into the sunlight. Should I help? But how? Tight-lipped, I stared, waiting for what would happen next. After a long time the process was completed, and I saw the lustre and delicacy of its newly lacquered wings, spread out to dry. Just so my dormant memories, illuminated and aroused by the stories of the grown-ups, began to emerge into a visionary brightness, heightened by fantasy, warmly coloured by awakened feeling, to become accepted fact. Who is to say that things were otherwise? The experiences we once lived through leave their slight trace, then find expression in words, and take on sense and form.

Among such quite legendary memories I should include the musical soirées my parents used to hold in my earliest childhood. Of course I could not *remember* them, but they mingled with the trivial details of my own life which had a particular meaning for me, and so were not forgotten. Occurrences were thus transformed into things I had apparently experienced myself—the remembered facts of my childhood.

For instance. Someone tiptoes into the dark nursery where two boys are fast asleep, or meant to be. Although they come in quietly, they carry a lighted candle. (There was no electricity in those days.) That moving light woke me and I clearly saw some terrifying, monstrous *thing* slip from corner to corner and down the opposite wall, where it crouched on the floor. At the same time, some bars of music sounded next door. Breathless with terror, for a few seconds I couldn't cry out. In vain they reassured me that I had imagined it all, that a hand shading the candle had thrown a shadow over the ceiling. In vain they even tried to recreate the same effect. It was pointless. My memory retained for ever the sight of an incomprehensibly frightening, shaggy something, and loud music: beast and music fused. The truth of our domestic musical evenings was learnt only long after.

Other sights confirm the general tenor of our early family life, spent in a cheerful, Bohemian confusion of frequent gatherings. The big bottles of clear or greenish glass, standing in our lumber room many years later, were probably relics of those days. Uncomprehending, I would read their labels, syllable by syllable: 'White (or red) table wine', and the quite mysterious addition, 'Court of HIH'. There was a mock seal in high relief, very convincingly done, down to the droplet of glossily hardened sealing-wax. Since I saw such red, stamped seals in reality on my father's letters, I could appreciate the sharpness of these imitations. Maybe I would have forgotten all about the labels, bottles, and HIH, had it not been for the sly adults, bent on making a fool of me. They called these bottles, so huge to me, 'quarts'. But I knew from my own experience exactly what a quarter meant. After all, how many times was I coaxed to finish an abandoned meal with the wheedling 'Come on, have another little bit, just a *quarter* of a spoonful' or 'a *quarter* of a bite' with such emphasis on that boring word *quarter*, that it clearly must be small, even in comparison with something as minuscule as Mamma's cutlets! And now what! Could they really make me believe that those enormous bottles, almost as big as I was, were just 'quarts'? So they were remembered as a fact of great importance, joining the other 'facts' which fused with the general, incomprehensible impressions of my life, among the all-important smells and sounds. Music itself took possession of me, without my understanding what it was or where it came from. I was an empty vessel into which snatches of melody were poured, day by day.

Mother played in the next room. When she was tired and broke off for a while, the music seemed to go on, as though the walls, furniture, and even my toys, were soaked in sound. Of course I could understand nothing of it, although I had my own imaginative impressions. Some melodies whispered to me; others were demanding, powerful and menacing. Some thundered in blizzards and black clouds, like a storm frightening and enticing me, so that I wanted to howl in exultation. It was all different. Sometimes quick and light, like a ball rolling downstairs; sometimes winding and unwinding like treacle poured from the spoon in a fine, soodling stream, turning elaborate curlicues and figures of eight on your *kasha*. My nanny disapproved, because, she said, you shouldn't play with your food. But I drew the patterns of sound anyway.

My brother, who had beaten me by three years into life, once explained that Mamma was riding with a sick son (rubbish again—she had no boys but us, let alone one who was ill!), and that he died in her arms before they reached home. At that moment the music broke off in two loud chords like a shriek.

I don't know how to explain the appearance of a man (later a familiar visitor) who seemed to be on first-name terms with music. Everything about him was odd, beginning with his un-Russian name, which, to my ears, seemed to fall apart. The grown-ups often spoke like that—the first bit was the name, the second, some explanatory addition to the name. But here both bits sounded very peculiar—'grzhi' and 'mali'. He looked funny, too, splitting in half just like his name, the top always black, the bottom dark and pale-grey stripes. What was more, a forked tail like a beetle's dangled behind him. In those days I couldn't make out whether this wonderful apparition was the cause or effect of strange sounds that didn't belong to Mamma. These quite alien sounds plaited together with hers, as though Mamma was walking arm in arm with him.

Then they would part abruptly, and Mamma would stop playing. Was she waiting for him to find his way to her on his own?

Later he became very dear to me, not because of his swallow-tail, but because of his beautiful playing. He turned out to be a first-class Moscow violinist, the Czech Ivan Voitsekhovich Grzhimali. Like the cellist Brandukov, another musician often performing in our home, Grzhimali made his way from the legendary garden of my childhood into the world slowly opening up around me. At that time, though, many others also came to play, or to sing, most beautifully; to talk and argue in real human voices, to smoke and not to smoke ... Together they made up that special, grown-up world outside our own, and, with Mamma, created the musical aura which fascinated us two small boys.

Gradually I passed from this kitten's blind world to sight. A new and not always better spirit was in the air. When I was four or five, the frame of things expanded so much that, even in our own nursery, many novelties had to be assimilated, as though we had moved into a new town. The sounds remained; the smells of our father's work persisted, but now 'the piano' and 'the easel', and many other things found their established places in my new life. Even our clothes grew up with us. On particularly grand occasions I began to wear a real sailor suit, with long trousers and a square, white-edged collar.

Leonid Pasternak and Rosa Koffmann during their courtship. Odessa, c.1886.

The young Rosa Koffmann at the time
of her first concerts. Odessa, c.1875.

Anton Rubinstein. Photograph dedicated to Rosa
Koffmann, with a musical quotation on the
reverse. Odessa, 1882.

Alexander and Boris, aged two and five, with their nanny, Akulina Gavrilovna. Moscow, 1895.

CHAPTER 2

LIFE IN THE WING

OF course it was not just a matter of long trousers and sailor jackets. Rather, it was that the amorphous gradually began to acquire a precise outline. It was as though I started meeting people long familiar to me by hearsay, identifying them by face and name for the first time. This one, for instance, was Pyotr Petrovich—and that one, with the hooked nose, Ivan Ivanovich. I could no longer mix up one with another, and no one could turn into someone else any more. If I was told Ivan Ivanovich was coming, even before he arrived, I knew exactly whom I would see.

A similar personification of things also took place. In mid-thought I used to be interrupted by some melody, heard from my earliest days, not once but many times. Only in that instant did it identify itself, almost forcing me to cry out: 'Good gracious! Surely that's . . .', just as people exclaim: Ah, Ivan Ivanovich, is that you? So the melody discovered its name and patronymic from, say, *The Demon*, or *The Queen of Spades*. It was as though everything, but everything, began to introduce itself: how do you do? I'm so-and-so!

Now I knew by name almost all the pieces and composers played by my mother and her friends. I no longer got confused, who was galloping through the night forest with his dying son. The odours of paint and turpentine were less interesting now than the easels, stretchers, and canvases with their particular smells. I knew now what was what, and what it was called.

When I was about two years old the family moved to a wing in the School of Art where my father taught. Our life cannot have changed materially from how it had been in the Lyzhin and Svechin households. My father continued to consolidate and expand his artistic career. There were no obstacles here: all the 'Creative Anguish', so much discussed in my childhood, was the theme for one of my father's earliest pictures, and nothing more.

My mother was just as intent on perfectly fulfilling her family duties, which were never questioned, once they had been assumed. In our new household the piano continued to sound. But now we watched her life with greater understanding, observing a division between 'work' and 'music'—which was not work. If there had been submerged anguish here, we would surely have been aware of it, even if only in her music's yearning. But no, she seemed uniformly tranquil, busy, and good-humoured. Even my older brother, who could see more than I, noticed no suppressed desire to reverse her decision. Yet, even now, I cannot be sure, and doubts often trouble me. Perhaps that lost concert career was the cause of secret tears, a perpetual repression of her unique being? Who knows? Maybe she tried, painstakingly, to hide such suffering even from herself?

It was quite clear to us that Papa was an artist, that he taught art at the School, that it was something he did for everyone, not himself alone. The adults called it a profession, but even without using such a long word, we knew exactly what it meant. Everything our father did was part of his profession. Nor do I mean by this to pin him down, like a lepidopterist, as an art-historical specimen in the glass cabinet of some entomological collection. My father's profession was not merely the means to our family's material well-being. It obsessed both my parents —after the exhibitions had closed, after the reviews were read, after the visits and discussions. It was, quite simply, my father's *raison d'être*.

And what about my mother? What gave her life meaning? She too had her recognized and respected function. A person of infinite goodness, she devoted all her strength to the family's complicated and contradictory machinery, so that it ran smoothly, at full steam, never jolting, or jumping the rails. My father could ignore the machine altogether. It was his job to paint others, and while they sat and posed, he laboured at his easel all day long. He ran backwards and forwards constantly, observing from a distance, darting up to dab at the canvas, then backing into the recesses of the dining-room once more. This was evidently his business, this scuttling to and fro, faithfully transferring the essence of his subject to the canvas. To relax and entertain his sitter, my mother often played, or made conversation. Like a personal secretary, she took part in all my father's affairs, his arrangements and correspondence, relieving him of everything that could disturb him and leaving him with only one passion, his work.

And when everything was done, and she could rest, she was suddenly transformed from a stoker or engine-driver to quite another being, a mother of sounds, a wonderful pianist. Then she could have driven the

whole machine off the rails without a second thought, throwing herself
into the world of Erl-Kings, undines, and elves—the ballades and
nocturnes of Chopin.

The courtyard of the School (or rather its three courtyards, comprising a
single estate) made up a large plot of land, even by the standards of those
distant times. Of the three, the first and largest was pre-eminent, with a
big garden surrounding it. Judging by the size of the poplars at its edges,
this garden had been established long ago. It was enclosed by a high
fence of smooth sharpened stakes, painted a pleasant reddish-brown.
Little red-sanded paths and squares, furnished with benches, were cut
through the lawns, and although it had neither beds nor flowers, it was
well cared for. Here a decorous silence reigned, in accordance with the
stern respectability of its style.

Adjoining the central yard was a long, thin back yard parallel to our
wing, which was particularly attractive to us boys because of its outhouses. In the furthest of these was a byre, where the director's cow was
kept. Although we never saw her, a glum lowing was sometimes heard,
and occasionally her blackened, dungy litter was shovelled straight on to
the clean snow, filling the frosty air with thick white clouds of steam.
The middle shed was filled with junk and didn't interest us. Almost
opposite our nursery windows stood the third and roomiest outhouse,
built of unplastered bricks and with big doors.

In this, for us the most fascinating of the outbuildings, huge flat chests
were kept. All through the winter they appeared from somewhere,
stacked upright on sledges. They were made of fresh, well planed and
jointed wood, boldly marked with big, black, long-stemmed goblets and
exclamation marks. Four, or even six of the School's caretakers would
strain to lift them one by one and, stepping delicately, disappear with
them into the shed. Then the doors were closed, and the heavy padlocks
fastened, till the next sledgeload arrived. Some secret lingered here,
although the whole process, repeated from year to year, had long ceased
to hold any surprises for us. It wasn't the chests' disappearance into the
dark that was so exciting: the climax came with the spring. Then the big
doors were thrown open and each crate in turn was carried out into
bright sunlight, to be carefully leaned upright. The lids were unscrewed.
Inside were great dark canvases in massive gilt frames, swagged and
garlanded, blazoned with pot-bellied apples and pears, that sent tiddly-
winks of sunlight skipping across our nursery walls. We felt a pang of

envy; Papa's pictures never had such posh and portly frames. All this magnificence made up the Wanderers' annual Spring Exhibition, which was displayed in the School's classrooms during the vacation. We had reason to be proud that we were the first to see the pictures, long before the opening, as, in the slow tempo of a funeral procession, they swam past us, swaying slightly in the hands of two or three pairs of pallbearers.*

The third yard, fronting the other two, had its own attraction—a large, relatively high square mound with sloping sides, bright with thick grass and mature trees. I remember a birch under which a long table and bench had been firmly driven into the earth. This mound took up almost the entire space between the surrounding buildings, in summertime making the yard look more like the outskirts of a village than the courtyard of a city house. It was known as the 'Swiss' garden. Not because its little plateau looked like a fragment of Switzerland, but because of its population, largely the children of the Switzers, or School servants, porters, nightwatchmen and doorkeepers, who lived in the houses round it.

We often used to come here to play with them. Wintertime was particularly noisy; the sides of the mound turned to ice, and toboggans could slide down them almost to our front door. The toboggans of those days were different from the Swedish sledges on sale now: they repeated in miniature the structure of real Russian sleighs, and were built without a single nail or metal fixture, not even runners. Wood and bark alone held the parts together, cunningly linked by cross-piece and binding. They were beautifully made! For the little ones a special plaited reed basket was attached—a snug, drowsy nest to curl up in. These toboggans were sold on most Moscow squares, like our own Turgenevsky Square, near Erman's Emporium, where we used to buy all sorts of household and pharmaceutical necessities, candles, and perfume. We came here many times with our nanny, returning home with her harnessed like a horse, dragging me in the new toboggan behind her. So we crossed the square, turned down the empty Myasnitskaya, into Yushkov Lane, and back into our own yard.

---

* 'Every spring the Travelling Exhibition was held in the College show rooms. The pictures arrivéd from Petersburg in the winter and were stored in sheds—there was a row of them outside our back windows. A little before Easter the crates were brought out into the yard. The College servants prised them open and unscrewed the heavy picture frames from the boards; then each picture was carried by two men across the yard to the main building. Perched on the window-sills we watched excitedly. That was how we first saw many pictures by Russian masters, which today are famous and make up half the contents of the public galleries and State collections.'

Boris Pasternak, *An Essay in Autobiography*, p. 36.

One day, instead of taking me into the garden as usual to play, my mother led me down to the Yushkov Lane gate. She turned aside abruptly before we reached it, into the doorway of a high, five-storeyed house of naked brick. We climbed up a long, light stairway with many turnings, finally stopping in front of a white door. Holding me by the hand, my mother pushed the door with her foot, and it swung open noisily, to let us into a wide corridor with dirty unstained floorboards and dingy wainscoting painted what the adults used to call 'government grey'. At one of several identical doors covered in brown oilcloth, my mother stopped and pulled a handle, just like the one on the front door at home. I heard a bell ring lightly. My father opened the door, and I was taken through a narrow entrance hall into a vast, high-ceilinged room empty except for us.

Everything here was unfamiliar and fascinating, except the strong smell of turpentine, oils—and, besides, the most appalling dust! There was dust everywhere in a thick layer of lint that had evidently lain undisturbed for years. The first thing to attract my attention was something I had never seen in my life before: a vast window—if a wall made entirely of large panes of glass could be called a window. From there my eye wandered to the grey floorboards, dusty as those in the corridor, dusty as the mass of trash, quite unlike real furniture, filling the room. Here, too, was a second dark brown floor on stumpy little legs, with an armchair set aslant on it, flanked by a one-legged occasional table. Both armchair, table, and everything else standing on this little stage was chalked in place. Woe betide you if they were shifted by a hair's breadth!

My attention was next caught by a cherry-brown cotton blind, bleached pale on its reverse. It was made up of several pieces, running on rings so that it could be moved both up and down and sideways. But apart from its original function of shading the room from excessive light, it evidently had the secondary job of a cleaning rag for brushes and those light, flexible knives my mother often used to scrape fine little petals of dried oils from Papa's palette. You could see that hands, too, had been smeared clean on the blinds. The clutter entirely choking the whole enormous room was especially impressive. It was difficult to turn round without knocking against something, and as I was forbidden to touch anything, the room ceased to interest me much.

Yet I had some experience from our own home. I knew, for instance, what was in those flat wooden boxes—and there were quantities of them here—flung around, their brass catches open or closed. Inside, lay small sticks of equal width and varying shades in packed rows on beds of cotton wool, now dirtily multicoloured; you could draw with them in fine, bright lines, if the grown-ups let you.

In that vast room the unchanging, characteristic smell reigned undisturbed, as did the equally idiosyncratic silence, evidently the consequence of all that dust. After our small but brilliantly clean and orderly flat, vibrant with happiness, I was oppressed by the dust, silence, and monotony of this room crowded with junk. It was much nicer to be lifted on to the window-sill, which was wide as a table. I pressed my nose against the clouding glass, to stare at the yard opposite: in the garden by the church some children were absorbed in a game. I watched the pigeons settling on the roofs, idiotically bustling about, busily nodding to one another. The cats moused after them, nearly always to no effect; the pigeons clattered to their wings and disappeared.

Many years later a forgotten pastel sketch, taken from the window at this time, was found in my father's archives. It is a view of the church garden, in deep autumn, with red roofs above the crowns of the trees and rosy clouds glowing in the sunset behind them—a beautiful range of colours! According to the label on the back, the sketch was exhibited in 1904 by the Union of Russian Artists. It hangs today in the flat of my deceased brother, in Lavrushinsky Lane.

When I still played with my brother, our favourite game was the arrangement of 'exhibitions'. Boris, of course, was leader and master-theoretician, but we shared the preparation and understanding of the game. Each independently set about producing a range of drawings using pencil, crayons, or water-colours. By avoiding any preliminary discussion about subjects and the manner of execution, we managed to achieve a considerable variety of styles. The whole thing was taken immensely seriously. Our themes and techniques derived from the Wanderers' repertoire—simply because of our familiarity with their annual exhibitions, and not in any satirical spirit, although the atmosphere at home was critical enough. Just such a picture turned up in my father's papers. On a page torn from an exercise book I had drawn a plate of melon rinds, signed it 'Myasoyedov'* (who knows why?), and called it 'How tasty were the melons'. It was numbered on the back.

---

* A genuine artist (1835–1911), and member of the Wanderers.

Everything just as it should be, and just as we'd often seen it. Also on the back, in my father's hand: 'Shura's drawing, 1897'. When we had assembled enough pictures, we put together a catalogue, and hung the exhibits on the walls of the nursery. Then all the inhabitants of the flat and any chance visitors were invited to the *vernissage*. We were very fond of this game, often returning to it, and drawing new pictures every time. The adults had nothing to do with it until the exhibition was mounted, and if they looked into the nursery prematurely, we shouted at them to go away.

Equally common was the game of chemists, derived from the colds my brother and I often had, although we weren't particularly delicate. Then our old doctor would appear with his little case, unfailingly cheerful and ready to make us laugh; he would ask us the same questions in the same order; we knew the routine by heart and answering was easy. After the questions, the examination: he tapped with fingers or a little hammer; he listened through a bone trumpet, and—the worst part—thrust a silver spoon down our throats with the injunction to say 'A–a–a–a–ah!'

The game repeated this ritual, in all three roles of patient, doctor, and chemist. As in the exhibition game, everything was taken seriously, and the skill lay in the accuracy of the replica. It didn't matter that our wooden building blocks, columns, and bars, had to double as pharmaceutical pots and phials. The main thing was that they should be used as they were in reality. For this reason, when Boris wrote out the labels and prescriptions, he did it with such care that in our eyes they became incontrovertibly authentic. And when I was the chemist I grated and pounded the pretend powders in pretend mortars just as they did in Erman's Emporium. I couldn't understand a word of Boris's abracadabra Latin, although all those acids and powders sounded even more convincing than in plain Russian. Our own experience took us as far as the dosage of medicine in grains, and the word 'grain', however mysterious it might be, was comprehensible enough in the familiar form, 'Three grains to be taken night and morning'.

What attracted us to such a strange game? Probably the process itself. Our transformation into adults—doctor, nurse, and chemist—went beyond the bounds of play. At that time Boris was eight or nine at the most. Everything was written carefully, and, for his age, correctly. One such prescription turned up with my picture of melon rinds, and both were carried off by my brother, together with other papers, when my father's archive was divided between us on Boris's move to a new flat.

Among our family photographs I clearly remember one plain post-card. (Would that it survived today!) The silhouette of a young woman in profile, wearing a large, ostrich-feather hat, was glued on it. This was an old friend of ours. The card was addressed to me by my brother, who had been sent to stay with her family in the country while he was in quarantine. On the card Boris informed me in adult, authoritative tones that his story was nearing completion, and reminded me that the two commissioned illustrations should not be delayed.

This too was a reflection of reality. That year my father was illustrating Tolstoy's *Resurrection* for the magazine *Niva*. The publisher, F. Marx, often sent my father similar instructions.* My brother was producing his own journal in tandem—a plain school exercise-book whose cover advertised prose, news items, puzzles, and brain-teasers. Orders for illustrations were usually sent to me, not because my brother couldn't draw them himself, but because I couldn't write. This particular postcard referred to a sentimental tale about stray dogs, which were normally impounded if they had neither collar nor identification tag. I had to draw a group of dogs languishing in a cage. I can see the illustration now, a bit mistily perhaps, but I remember the dog-hero perfectly. The second illustration was meant to show the moment when a kind little boy set the whole pack free.

This card also stated that the author was preparing a new work about the life of the Red Indian Cherokees—a story I've forgotten, although I can recall another of my brother's compositions, about a Japanese fisherman and his catch of sea-cucumbers. Boris must have found out about the Japanese from a book called *Japan and the Japanese*, interesting mainly for its illustrations. It vanished after my sisters grew up. His journal also failed to survive.

Of course our childhood was not only passed in these games, but others more generally known, like 'Cossacks and Brigands'—a noisy

* 'The novel appeared, chapter by chapter in *Niva*, a periodical edited by the Petersburg publisher Marx. It came out regularly and on time. My father worked feverishly to meet the deadline. . . .

To save time, the drawings were sent off by hand as occasion offered. The guards on the express trains to Petersburg acted as messengers. My imagination was impressed by the sight of a uniformed guard waiting outside our kitchen door, as on a station platform outside a railway carriage.

Joiner's glue sizzled on the range. The drawings were hastily sprinkled with fixative and glued on sheets of cardboard, and the parcels, wrapped up, tied and sealed, were handed over to the guard.'

Boris Pasternak, *An Essay in Autobiography*, pp. 37–8.

affair that deafened all the Moscow squares and gardens. There were innumerable table games, too. I remember one most clearly. It followed the usual pattern of chance rather than skill, but something different gripped us here: not the uncertain excitement of hazard, but anxiety for a happy ending. It was called 'To the North Pole'. Four explorers, Nansen, Peary, Andrée, and Scott, had to overcome a series of obstacles. There were four small olive-wood figures: two balloons with gondolas in their respective national colours for Peary and Andrée; Nansen's boat, the *Fram*; and for Scott I forget what, huskies, maybe, or dog-sleighs. We already knew the fate of each, and, feeling for them all, played seriously, without laughter. For some reason my sympathies for Nansen were most acute, and the knowledge that he had been 'crushed by ice' sounded in my ears with particular, melancholy finality.*

---

* The author's memory has betrayed him. The *Fram* was specially designed to resist crushing by ice, and in an expedition from 1893 to 1896 successfully drifted part of the way to the North Pole anchored in the Arctic ice pack.

CHAPTER 3

THE END OF THE WING
AND THE GARDEN

ECHKIN'S establishment! Who can now remember that symbol of ancient Moscow in its lordly, fantastic days?

Memory really does demonstrate chain reaction in its most perfect form. One explosion of recollection promptly sets off another, that in its turn a third, and so on, carrying you back and back into the debris, till suddenly you shake yourself free: Good Lord! Where was I wandering off to? It happened to me just now. I had no intention of describing Echkin's establishment; in fact, I'd quite forgotten it. But, while pottering about my childhood, remembering my mother's care for us, our spotless flat, and her grand tidying sessions, I suddenly heard, as it were, her habitual reference to some stables or other, and, *voilà*, Echkin's establishment . . . Let me return first to the tidying-up.

When I grew old enough to help my mother (even if my help was mainly to stay out of her way), one of our jobs was to sort my father's chaotic accumulations in the drawers of desks and cupboards, heaped any old how over his big working table—stacks of envelopes, scraps of paper, newspaper cuttings—all so much rubbish to my eyes. My mother, though, read through the lot painstakingly and honestly, sifting it into tied bundles which she marked with thick red, green, and blue crayons. My job was to put them away as she instructed. Exhausted, she used to sit back, sighing something about Eugene's stables. Eugene was well known to me, as was the word *stables*. The words in themselves were not remarkable, except in this linked formula, especially as my mother for some reason never quite got the name right. But I knew perfectly well that Eugene had no stables and where could he get them from, anyway?

In spite of an altogether ogrish blue-black beard that grew practically from his eye-sockets, Eugene was a gentle, honest man who often made my brother and me laugh. On his regular days he'd appear in the kitchen with our super-clean, beautifully ironed laundry in a huge two-handled wicker basket which he steadied on his head with one hand. Under the basket he wore a ring of soft black felt shaped like a croissant. As he came through the door, he would clear his throat with a significant cough, as though performing some preparatory rite of entry, then take croissant and basket off his head and place them on a stool. These rituals observed, he would greet everyone with a deep, respectful bow. When my mother was ready, he knelt before the basket with the same ceremony, extracting the exquisitely ironed and folded linen, pile after pile, while my mother, with equal precision, took it, checked it, and laid it aside.

Every grown-up knows perfectly well that if someone humps around a basket like that, piled high with heavy washing, and carries it a long way, *and* loses his breath, *and* has fits of coughing—then he obviously can't have horses. If he had a horse, would he walk about with a great load like that on his head? Of course not. And if he didn't have horses, then he couldn't have any stables either. As, of course, he hadn't. The only way to make sense of it was that Mamma was making fun of me. And yet, I heard the words, 'worse than the Augean stables' not once, but many times, quite distinctly.

Which is why I thought of the real stables. The proprietors of this popular establishment were Echkin and Sons: their single-storeyed house of Empire design stood right at the beginning of Karetny Ryad. By the time I came to know it, it had suffered changes; the plain, small but attractive windows had been replaced by two large sheets of plate glass, at that time a novelty in Moscow. Between them were two huge gates made entirely of glass, instead of the usual front doors. A sign ran the length of the house, just below the roof, proclaiming in gold letters embossed on black: *Echkin and Sons, Coachbuilders*, and beneath, in smaller letters, *By royal appointment to the court of HIH*.

Passers-by were immediately attracted by those enormous windows, so unbelievably clean and transparent that the glass apparently relinquished its protective function, and visibly ceased to exist. Yet it was the contents of the windows, rather than their miraculous, self-effacing glass, that stopped the pedestrians in their tracks. At each window stood a coach, real as could be, as if just ready to go. Its beautiful black lacquer and silver handles glistened in the sun; the delicious thick leather reins and harnesses looked good enough to eat.

One window held a wedding-coach, its interior all of white. Upholstered in shining white satin, it gave an impression of great coolness and freshness in contrast with the bright black carapace. The curtains had white silk fringes; the buttoned-down pillows and bolsters were white; even the window straps were gleaming white leather. Everything was fresh, light and festive, like just-whipped, still frothy cream. An elegant black coach stood in the other window. This too was virginal, unscratched and unscathed, divinely glossy and young, unlike the battered hackneys that traded on our streets. But when my mother or nanny took us past these windows, we were attracted to another marvel—a colossal stuffed bear, the size of a grown-up, reared on its back legs, one open paw raised for a murderous cuff. Nothing but the glass stood between us and its bared teeth, dyed red gums, and muscular tongue, the living symbolic protector of all coachbuilders and the carriages they displayed.*

The most wonderful thing in the world would have been to clamber up into the coach-box, and perched on that soft, wide, comfortable seat to fancy myself the master of coach, passengers, and, above all, its lathering pair of horses, galloping far away over the boundless steppes. If it hadn't been for those deceptive windows, I could have put out my hand and stroked the coaches' palpable smoothness. That was true happiness: the concrete reality, materially evident, incontrovertibly tangible —a far cry from the non-existent Augean stables of my mother's impoverished imagination.

My mother often used to take me visiting. These variations on the daily routine were a great treat, carrying me into the novel world of unidentified and unfamiliar experiences, so much more interesting than the world I already knew. One acquaintance was an old lady, a close friend of my mother, in spite of their difference in age. Her calls were frequent at first; they grew rarer when both moved to different parts of town. Yet the friendship didn't wane, although in time it dwindled to my mother's one-sided visits, as her friend became too old to go out. At first I knew Mamma's frequent guest as Sofya Grigoryevna. I couldn't understand the much more important fact, that she was the sister of Anton Grigoryevich, or, as he was simply called in our house, Anton Rubin-

* 'My impressions of my early childhood are made up of terrors and delights. They ascend in fairytale colours towards two central images which ruled my world and gave it unity: one is of the stuffed bears in the coachmakers' windows in Coachmakers Row.'
Boris Pasternak, *An Essay in Autobiography*, p. 30.

stein. For some reason this name was always set in opposition to another, that of Nikolay Rubinstein.

Now, when my mother told me to scrub my nails, because we were going to see Sofya Grigoryevna, I knew exactly where we were going and who this old lady was. Eager, a little anxious, I hurried through the distasteful business of tidying myself up, and was ready to go well before my mother.

In those days it was a long way from the Myasnitskaya to Dog Square, and we took a sleigh, in itself always a holiday occurrence. The name Dog Square should have suggested something as depressing as a dog's life, but in reality it was a retired, pleasant little square, whose insignificant and irregular shape gave it a domestic quality unlike the civic pomp of the larger squares. It no longer exists, having made way for an imposing avenue, but in its day it seemed a solid witness to the unshakeable stability of the old town. There were many such squares in Moscow then; they have all gradually disappeared, taking with them a characteristic aspect of the vanishing city. Everything here was scaled for the individual, not the crowd, as in our bustling central squares today. Just two or three benches, a memorial statue or a modest fountain with its single weak jet trickling into a stone basin, and all the enveloping peace of the countryside.

Dog Square was surrounded by a number of those detached, single-storeyed old houses, often built of wood and plastered to suggest stone, that were common to Moscow back-streets until recent times. Sofya Grigoryevna lived nearby, in a larger house of quite different character, three or four storeys high, jerry-built of naked, unplastered brick—one of the first of those faceless tenement-blocks littering and obliterating old Moscow, that began to appear at the end of the nineteenth century. It was built in a style completely indifferent to architectural beauty, and designed instead for profit, for the maximum number of rentable flats it could contain. The whole block was intended for families on a low income. Sofya Grigoryevna lived on one of the upper floors, probably in one of the cheapest, two-roomed apartments.

That quiet, welcoming Dog Square hardly deserved its name. With more justice the stairs we went up might have been called Cat Steps. We clambered up in the dingy half-light of a single lamp and the overpowering stench of tom-cats. Cats scattered like mercury from under our feet at every step, bounding to the next landing to watch our approach, and bolting off again. This gloomy, steep stairway with its plain iron railings was more like our back stairs than the wide main entrance of our wing, and this mean impression persisted on our admission into a tight little entrance hall.

Our hostess led us into a small, surprisingly fresh and comfortable room. There was no smell of cats here, only the indefinable odour of poverty. In contrast to our spacious flat, there was a low ceiling and one narrow window. Pieces of attractive, antique red wood furniture jostled each other, quite evidently in excess of need; their careful preservation, the neat polished floor, tasteful curtains and white blinds all showed the character of their owner. The walls were most striking; they were smothered with photographs of eminent people, signed and affectionately dedicated to Sofya Grigoryevna. Everything combined to create an atmosphere of quiet good breeding, in spite of our hostess's evident poverty. Perhaps for the first time, I encountered here that poignant combination of material indigence and spiritual beauty unaffected by age, evoking my passionate admiration.

Sofya Grigoryevna gave us coffee and started a lively conversation with my mother, full of the names of music and musicians already familiar to me. Fearing I'd be bored, she gave me some book which I looked through politely, glancing surreptitiously at my hostess and her surroundings. She appealed to me at once: I liked her sternness, her fresh though hoarse voice, and her quick, dignified movements. She sat with my mother at a table to one side, so that I could watch them unobserved. Their conversation, the reminiscences it aroused, clearly engrossed and enlivened them. Half-listening, I looked about the room, and the mass of photographs on the walls. From every side a hundred Antons and as many Nikolays of varying ages and in different guises stared down at me. I recognized them from a few pictures at home and could distinguish who stood, who sat, who leaned against a piano or a desk. The Rubinsteins apart, there were many others, shaggy-haired, whiskered or bearded, in frock-coats or tails. Signatures sprawled half over their faces, ebullient with flourishes and dried, inky splashes for full-stops. Then there were smiling, fashionable ladies, hatted and bare-headed, young and not so young, with similar signatures set aslant but well below the shoulder-line, tenderly avoiding the pretty faces. Everything was stern, although the photographs smiled: with absorbed attention I stared at this exhibition of *fin de siècle* eminence.

When my mother got up to go, she was asked with genuine friendliness to stay a little longer. No, no, it was late already; we had been an hour at least. I was astounded! Had we really sat there so long? And now, if I concentrate, I can see that room once again in every detail, and our hostess too, with her beautiful head, grey hair smoothly drawn back, and her tall, erect figure, so lightly threading her way through the furniture.

This figure dominated by furniture and photographs remained in my memory as a fact whose significance only emerged later, a long time after Sofya Grigoryevna and her surroundings had ceased to exist. She was crushed, that was evident enough, not by financial necessity, but by lack of attention to herself and lack of room to breathe. Her every movement embodied her strong sense of self, the dignity of a person unbroken by adversity. Struggling against material want, this old lady succeeded in preserving and transmitting the spirit of an entire world untouched by time. Moscow's cultural history at the turn of the century—the world of music, theatre, the arts and her two dead brothers—lived on in the photographs, signatures, settees and chairs. Naturally enough a child could not entirely appreciate such things. But the difference between this and my daily life was sufficiently powerful to impress on me, uncomprehending as I was, the memory of a thing never to be seen again.

The School garden I described earlier passed the last of its hundred or more years in my presence. I must have been two or three when it ended its long and respectable life. Any memories independent of my parents' or nanny's suggestion are therefore most likely to concern its final brief moments.

The rest of my recollections are linked with the marginal phenomena of the garden's life—the smell of damp, heavy sand after watering or rain; the wonderful, reddish-green, soft fat caterpillar-catkins unexpectedly littering its paths and lawns; the fine unmistakable scent of sticky young poplar leaves, and the freshly-shed, dry rusty cowls of the buds, blue with dust. It is strange that I should forget much of our own life there; try as I may, I cannot remember by what gate we entered, or how we reached the little area where my mother or nanny let us browse. Nor can I recollect how its goings-on appeared to us when we stared at it from our dining-room windows, although we must have done so many times a day.

And then, the familiar signs of recurring spring—the long switches of pruned poplar branches, with their thick, delicious smell of young sap—turned out to be omens of the garden's misfortune. That dignified, ancient and kindly place was destroyed, in order to make maximum use of the land hitherto wasted in an apparently unfunctional garden hardly needed by anyone. In exchange for the ghost of a park, the last surviving phantom of an old country estate, they dug out an underground studio for the plaster casts required by the School's drawing classes.

When my brother described this period in his *Essay in Autobiography* (earlier entitled *People and Places*), he spoke of rats drowned by spring rains and frogs driven into asylum in the foundations, finding glimpses of nature everywhere, even in the city's onslaught on our dear garden. In all honesty, however, I cannot recall any such prematurely perishing rats or jolly frogs.* For me the garden's general decay was infinitely more depressing. It all started with the gigantic, helpless poplars, axed, then lopped to their very trunks. I remember too the viciously disrupted order of the sedate garden, which had seemed eternal to us when we walked in its coolness and calm. Spindle-shanked, cachectic ponies, whinnying weakly, passed freely through the broken fences as though into their own back yard. Behind them were harnessed stubby carts, which left their mean tracks everywhere, along the paths and over the trodden lawns, scoring the helpless garden with wheel-tracks, trampling it to death. When was there a chance to notice the rats and frogs! As the last barrows left, the children of the yard took the formerly forbidden realm into their own possession.

Probably at this time and forever afterward, the encroachments of self-satisfied suburban civilization on the quiet dignity and comfort of old Moscow, its hour past, instilled in me a deep, unyielding sadness. I think of station partings, and of friends who will never return. The older I grow, the more such friends leave Moscow. The dear, detached Muscovite houses pass away; they die; those beloved but unnecessary little yards turn into wastes. They are buried under characterless multi-storey blocks wholly alien to our city, or, worst of all, they are barricaded off from the life of the street by vast hoardings plastered with notices.

* 'It was decided to build and let many-storeyed blocks of flats on the College grounds, and glass-roofed premises suitable for exhibitions on the site of the garden. At the end of the 'nineties the sheds and outbuildings were pulled down, the garden was uprooted and deep trenches were dug in the ground. The trenches filled with water and in them, as in a pond, dead rats floated and frogs jumped and dived in off the banks. Our annexe was also scheduled for demolition.'

Boris Pasternak, *An Essay in Autobiography*, p. 40.

The basement replacing our garden was soon fitted up as a plastercasting studio (perhaps originally intended as a temporary measure). The underground studio was illuminated by four pairs of skylights, set level with its asphalt roof, to facilitate the clearing of snow in winter, dust and dirt in summer. The square windows were made of those thick, glass bricks which were just coming into fashion; as well as daylight, the studio was also provided with new-fangled electricity, instead of the usual risky kerosene lamps. In the early dusks of winter and freezing evening fogs, fountains of yellowish electric light beat upwards from the skylights; snowflakes drifted into the funnel of light, waltzing down its bright beam. These inverted cones of light were for us a living illustration of Jules Verne's *20,000 Leagues Under the Sea*: in our copy, there was a primitive but (as it was then called) 'suggestive' drawing of the submarine *Nautilus*. Its main impact lay in just such a cone of light cutting diagonally across the blackened page. In fog, fine rain, and heavy snow, eight exactly similar cones sprang up, to end somewhere in the skylights' vague patches of brightness.

The asphalt covering of the dug-out was raised slightly above the level of the yard. A single steep flight of steps led down to a wide passage, partitioned off from the main room, where the workmen washed and changed, rested and smoked. In the studio itself there was a permanently damp, solid smell of wet clay, although the ventilation was in working order. I often used to call in here with my brother or friends, to watch old Mikhail Agafin, the master-moulder, at work. We should, of course, have called him by his full name, but alas! that somehow never occurred to us, and he was known to everyone simply as Mikhail. He was a great connoisseur of plaster-casts and their originals, and when he wasn't too busy, he enjoyed showing us the casts from different ages. His overseer was the School's Professor of Sculpture, S. M. Volnukhin, a mild, grey-haired old Russian, with a broad spade beard that he tugged, sucked, fingered and ceaselessly tormented as he chatted to us about classic statuary. Interesting as it all was, the unpleasant stench of wet clay drove us away, bursting like bullets back into the clean air outside.

Mikhail's studio was out of bounds when Prince Paolo Trubetskoy used it to make casts of his own work. This sculptor, a Russian prince Italianate, had lived so long in Italy that he translated his name from the Russian Pavel to Paolo. In the School's corridors he was mockingly referred to as 'Prince Paolo', or 'Prince Trubetskoy'. But the Director of the School, Prince Lvov, a generally respected man of simple manners, was known in affectionate abbreviation as 'the Prince', with no danger of confusion. If anyone asked, 'Have you seen the Prince?', he was promptly told: 'The Prince is in the Library', or 'The Prince has just stepped out', or 'I'm sorry, I haven't seen the Prince today'.

Prince Paolo had only recently arrived from Italy, where he'd passed most of his life and made himself a considerable reputation. According to Mikhail, supposedly from Trubetskoy's own account, in Italy he had learned to make immediate casts of his clay models, at every stage, before the arid Italian air dried and distorted them. Wet rags apparently made no difference. More than that—it seemed that in his Italian studio Trubetskoy had rigged up some kind of special shower to maintain the required plasticity in his materials. In Mikhail's words, at least, a perpetual drizzle clouded that unvaryingly damp studio. Trubetskoy was accompanied by a cheerfully energetic Italian assistant called Robecchi. On fine days in winter and summer Boris and I used to cram our faces against the dining-room windows, shouting a running commentary to one another as the young Robecchi practised riding his bicycle on the studio's asphalt roof. But this was nothing ordinary; it was trick cycling of the highest degree! What couldn't he do? He not only rode 'with no hands', as we called it, but on the back wheel, rearing the front into the air; he could even cycle back to front. Skimming over the smooth asphalt roof at incredible speed, by some miracle he turned himself upside down and rode on, for whole seconds that seemed like hours to us. It was marvellous watching the fluency of his tricks, performed so light-heartedly, as though there was nothing to them. Some he worked over, again and again, perfecting their cleanness of line. While training, he used to drive everyone off the platform, and then young fans and even adult passers-by would hotly discuss the spectacle, exchanging comments with Robecchi and among themselves.

The temporary studio where Trubetskoy worked with Robecchi adjoined our wing: he only built his own large, light studio some years later, at the very turn of the century. Attached to it were separate stalls communicating with the workroom and the street, where he kept various animals to sculpt and draw. I loved coming here with my mother, to stare at the 'zoo'; one northern stag in particular sticks in my memory. It was massive, to my childish eyes, with antlers flung wide and a frenzied, bloodshot eye that used to terrify me; I was convinced it wanted to scorch me to cinders. Once there was a single-humped camel whose beauty and expressive desert yearning filled me with wonder: two-humped camels lack this haunting quality altogether. More often there were dogs—rough-coated wild ones, lithe borzois, a fox once, and even a wolf. Coming home down Yushkov Lane I always looked in through Trubetskoy's clean, bright windows, to see what new inmates had arrived, and what this fine artist and great sculptor, so Russian and yet so un-Russian in appearance, might be doing.

The decision to build the underground studio carried in its train the fate of our own wing. As soon as some old classrooms had been transformed into new living quarters for our family, we moved out of the wing and its destruction was hastily begun.

Just as we felt tender about the garden, so we now suffered at the depressing sight of our wing's savage annihilation. But that, it seems, is man's nature: at once a zealous and wonderfully successful master where his own profit is concerned, he mingles indifferently with these gifts his passion for destruction.

First the iron roofing was stripped away, and its regular, smooth sheets, screeching, grating, and buckling as they fell, clattered to the ground, their crumpled remnants ringing. The doors went; window sashes were flung down on the general mound of rubbish, together with carved wooden fittings whose sense and value were lost.

As the bulk of the building dwindled, the pile of debris grew, until the inevitable day came when demolition men armed with sledge-hammers and crowbars appeared. Silhouetted on the walls, a naked well-shaft which was all that remained of our wing, they looked like stonemasons chiselling the decorative frieze of some classic Colosseum. But instead of embellishing, these figures smashed up the lintels and door-jambs, so that, day by day, the walls were reduced to solitary piles reaching skyward, and the flat expanse of masonry piers stretched between them. Freshly broken, pinkish-red bricks with pallid streaks of lime contrasted with the dark tone of the piers' outer walls, intensifying the general ugliness of the scene. But even the piles were not to stand long. The waste ground was roped in. One morning we woke to find a crowd of labourers in dirty shirts, shod in bark sandals bound with rags, loitering in the enclosure. After a preparatory rest, they were divided into groups, each equipped with a strong rope, looped at one end over the tip of a pile and drawn tight. When every pile was lassoed, leashed, and collared, the last act of the drama began.

With a chorus of shouts and groans, each group seized hold of a rope and began an apparent tug of war. In rhythmic accompaniment to the chorus, the rope would pull taut, then liquidly slacken, drooping with its own weight. Gradually, as though yielding to the chorus, the pile began to sway, still nobly withstanding brute force. When it was seriously loosened, and seemed about to drop, the chain-gang themselves ran out of breath; the rope sagged once more, and the pile, patently shaken and half subdued, still reared above them. But now, to the rhythm of a repeated 'heave-ho', the pile, with a pathetic cracking, lost its balance and—as though fleetingly struck by the vanity of resistance and life itself—trembled down its entire length. Bowing stiffly to us for the last time, it dropped once and for all in a slowly accelerating curve, drowning us with the roar of its descent, a cloud of dust and broken brick, and the sudden aftermath of unexpected silence. So they fell, one by one.

That evening, when I passed the yard on my way to Yushkov Lane, only a funeral pyre of brick-dust, rubbish, and the boulders of half-demolished piles mutely reminded me of our living home. I stood and wondered how different it had all become. Although nothing told me so directly, I felt quite clearly that a definite period of my childhood had come to an end. The disappearance of those apparently inessential things—a garden, a yard, a wing—seemed to me an irreparable loss.

CHAPTER 4

THE NEW FLAT

MYASNITSKAYA, No. 21—the address is short, but its history spans at least two centuries, in which it suffered many changes. In the time of Peter the Great, this part of the Myasnitskaya—the 'end', as it was called—was known as the Frolovskaya, from the church dedicated to Frol and Lavr, patron saints of horses, which stood in a nameless blind alley running off the main street. A large estate, with a park and gardens, bounded on one side by this cul-de-sac, and on the other by the Frolovskaya, is said to have belonged to Count San Donato Demidov, or, according to other sources, to the Mamonov family. More certain is the fact that in the second half of the eighteenth century the estate was broken up, and the corner between the street and blind alley (by now a thoroughfare) passed into the possession of a great society host and gentleman, the General of Infantry and Fusiliers, Chief of Staff I. I. Yushkov. From that time until our own day the nameless side street was called Yushkov Lane.

For this gentleman a large, stone, two-storeyed palace was half adapted, half built, possibly by the architect Bazhenov, at the end of the eighteenth century. Only the corner rotunda survived unmodified to our time. The rest of the building was spoilt by extensive alterations, particularly after the mid-nineteenth century, when this building, and part of the adjoining gardens, were let to the Moscow Society of Artists and its Art School. From then on, the building was intermittently adapted to its needs. The Society was renamed the School of Art, Sculpture and Architecture shortly after its establishment.

The main nerve of this building, its spirit and inner *raison d'être*, as it were, was without question the corner rotunda, with its wonderful circular hall, the culminating corner piece to two suites of chambers opening off it to either side. Externally, the significance of the rotunda was further stressed by its façade, embellished by a loggia and a free-standing colonnade. It was a fairly typical example of Bazhenov's work, often repeated by his students and imitators in a number of Muscovite private residences.

Nevertheless, the architectural axis was emphasized by a main outer stairway, a central part slightly brought forward from the rest of the façade, with more richly decorated windows, an antechamber within, and even a second 'entrée', as it was called, with a well-conceived and executed marble stairway up to the first, principal floor, with its suite of imposing chambers leading to the rotunda.

From the side of the park and garden the palace was constructed with an even more emphatic symmetry pinning the entire composition, both palace and park, to a central pivot. Here the dominant force of such a composition was clearly felt. Everything went away from the central point and returned to it, both the exit from the building into the park, with its wide main stairway, evidently once flanked with statues (long extinct by my time), and two side wings, identical in size and finish, completing the composition; likewise the two corners, each curving around an equal radius, connecting the central block to the two wings, and, finally, the two central windows over the entrance doors, equally distinguished from the rest by their different proportions and more elaborate carvings. This symmetry was evident after all the alterations the palace suffered in its lifetime, reducing it in the end to something unremarkable, even second-class. It is to the architect's credit that the clarity of his original composition survived all its vicissitudes so well.

It used to be rumoured that the palace once accommodated a masonic lodge. The rotunda built out on a limb, rather than at the building's central axis, was explained in these terms. This opinion was stated so categorically that when we grew up we accepted it as a *donnée*, to be neither contested, nor wholly believed.*

I haven't lingered idly over this account of the palace's symmetry and its curved corners on the park side: they help to explain the peculiarities of the flat specially adapted for our use on the third floor of the School. Our flat was crammed into the tail-end, some former classrooms being adapted for us, with minimal loss to the School's teaching area, and

* 'The building was old, beautiful and remarkable in many ways. The fire of 1812 had spared it. A century before our time under the Empress Catherine, it had been the secret refuge of a Masonic Lodge. One corner, at the intersection of Myasnitskaya and Yushkov Lane, had a pillared, semi-circular balcony; part of it formed a recess and communicated with the College hall. From it, you could have a clear view of the Myasnitskaya running into the distance towards the railway stations.'

Boris Pasternak, *An Essay in Autobiography*, p. 32.

minimal concern for the future life of the impromptu flat's inhabitants. But this tail-end was not the normal section of a right-angle; rather, it was the wisp of a curving tail, as of a whippet, say, or a husky.

The imposing classical symmetry of the building was turned directly against us. What could we do about that? Here you could see the law of dialectics in action: the beauty of the general plan necessarily entailed the private quarter's bizarre, one-sided crookedness.* Because of the curve of the outer wall, all the partitions between the rooms met it either at an acute angle, instead of the conventional ninety degrees, or they set off, fan-like, at a wide rebound. The core of the flat, remaining after various respectably sized and shaped living-rooms had been partitioned off, was large enough—bigger indeed than might have been necessary for two flats—but an extraordinary shape. The bathroom was an elongated triangle. The large kitchen was geometrically unidentifiable. The lavatory floor was raised by two steps under the pedestal, presumably allowing the soil-pipe to slope at the proper angle. The stairway to our flat was not a main stair, nor yet a back stair, fulfilling both functions and looking like neither—resembling, indeed, no stairway in any household at any time.

It must have been built long before: one would scarcely find anything like it nowadays. Since it took up the corner square of the building's wing, the stairwell was huge, while the actual stair, though wide enough in itself, seemed in contrast precipitously narrow and flimsily tacked on to the wall. The open-work iron banisters intensified the feeling of insecurity. It was terrifying for us children to stare down into the emptiness, particularly since the high ceilings of the grand residence meant that our third floor was equivalent to a modern seventh or eighth. The back entrance to the director's flat was the only other door on to the stairway apart from ours, opening out somewhere on the first floor. Consequently, very few people came here; at midday and dusk it was deserted. Instead large numbers of pigeons were free to come and go,

---

* 'That winter, two or three classrooms and lecture halls in the main building were converted into a new flat for us and we moved into it in 1901. As one of the apartments from which it had been carved out was round and another still more fancifully shaped, our dwelling for the next ten years had a bathroom and a box-room which together formed a crescent; the kitchen was oval and the dining-room had a semi-circle bitten out of it. There was always a muffled din coming from the passages and workrooms outside, and from the end room Professor Chaplygin could be heard lecturing on heating methods to the architecture class next door.'

Boris Pasternak, *An Essay in Autobiography*, pp. 40–1.

flying in through the broken glass of an upper window quite beyond the reach of any human being. In my own memory that window stayed unrepaired a decade or more. When the whole flock suddenly rose from the cornices, raising the dust with a crepitation of wings, a stranger could be seriously frightened, particularly in the evenings, when the stair was poorly lit by the two lamps over its only two entrances.

Then there was another curious thing. In the unusually thick longitudinal inside wall of our flat, running down one side of the corridor between the dining-room and the bedrooms, there were two large niches, in which two wide cast-iron cylinders, like cannon, stood on end, closed by heavy, tight-fitting lids on hinges. Their function was a mystery to us. In winter storms in our childhood we used to be startled by explosions, shrieks, and groans clearly vented from the depths of these infernal chimneys.

As there were no Dutch ovens in the whole building, the house must have used some early form of central heating (pre-dating the hot-water system of our own time) which must have required thick walls to accommodate its pipes; the iron cannon set solid in the walls were evidently its outlets. Not knowing what they were for, I used them in 1905 to destroy certain incriminating papers which I set alight in the cannon mouths. I was taken aback by the speed and deep-toned booming with which a gust of air carried off the blazing scraps to vanish in the darkness.

Passing through the entrance of our flat, you came into a small corridor, illuminated by a single window. The actual entrance hall, where we took our coats off, was half-dark, lit only by an internal window over the kitchen door. The pleasantly polished wooden box of the wall-telephone later appeared here. In order to call the operator, you had to turn a little handle on the right of the box quickly and persistently, till a melodious female voice seemed to reach you from another planet: 'I'm listening'. The telephone was a novelty then. The bells gleamed on the cabinet's back wall, which was sloped like a desk for you to take notes. The earpiece hung on the other side by a little hook; the mouthpiece you shouted into stood on a movable bracket. I can still remember our first telephone number: 15-76.

Every room had its own peculiarity. The dining-room flaunted enormous square windows occupying the whole of one wall. The wall's unusual thickness, three or four bricks deep, allowed the window to fit into this embrasure without distortion, in spite of its size and the wall's broad curve. In the kitchen the rest of the window was half obscured by the partition separating it from the dining-room. We shared the drawing-room with a wide water-pipe crossing the ceiling, which served our flat and the neighbouring classrooms. It was usually drenched in condensation and dripped democratically on the piano, the furniture, and the occasional guest. (Later it was lagged and boxed in.)

From the different rooms we had views in every direction. The dining-room window looked out over the Moscow roofs, the Lubyanka, the Kuznetsky Bridge and beyond, with the Polish Roman Catholic church forming a large, complex perpendicular in the general view. This church was especially beautiful in the evenings, when the sun slipped behind its massive silhouette. Suddenly catching fire almost from within, its outlines would be doubled by a halo, as though the already invisible sun was sprinkling it with gold. It was lovely, too, on moonlit winter nights, when it rose like icy breath, luminous against the dark sky.

But the dining-room from which it could be seen was not a part of our childish life. We came here only at fixed meal times; for us it was an interesting, transitional stopping place. We came and went, just as a long-distance train waits a few minutes at a station; the passengers jump out, some race off for hot water, others for snacks, shouting remarks to one another and munching as they run; at the triple chime of the station bell they scatter back to their carriages again.

Settling gently on its springs at every jolt of the rails, with a mild squeaking of irregularly colliding buffers, the train sways slowly past the buildings. Along the sand of the open platform blinking slants of sunlight interleave the long shadows of carriages hurrying to escape . . .

So at different times of the day and year we saw but did not watch the cupola. It was a part of the window, not our lives. However beautiful it might be, we left it behind us when we walked out of the room, and thought no more of it.

The living-room windows were less interesting. They looked out on a narrow yard behind the shop on the ground floor below us – a shop now known for its somewhat tasteless, pseudo-Chinese façade. At that time it belonged to a well-known tea-merchant, Perlov and Sons. On warm spring days, when the windows were thrown wide, the aroma of coffee and tea would overwhelm the room, as huge bales, sewn in soft, closely woven matting, were unloaded and unpacked in the yard below. In wintertime the oriental fragrance could not reach us. Even if we climbed up on to the window-sills, we could see nothing of what went on below, but there was really nothing to see. The monotonous work was well known to us, and the windows had nothing visible to offer.

But the windows on the third side! The ones looking out on the Myasnitskaya, the Old Post Office, and the wonderful sculpture—you could call it nothing less—of the Menshikov Tower! That side played the largest of large parts in our life and probably because of that, when I name the Tower, to this day I feel a rush of joy, just as when I speak of my mother and father or our dear old nanny, a much loved member of the family. Until now I have described the past in the name of all four of us children. I am sure that my sisters, and above all my brother, had he not died before me, would agree with what I have said, supplementing it perhaps, but not correcting. Yet in describing the Menshikov Tower, I must speak for myself alone, of my personal feelings as for a loved and living being.

It is not difficult to find illustrations, full descriptions, even structural analyses of this exquisite church in any Moscow guide-book or architectural history. But none of them have noted how changeable, though uniformly beautiful, its individual spire appears, lapped in the milky-pink, mother-of-pearl mists of winter dawns, or the rich damson of the setting sun, or drenched by the full moon, all its silvered details shot with turquoise and gold. It was solidly stamped in our memories like brass five-copeck coins, with their embossed eagles, or majolica tiles bulging with bright, gaily-painted flowers and swollen scrolls.

In my first year at school I fell ill with diphtheria. In those days the illness was sometimes fatal and the word itself, 'diphtheria', sounded ominous to me. My brother Boris was sent to stay with friends. In our playroom I felt lonely and scared, although the door into our parents' room was permanently left ajar, and in the first anxious nights one of them sat with me in an armchair drawn up to my bed. They told me later that I had had a high fever and very bad throat. Most of the time I was semi-conscious and delirious.

Of course I can't remember what feverish dreams I had then. But even now I remember distinctly the apparition of the Menshikov Tower, which stood exactly opposite, almost in the middle of our window. It was, precisely, an apparition, suddenly and weirdly rising up in the hushed, secret glow of night and a deathly moon. As I surfaced fleetingly from wanderings to a reality that seemed like the continuation of my dreams, I clearly saw the looming outline of *someone* beyond the window, yet moving about the bright squares on the floor of my room. Like a figure out of Goya, it stared at me—intent, forbidding, finger to its lips, wordlessly demanding prompt and total self-surrender. The Menshikov Tower stood at my side, whispering to me in omnipotent silence.

Even the homely sounds around me—the regular breathing of sleepers in the armchair and the room beyond, the creaking of shelves in the cupboard, the airy chink of disturbed glasses and the dry, attentive gnawing of mice somewhere beneath the floorboards—all seemed to intensify this sense of inaudible, universal dissolution. And, like a magic sign, an incantatory hieroglyph, at that moment I saw beyond the windows a motionless pillar of light, steeped in the moon's lifeless pallor, the most hushed and still of all existing things.

Was it just the rambling vision of a sick child? A mere hallucination? In that laconically simplified glimmer of blue-green light and stark shades, the Tower manifested itself as empress of the night and my own life. She reigned, as cold as an ice crystal, secret as thought. Everything stiffened and grew chill. Time ceased; shadows did not shift. I would turn away, shut my eyes, hide beneath the blankets, but the magnet of the moon drew me out to gaze, half-upright and entranced. It seemed that no more elevated, exquisite being could exist. She was sovereignty incarnate, the conductor of an oratorio, the inexplicable essence of beauty, drowning me in light like one of her chosen ones. How could one forget such a thing?

On winter nights, when I was wakened by the sobbing whine of the blizzard, the window-panes would suddenly ring out, shaken by the snowstorm's violent gusts. Someone would start up a dismal moaning and booming in the pipes. Snow dashed against the window, as though flung by an angry hand; clouds chased across blackened sky. Light and dark poured into each other, and the Tower set sail to meet them, an ice-breaker slicing through the packed, jostling floes. After a brief tussle, she would ride out triumphant into the wastes of darkness. Single clouds massed and sallied, but she surged on, breasting the onslaught. The chains of her cross, the taut shrouds of a frigate, sang and wailed in their weakening throes as she cut through the ice-clouds. Another wild burst of wind; another swivelling rush of snow; once again someone turns and grumbles, moaning, and I am ready to shout with the exultant surge of strength, as, yet again, the Tower in the windows masters the unforgettable night's confusion.

But how different she was on frosty mornings, young and rosy in the mists of sunrise. With day, her three-dimensional, sculptured form was reborn. Her lacy cross, delicately chained to the dome, pulsated in the early morning light. Airy shadows stretched like acrobats from wreaths and garlands, leaping from vase to vase and scroll to scroll. Flights of doves and sparrows played over stucco, pediment, and pilaster; everything began to shift and fuse in the gentle pinks and insubstantial pale-green shadows.

The cleanliness of the sky's colours, and the transparent brightness illuminating her walls were only possible in these early hours. How lovely she was on such mornings, almost blushing with shame at what she had done the night before! How I envied my father, as he lightly transferred her with his little pastel sticks on to the smokey-blue paper, imposingly named after Ingres. Pinned to the wall, the sketch's composition sounded like a melody long after, while beyond the windows the spectacle had faded, leaving only the suddenly ponderous, boring basic structure. Chipped, grey and peeling, by day the Tower meant nothing to us, until the light of the sun setting behind our house sprayed it, like my father's pulverizer, with life-giving rays. For the thousandth time everything changed once more, and the Tower was transformed into a heavily powdered lady-in-waiting at the court of Catherine the Great. In vain the last, barely distinguishable shadows lingered. Retiring to rest with a light yawning and a shiver of her naked shoulders, she shrugged around her a dusky stole. As the sun sank, her resilient form slackened, losing its lustre; robbed of her shadows, she turned to flat cardboard.

The end comes quickly. Yellow patches of light flare up here and there in the windows of the Post Office. The street lamps are lit. The Tower withdraws to her own peace, suddenly melting into a grey nothingness, till the sky darkens and her naked stucco-work tiptoes out in a misty whiteness, whispering to us of her continued existence. But in that hour we too cease to think of what is passing beyond the windows. Drowsily going over the events of the day, nothing now can touch us . . . And we are sleeping soundly, as only little children can.

CHAPTER 5

THE MOSCOW OF THOSE DAYS

WHEN we settled into the main building of the School in 1901, we unexpectedly found ourselves in a wonderfully atmospheric part of old Moscow. Every day for ten years its beauty passed through the windows and into our childish life, changing its expression with the changing times of day. So ten years of our childhood were fed and fostered by the magnificent architectural panorama standing before our eyes, now vanished for ever.

In the seventeenth century the plot of land later passing into the possession of the Moscow Post Office was part of a large estate: it stretched along the walls of the White City, from the Myasnitsky to the Pokrovsky Gates. More precisely, it is known that this part of the estate was bought by a 'low-born minion of fortune', Menshikov, the 'princeling'. In the very first years of the eighteenth century he commanded the master-builder, Ivan Zarudny, to erect a palace and a church 'beneath its bells' dedicated to the Archangel Gabriel. The church, better known as the Menshikov Tower, was consecrated in 1707. By that date the palace had probably also been built. Zarudny set the church and palace in the heart of the estate, evidently foreseeing a possibility, in the distant future, of realizing an architectural composition in depth, which always holds great advantages over the flat façade. Jumping far ahead, I must note that we found just such a spacious composition in 1901, when we first looked out of the windows of our new flat.

The favourite did not enjoy his part of the estate for long. After his fall it passed from hand to hand, evidently without any structural alterations, until at the end of the eighteenth century it was bought from its last owner by Ivan Pestel, the Director of the newly founded Moscow Post Office. Not long after, it became necessary to extend the building for the first time. This was done most successfully by an architect whose name is unknown to me. Sensing the dominant presence of the Menshikov Tower in the panorama, he did not simply add upper floors to the palace, which might have been the simplest and most economical solution to the problem, but chose to construct two single-storeyed side wings, at right angles to the existing building. In this way he preserved the relationship in height between the palace and the Tower, and increased the Tower's visibility by clearing the intervening outhouses which had grown up in Menshikov's time. In this way, also, he turned the formerly amorphous garden into the geometrically correct figure of a *cour d'honneur* opening out on to the street. This courtyard completed the composition, giving it a finished, ceremonious character.

A *cour d'honneur* combines the two opposite functions of separation and unity, distancing and drawing together simultaneously. A building set flush with the pavement is a vertical boundary to the street's width, turning it into a corridor. The *cour d'honneur* breaks up the street's usual line, widening and liberating it. More than that: although such a courtyard is always separated from the street by railings, the eye, sliding past the other houses, is forced to pause, following the buildings leading back into the courtyard. This depth of composition also allows for a multiplicity of planes—the plane of the palings, the courtyard or garden, the back-drop, even the occasional intervening flats. However modest the architecture, such a capacious composition is invariably richer than the most highly ornamented flat façade.

Throughout the nineteenth century the architects extending, modifying, and adding new buildings to the Post Office zealously cherished its panoramic structure, which was so easy to read in reality, and yet has never been noted in written accounts. Like a relay baton, it was carefully passed from hand to hand, until in 1910 they began to build up the main courtyard, exchanging it for a flat, tedious façade obscuring the spire of the Menshikov Tower and the spacious recess of the original conception. Thus the new century got to grips with its heritage, and destroyed what should have been preserved for its descendants.

On the first plane, following the line of the street, was an excellent black hammered iron railing of fine design, almost one storey high, like a bowstring tightly drawing together the two free ends of the building's wings, which extended to the edge of the pavement. At either end the railing was interrupted by a driveway, with gates of similar design, nearly always flung wide. The drive of fresh, bright-yellow sand bent in a smooth arc from the entrance gate to the Post Office's main doors, and on to the exit. Running alongside the railing between the gates, part of the former garden had survived, with its mature limes and thick lilac bushes; a low fence on the palace side repeated the avenue's curving sweep. In this way the main courtyard was broken up into intermediate planes with their repeated motifs.

The uncomplicated building embracing the courtyard and garden was discreet in its decoration; in every respect it was a standard example of government offices of intermediate quality. Nearly all buildings of this kind were on two storeys, the ground floor accommodating the low-ceilinged offices, while on the first floor there were a number of reception rooms and studies for the highest-ranking personnel. This upper floor was light and airy, with ample sunlight solid on the herringbone of wax-scented parquet. The furniture was neatly lapped in grey slip-covers. Inside and out there was an atmosphere of quiet severity, befitting the importance of government offices and morning-suits.

The crux of architectural compositions, so diligently sought out and underlined nowadays, was unemphatic here. The architect admitted neither porticoes nor the embellishment of windows and doors in the central part of the façade. Only a plain iron awning, painted the standard green, and supported by two pairs of cast-iron columns, sheltered the main central doors. And yet, remembering the palings' delicate design, the buildings' good proportions, and, above all, the perfect relationship of the whole to the Menshikov Tower, I begin to respect the author of an ensemble so successfully marrying recent extensions to architecture of long standing and marked character.

This architectural complex was gradually overgrown with new buildings, distributed further along the line of the street. On the corner of the plot, the block of the Telegraph Office grew up, with a large clock-face set in its wall, and, beneath, the doors to the public halls on the first floor. A wide outside stairway of white stone led directly to the entrance, with an extensive upper platform paved in large squares of the same stone. A large crowd of people milled around here, not all of them with business at the Telegraph Office. Today neither stairway nor entrance exist. In the Thirties they were dismantled and the doorway bricked in.

The employees of the Post Office had to speak French (German and English were not compulsory). We knew this from the young man serving as hall-porter to the Director of our School, Prince Lvov. During frequent encounters on our shared stair he told us that the Prince himself, and his eldest daughter, were terrifically helpful preparing him for his French exams. We often met him after that in his new uniform of postal employee.

The new buildings running down the side of Clear Ponds Boulevard were divided by a wide entrance. The ringing of a handbell warned passers-by of service vehicles driving out. Later this was replaced by an electric bell, and, in the end, an automatic light. In the first years after our move to the new flat, we often used to watch the arrival and departure of the various wagons, carriages, and sledges, when we walked down the boulevard or past the Post Office. They were all distinguished by dark-blue paintwork and a sign like a coat of arms on the side—a white, diagonally transected rectangle, symbolizing an envelope. Soon after our arrival the main Moscow tramway, which followed the ring of boulevards, was extended by a branch-line into the Post Office yard. Its little, horsedrawn carriages were also painted dark blue with a white envelope; the Post Office employee sat on a folding seat next to the driver, while a Post Office guard paced the back platform. They all wore black greatcoats with navy piping and button-holes, and black-holstered revolvers slung on a blue cord.

Special, closed, windowless carriages with the usual paintwork hurried in and out of the courtyard from the stations and trains. Everyone knew they transported valuables and money. Back and front, lower ranking military personnel sat fully-armed. The horses were driven at a furious gallop. By the side of the driver, and at the rear of the train of carriages, hung handbells which were rung without interruption.

On the wide balcony and open stair of the Telegraph Office were the now extinct errand boys, called Red Caps. Rain or fine they crowded the stairs, in cold weather dancing up and down the steps to keep warm, leaving only a narrow passageway for the Telegraph's legitimate visitors. At first glance they looked like a miscellaneous crowd of layabouts, but this was deceptive. They were united by comradeship and by their common origin, evident in the flat red tops to their caps (hence the name). Their black, uncockaded hat-bands, like those of doorkeepers and postmen, carried a brass, numbered disc, on which the word 'messenger' was stamped. The Red Caps were members of a highly ramified guild that specialized in running errands. They were sent to buy theatre and train tickets, to deliver flowers, urgent messages, or parcels to the door. Through the organization of the co-operative, they were even trusted with simple financial errands, such as visits to the bank and Post Office, and trips outside town. The safety of the client's valuables was guaranteed by the co-operative and backed by its funds. For this reason each Red Cap had his own number: it was for him a kind

Boris and Alexander with their mother. Sketch by Leonid Pasternak. Odessa, 1899.

Leonid, Alexander, Rosa and Boris Pasternak. Odessa, 1897.

Boris, his cousin Zhenya Freidenberg, Alexander and Rosa Pasternak. Odessa, *c.*1898.

The School of Art, Sculpture and Architecture, Myasnitskaya, No. 21. The Pasternaks' flat is on the second floor. The Church of Saints Frol and Lavr is on the right. Moscow, *c.*1900.

Ice-cutting on the Moscow River, with the chimneys of the tram station in the background (see also p. 183).

Boris and Alexander playing chess. Sketch by Leonid Pasternak.
Moscow, c.1903.

Lydia and Josephine. Drawing by Leonid Pasternak.
Moscow, 1908.

of passport. Such messengers were easily picked out of the thick of a crowd by their bright headgear. Since they worked according to a set tariff there was no danger of being overcharged; undercutting prices was also against their interests.

There were different guilds for different trades: the messengers; the specialists in the packing and transport of furniture; station porters. These last had their own distinguishing characteristic: a white apron with a bright oval number-plate dangling on a leather strap. Across the apron they wore a black leather thong with a similar numbered tag. They were athletically built; after all, they had heavy luggage to carry, since in those days there were no handcarts, and the trolleys were reserved for unaccompanied baggage. When there were many heavy pieces to carry, the porter threaded his leather strap through the handles of the cases, grips, and bundles, slinging them all across his shoulder, and, picking up anything remaining in his free hands, he would toil after his customer. Despite this heavy, rather dirty work, the porters always wore clean aprons and maintained a benevolently dashing appearance. Since they were sometimes sent to buy tickets, deposit trunks in the luggage van, and so on, they made life much easier for the passengers, who in those days were nearly always overwhelmed by mounds of baggage and quantities of children.

On our wide window-sills, we could happily watch the life of the Post Office for hours on end. People of all classes came and went— thickening into clusters, thinning out into a long chain, one by one like flies. Some were quick and decisive; others dawdled, still thinking out what they had to do. Sometimes they lacked anything distinctive and bored us; others made us laugh at the funny way they walked, waving their arms about, as though they were arguing, or trying to impress a point on themselves. It was surprising how they all followed the same invisible, narrow track, although the path was wide enough. They walked in a neat defile, and anyone overtaking the rest seemed to be rudely disrupting the system. Later we joined them, as our parents sent us on minor errands, to post registered letters or parcels. The dispatch sections we visited were on the dim and stuffy ground floor. It seemed as though it had accumulated over the last century its powerful, persistent smell of melted sealing-wax, glue, fresh hessian in which smaller parcels were sewn, the heavy odour of a permanent crowd. The employees serving us were uniformly dressed in black, high-collared jackets with dark-blue piping and epaulettes. They did their job swiftly and silently, with the accuracy of long experience, which combined with the characteristic smell to create an atmosphere of conscious seriousness and importance.

There was no entry from here to the first floor, but of course none of the general public had any business in the formal reception rooms and offices of the higher officials. In one wing were the flats belonging to the Director and his assistant, both of whom held a civilian rank equivalent to that of a general; they were always addressed as 'Yexsy', meaning 'Your Excellency'. But they didn't interest us. In winter what absorbed us was watching the pedestrians' footprints pitting the snow of the yard, and creating, here and there, black holes of wonderfully smooth, slippery ice.

Inconspicuous to those below, they looked to us like bottomless water-holes in a bright ice-field, hurting our eyes with reflected sunlight. Mean kids that we were, we loved watching how the people hurrying to the Post, their minds on far other things, were suddenly, grotesquely transformed into virtuoso acrobats performing an intricate sequence of leaps, pirouettes, and *salti mortali*, ending—alas!—flat on their backs. Most often they fell, one after another, in exactly the same place. It was as though there was a trip-wire automatically twitching their legs and arms into unnatural, spasmodic jerks, culminating in the body's pre-ordained collapse. For us the quick, kaleidoscopic succession of fall after fall was funniest of all. We used to bet on who would succumb to the tumbling mechanism next, and where, and how. It was a great disappointment when our chosen victim turned out to be steadier on his feet than we had decreed.

The winter day on which the Post Office was visited by the icon of its patron saint was an important holiday. For some reason it always seemed to coincide with sharp frost. From early morning a notice appeared on the Post Office gates, proclaiming that it would be shut between such and such hours, and everyone knew why.

Gradually the courtyard grew empty. The fresh yolky sand shone on the unfrequented pavements. The yard-keepers in their laundered and ironed white aprons earnestly swept the new snow across the deserted yard, making it white as a newly laid tablecloth. At a precise moment, they put their brooms away and lined up at the entrance gates; after a short interval a coach of antediluvian design, drawn by two pairs of equally antique horses, lumbered into the yard and up to the main entrance with its green iron awning. Mounted on one of the leading pair rode a young boy, known as the *vorreiter*. Behind him the coachman sat high in his box, flanked by those of the suite who couldn't be crammed inside the carriage. Everyone arriving with the icon, including the coachman and his boy, were decorously hatless. But, because of the intense cold, they were all wrapped up like little old women in warm scarves, or those hoods which no longer even exist. They were once the ordinary adjunct to every winter uniform, and soldier, cadet, and schoolboy all wore them in their own distinctive styles.

The yard-keepers ceremoniously bowed and crossed themselves as the icon was unhurriedly lowered from the carriage and passed respectfully from hand to hand, slung on straps and towels. When it reached the ground, its religious following took over, carrying it, slowly swaying, through the wide doors of the Post Office. We knew that, once inside, it would go from room to room till it came to rest in the private church, where a long service would be held. But for us there was a corresponding break in interest. Still crossing themselves, the yard-keepers relaxed, put their caps back on, and dispersed, spitting. The coach emptied as the helpers went indoors to get warm. Old, black, ripped, inadequate horse-cloths were thrown over the horses, who were white with rime; as a treat nosebags full of oats were hung about their necks. They stood, dreary heads drooping, now and again shifting their legs thoughtfully. The nosebags, pocked by the statutory bite-holes, leaked a thin trickle of oats on to the snow as the horses tossed the bags up or shook them, nuzzling after a bigger mouthful of feed. A banquet began for all the sparrows of the yard, then the pigeons and the jackdaws, till the horses steadily munched on in a mass of surging and subsiding wings. With jerky steps, a crow would edge up from nowhere, head cocked, reconnoitring the restless bustle; deciding against the food, it would hop to one side just as seriously and gracefully as before, flying off with heavy, slow wingbeats and a disgruntled caw, to settle on the low branch of a tree.

The Post Office of those days is long past. Few remember it now; most can never have seen it. Let my description serve as its belated funeral lament, and a deserved epitaph.

CHAPTER 6

IN MEMORY OF MARSHAK

ANNUALLY, on our return from the summer holidays, the maid (a Dunyasha or Grusha) would whisper to our mother that someone had just arrived to welcome the gentry home. It was quite clear from her tone of voice that a treat was in the offing. In a few minutes two Homeric warriors would stalk into the room, each with a wonderful, pure gold casque in the crook of his arm—lacking a horsehair mane, perhaps, but crested for all that. They looked exactly like the Hectors and Agamemnons I had often seen in my father's library books and the plaster casts of Mikhail's underground studio. But these were to me infinitely preferable, living, moving beings. Black-jacketed, black-belted, fiercely bearded they came, their brass buttons, buckles, and helmets brightly scoured with brick-dust, their boots redolent of wax and tar; instead of short sword and hand-shield, they bore long shafts of golden straw.

They would light this at one end and plunge it into our ovens, unlit end first. With a hollow roar, the brightly flaring bundle would vanish from sight, spiralling upwards in the draught of the flue. They explained to us that colleagues on the roof would judge, by the amount of time the flare took to reach them, whether a sweep was needed, or if the chimney could be cleared of soot by a quick blaze. A trifling little job, really, but executed formally like some arcane magical rite. And even during their short stay, our rooms became permeated by the light, pleasant whiff of smoke, and the rather less appealing smell of wax and tar. Wax and tar! The tar itself wasn't so bad, but it lingered deep in our throats, long after the fire brigade had left.

Taking their tip with a bow, they would put on their bright helmets, so melodiously ringing, so hot in the sun, and turn once more into the heroes of ancient legend. It is extraordinary that time, which brought with it the transition from horse and cart to the car, from kerosene lamp to electricity and the telephone, had no external effect on our firemen. The scene repeated itself for many years. When we moved into a third flat in 1911, they performed the same rites in the same magisterial tempo as they had done on the Myasnitskaya, and for centuries before that. Only we no longer saw Argive troops in them . . .

Childhood memories like these were caught, beautifully and accurately, in Marshak's fine poem, *Fire*. The first edition, well illustrated by Konashevich, made a great impression on all its readers—adults, perhaps, even more than children. I can still remember some of Konashevich's rich water-colours, and bitterly regret that of all my son's picture-books we preserved so carefully, this one failed to survive. Nor can I understand the misguided initiative by which the second edition was up-dated. It seems that Marshak felt bound to spoil his own work, as well as his illustrator's, just to keep up with the times. The new verses, robbed of their dated appeal, were bolstered by boring black-and-white pictures of contemporary firemen, evoking none of the first edition's warm feelings. Certainly we need the horribly squalling sirens (poor Sirens!) of the modern, high-speed fire brigade. And yet, the other *was* the picturesque old Moscow, in all its antiquated richness.

The distant shape of a watch-tower rises in my memory. Painted dark-grey, it has a balcony on struts, and some kind of horned spire. Round and round the balcony walks a fireman on the watch, like a wound-up toy, a sight perfectly familiar to Muscovites and provincials alike. At that time, the whole of Moscow was divided into twelve districts, each with its own fire brigade, named after its neighbourhood —the Tverskaya, Sretenskaya, Prechistenskaya. Each had its own district flag, type of tackle, and exactly matching horses. A military uniformity was painstakingly maintained, extending from stirrup and stable to boots and barracks, the size and organization of each brigade following a single pattern. Chief in the brigade, in the days before the telephone, was the look-out on his tower. Few houses then were more than two storeys high, or three at the most, so that the look-out could easily survey his region, spread out as it were in the flat of his hand. He was trained to distinguish between the smoke of an incipient fire, and the thousand innocuous spires drifting from the chimney-pots of a thousand Dutch ovens, burning throughout the winter months.

As soon as a fire had been sighted, the look-out would raise a single black ball on the flagstaff, which was clearly visible in every direction, whatever the weather. With serious fires two or even three balls were hoisted as an appeal for reinforcements to the look-outs of other districts; in particularly threatening or complicated conflagrations a black cube was also displayed on another pole, calling together all the brigades of the city. In the worst fires of all the *brand-meister*, or chief fire-officer, would ride out with his adjutant, while a single, ominous black ball and black cube were hung out on every Moscow watch-tower. This sequence of visual signals survived from the most ancient times. The dark silhouette on his balcony reminded me of the earliest sailors in their crow's-nests. And yet this wasn't in the God-forsaken wastes of the Russian steppes, or some forgotten suburb of the town, but in the very centre of Moscow. There was a barracks on Tverskaya Street, just opposite the house of the Governor-General (now the Moscow Soviet of Working People's Deputies, on Gorky Street). In this elegant building of Empire design, with a Doric colonnade stretching the length of its façade, were the administrative offices of the local fire brigade, still with its stables, stone barracks, and primeval watch-tower in the yard behind.

The pride of every brigade was not so much its scrupulous uniformity, as the speed and skill of its turn-out. They were a terrific sight—driving full tilt down the middle of a street suddenly drained of traffic and noise, the carters and drays drawn up dead, crammed out of the way against the pavement. This headlong gallop was an undisputed privilege unique to the fire brigade; in normal circumstances, of course, the city would never have put up with such speeds, when the cobbles sprayed sheaves of sparks and the clatter seemed to set the houses swaying. The very air began to smell of Wagner.

In this unforgettably powerful, well-coordinated turn out, every detail had its own important part to play—the exact match of the horses' coats; the perfectly maintained fan of their formation, down to the team's turning necks and their even, thundering bodies; the sustained drumming of their hoof-beats, the white-gloved driver, standing in apparent indolence, as powerful as the charioteer of Delphi. It all demanded supreme training, colossal stamina and skill, and yet it seemed to happen lightly, easily, almost of its own accord.

A mounted bugler led the way. The four-in-hand behind carried the rest of the brigade, sitting back to back in two rows, dressed in asbestos trousers and jackets, with helmets blazing on their heads. A fireman beside the driver continually rang the silver, clear-toned alarm bell, whose uninterrupted tocsin, at once dreadful and invigorating, travelled far down the suddenly hushed and emptied street, adding a potently romantic note to the massed Wagnerian theatricality. At the back was the water-pump. I still remember seeing the original primitive hand-pump—a large, red, right-angled tank, with four handles for the four men operating it. It was later replaced by a new nickel-plated boiler with a long-chimneyed fire-box, trailing black clouds of curdling smoke and thick drifts of sparks which looked, on night rides, like fireflies in autumn dusks. The stoker by the furnace fed it from time to time with chocks of wood from his stack. It was no different from the geysers standing in every bathroom of that time, including our own.

The bugler wore his copper trumpet tightly bound to his back with multicoloured cord, to stop it bouncing and bruising him. If the brigade went out at night, his second in command carried a flare in his left hand, its smoky flames beaten by the wind into the long, wavering tail of a Chinese dragon spitting fire. Like the revellers in a *Walpurgisnacht* they pounded by, bell chiming, hoofs in unremitting unison, the many wheels roaring over the cobbles. Hearing their approach the street would fall still as at the first roll of a distant thunderstorm, which dallies, drawing nearer, and then is unexpectedly upon you.

The chief city fire-officer, appearing at the worst fires on his black stallion, wore full regimental regalia, a small broadsword hanging from his sash, as a symbol of power only. His adjutant, hurrying up on a matching charger, would dismount, then keep a respectful distance beside him, his silver trumpet on its tasselled cord at his lips, ready to transmit his superior's commands. Their horses, harnessed and saddled for further sorties, were walked by one of the unoccupied firemen.

My way home from school crossed Theatre Square. Twice as a schoolboy I lingered with the crowd to watch the Nezlobin and the Maly Theatres burn to the ground. The shrill solo of the bugle was unforgettable, suddenly audible above the incessant din of the fire, now swelling, now withdrawing, smothered by the discordant howl of hot air and the splintering of everything the fire and its fighters destroyed. Its song of command was answered by the rough shouts of firemen near at hand. Huge cross-beams like lit matches leapt from the fire, spinning up in the draught, to tumble back into the terrifying bluster of an element broken free of all restraint. The gutted building turned into the bars of a giant grate, its prodigious blaze laid by titanic hands. How can words, lying so silent on the page, convey the din of cracking beams, bursting glass, the clang of metal girder jarring against girder, the scattered burst of explosions—and the overriding, even boom of an infernal hurricane, like the magnified bass of the great Conservatoire organ, bellowing with all the might of its inhuman lungs?

The warp and weft of flame, the black smoke—everything momentarily appeared to be a living force, risen up in defiance of man. And where open force failed to win the upper hand, sly cunning took over. Low tongues of beaten flame cringed like a puppy at our feet, to slip aside and spring up, mocking and dancing, in a tower of flame.

They say that the Metropole in flames was even more terrifying. That happened in the deep December frosts, when the water froze. Burns and falling masonry were bad enough without this unforeseen, elemental betrayal.

Everything now has vanished: the brass-helmeted train; the galloping rider at their head, a dragon uncurling from his torch; the frightened drays; the cobbles of the highway. No one will ever see that fire brigade again. And only those lucky enough to possess the first, superseded edition of Marshak and Konashevich's work can recapture it now.

CHAPTER 7

TRANSFIGURATION

WHAT of the city's genuine metamorphoses? The transitional days from summer to autumn and winter, and the even more wonderful change from the long winters to the longed-for spring?

In those days, winter turned even major cities into country villages, heavy with the slumber of deep, impassable snows. The city streets had to be travelled by sleigh like country turnpikes, and the countryside dictated its conditions to the town. Snow was vital in our childhood: it was cherished, much as it was saved in the fifteenth century, till the car gradually ousted the honest horse, and changed the city's winter face. In my childhood, though, the car was still in its infancy—a rare creature, lacking the strength to compete with snow and sleigh, feebly aping the barouche and landau in its form. Snow still reigned supreme.

While horse and sleigh survived, no snow was cleared from the streets—however ice-bound—to be transported to the suburbs and melted down as it is today. Heavy falls were carefully swept from the roofs and superfluous drifts cleared off the pavements; they were all collected on the streets where they were most needed, to create a permanently thick, fine carpet. After good falls like these, the sledges rode sweetly, and the steaming horses ran with pleasure, throwing up icy spray to either side. What a delight it was for us to set off on evening visits to the Christmas parties of our friends; how different from ordinary days! The town itself, with only the odd, unhurried pedestrian, seemed hushed, new, and strange. Kerosene street-lamps burned dim on their short, red-painted wooden posts. How familiar it all is, and how distant from us now! The lamplighter used to prop his ladder against the crossbar under the lantern. First he would take the glass off, warming it with his breath to stop it cracking. Then the lamp was lit, the wick turned down, and a soft, warm, rather dim yellow light sprang up round the lamppost. On the frosty, blue-black nights of a full moon, the street lay brighter between each lamp than beneath it; the snow seemed bright with finely shattered glass, or winking stars, tumbled into the blue drifts of a diamond-field.

These Christmas evenings we went by sleigh to our friends, clinging tightly to Mamma's cloak, lulled by the soft, monotonous slide over the snow. Invariably repeated and ever new, the yellow ring of light beneath each lantern would alternate with moon-blue snow, over which raced the frightened, fairy-tale shapes of our shadows, and us chasing them. Each lamp approaching in its turn fathered shadows, springing to life behind us. You only had to turn round, and see them—gigantic sweeping gestures of hand and wing overtaking us as the lamppost swam past, then dropping under the horses' feet. Tearing themselves free, they ran further and further ahead, till they vanished altogether in the shadows, only to be born again, behind us once more, as the next lamppost drew near.

Everything shone like the cotton wool sprinkled with salts of potassium chlorate, which we used to lay on the outspread paws of our Christmas tree; or like the spangly flakes of camphor, still clinging to the furs just taken from our huge chest of winter clothes.

That snow! Those star-sparks in the snow!

How everything changed with the snow's arrival! Not only the appearance of Moscow, but every single thing: the city, its people, and their very life, from streets and yards to homes and rooms! Such smells and sounds, our daily ways—were they all just yesterday? You only had to put on your fur coat, hood, and felt boots, to change to someone slow-footed and sedate. You went out to play in the yard as usual, and came home for lunch, to find everything suddenly hushed. Heavy dark blinds hung everywhere; the grey summer slip-covers were stripped off the furniture; thick carpets stole the sound of your boots. The trunk had been opened, the winter coats hung in the hall, filling the air with their thin clear pungency of camphor and dried patchouli twigs to keep off the moth.

There is the familiar, acrid smoke from the Dutch ovens, kindled for the first time, their brightly scrubbed brass doors ringing cheerfully as the fire draws well. The birch logs smell moistly of holidays— mushrooms, dachas, and the damp. How familiar these signs of winter's arrival: deep warm bolsters of cotton wool between the double windows; little glasses of dark yellow, oily acid nestling there. Dead, dried flies (where do they come from?) will appear later; as yet the cotton wool is still fresh and white. The window-frames are sealed for the long winter with satisfying, evenly-bulging ribbons of still pliable putty, whose white paint shines sweatily and smells of fresh linseed oil. So silence is created, the roar of the town excluded. The carpets, blinds, and softly uphol-stered furniture absorb the flat's family noises, the last whispers of sound. It is as quiet as if the town itself is walking on tiptoe, or in an old man's muffled, goatskin slippers. Like a muted instrument, everything sinks in velvety peace.

So, from year to year, from our earliest childhood, the city's great transfiguration came to pass. The snow's mild silence, the measured pace of life, the woolly, grandfatherly quiet, were the season's invariable marks. How much was given to us children on those sunny winter days, tranquil evenings, and magical moonlit nights!

Still, we can't go on like this for ever, sliding over the snow! Higher and higher, the sun rises over the town . . . A long farewell to all our greatcoats! But, for all its growing warmth, the sun cannot immediately conquer the snow: allotted days must pass, before the town steps out into the bright glaze of early spring.

Winter is marked by stereoscopic snow sharpening contours, in-cisively dividing not-white and white. A world of softly muffled sounds, of ponderously measured pace. The cheerful snapping of oven wood, and smells, smells, the smells of winter days . . .

Spring is water. Not the wet substance, nor the chemical formula, but phenomenon and action all together. Water wakes the dreaming town to life, carrying away winter's deadening when its function has gone. Slowness is anathema to it; spurring all things to a gay youthful urgency, it sets them running, gurgling, glimmering, dancing from stone to stone.

How is that to be explained? Why, very simply! In those days, as I said, cars were unknown. Cobbled streets and the medieval droshky, like the tarantas or unsprung wagon, must have survived from the days of Gogol to our times. Iron-rimmed wheels with heavy wooden hubs and spokes thundered over the cobbles. And then, that cobbled highway! Of all the towns in Russia, only SPB, or St Petersburg, had the new, soft and silent tarmac roads. Everywhere else the streets were paved with small, regular granite blocks of all colours—pinkish, greenish, grey-blue, bright yellow. When the rains washed away the dirt and dust, drawing colours from the heart of the stone, their chance mosaic was far richer than the asphalt's colourless monotony. The gutters running alongside the pavements were set with the same bumpy stones; the near-compulsory high sides of the pavements were also cobbled and marked out with stone posts vital in wintertime, when the sleighs, slithering everywhere, could easily ride up and hurt pedestrians. In spring and summer these dangers faded, as cart and carriage kept to the road. But for us those high-raised pavements had their own advantages.

At first, each battle won by the sun is lost at night, as the cold seals the water in a thin, icy crust. In all innocence, the morning pedestrians step securely on to the familiar, solid ice, only to crunch into the freezing puddle beneath. At first the lurking melted snow evokes a weak, good-natured smile. But the day soon comes when it is no laughing matter. Hidden no longer, the water breaks through the snow in gentle trickles at first, nosing their way through loopholes and byways to join similar rivulets. Still barely audible, scarcely seen, they run together, gathering strength, swelling into streams, and then—look, over there! —into a noisy torrent. On the many steeper streets of Moscow they hurtle downhill, scouring gutters, waltzing past diminutive reefs and shallows, spreading by snow-drifts into wide, icy lakes.

Old men of today will still remember going out as boys, their eyes alight with anticipation, their unsinkable galleon, an empty matchbox, clutched in red hands. We would take up our posts at the top of the street. Here, for instance, at the top of Prechistenka, where the pavilion was . . . In that priceless building (a *chef-d'œuvre* of the architect Bauvais, decorated with stucco mouldings by Vitali himself) an umbrella-maker had his shop. Without warning, the building was pulled down, as an 'obstruction'—a great stumbling-block its beauty must have been to somebody! Now, all that remains is its own special commemorative plaque—four huge hoardings, to this day proclaiming films seen and forgotten long ago. These incomparable hoardings celebrate the hallowed antiquities of time and offend nobody's visual sense. They have stood in its place for the last twenty years.

But to get back to my forgotten boy, anxiously lowering his vessel into the swollen waters of his imaginary Potomac. There she goes! caught headlong in the choppy flux, weaving past obstacles, vaulting the water-falls, whipped away. Like many other captains launching their boats before him, he runs down the gutters, guessing at what Scylla or Charybdis his ship will sink, to be washed ashore, soaked cardboard keel to the skies.

My God, how memorable, how dear were those marvellous days! What absorbing variety the town's transfiguration brought us! For the grown-ups, perhaps, they were just wet and inconvenient. After all, the clear torrents came after the town's rebirth. But before that?

Before the snow had time to turn to water, it went through a dry, granular stage, generally known as 'halva', for obvious reasons. God knows where all that discolouring grit, sand, and even clay came from. This halva covered the streets in a thick layer, bogging down the pedestrians, running high over the sledges' runners. Scarcely snow any longer, it melted to a lumpy, dark-brown stew. How could I fail to remember every detail of Theatre Square, weltering in this slush? It was the city's main square, a large parade-ground, strewn with sand and nearly always half deserted, not cut in two by the traffic as it is now. Carriages drove round its edge. The rest was cordoned off by a chain as thick as your arm, threaded through striped wooden bollards, and could only be crossed on foot. Sometimes it was used for the cadets' military exercises; in summer, horse fairs were held there. On dry days in spring, summer, and autumn the wind would whip up dust-devils which ran from corner to corner, to the intense irritation of the rare passers-by. The Square's ghastliness set it somewhere between the Mirgorod Square of Gogol's days, and the equally notorious Koziulka, whose miseries Chekhov experienced driving from Siberia to Sakhalin. Theatre Square was Moscow's impassable Kozyulka, and in the early days of spring it became the bane of Moscow traffic. For the pedestrian it was downright dangerous, and few braved the loss of galoshes and boots in its icy sludge (a diminished risk on other Moscow streets also). But for the poor dray-horses it was worst of all.

Only too often, as schoolboys, we had to shrug our shoulders and slope off, unable to prevent the unmerciful beating of those innocent animals. Sledges, grossly overladen with boxes, bundles, crates, and chests, biting deep into the uneven slush, would suddenly run aground, iron screaming against the flints. It was no joke getting them going once more. Some carters, swearing horribly, seized the shafts and tried to rock the sledge free. With even choicer obscenities, others grabbed whatever came to hand, and ruthlessly thrashed the poor horse. For all their joint efforts and blasphemies, the sledge refused to budge.

The horse braces its back legs, straining till a light shudder runs over its skin. Its front legs paw, slithering, for a purchase. Then a policeman comes up to demand an immediate departure—as if that wasn't the carter's prime concern! In a happy glow of self-importance, this protector of the peace in his turn beats the unhappy horse with the flat of his sword and yanks at the shafts. At long last it dawns on him that force is useless, and the carter is told to unload half his freight on to the pavement. Considerably lightened, the sledge tears free of the damned stone, setting our teeth on edge with a sharp screech and showering sparks—not for the last time. What could we tender-hearted schoolboys do? Routed by the carter's abuse and the guffaws of a gathering crowd, we would slink away.

The horses were noticeable for another peculiarity of that time: their hooves, normally blackened by an equine cosmetic of wax and tar, were scoured clean by the sandy sludge, restoring them to their natural colour of old ivory, sometimes with a pinkish tinge. To us, those indecently naked hooves seemed unaesthetic, somehow, even disgusting.

The town is already drying out. Sledges are no longer to be seen. Everything runs on wheels. The end is in sight. Petrified putty is chiselled in chunks from the window-frames. The inside window is opened and the window-sill swept clear with a cockerel's wing. A pail receives the desiccated husks of beetles and flies, incomprehensibly collecting in that hermetically sealed space. The dirty cotton wool is taken away; so are the blackened tumblers of once liquid acid, now thick as ointment. The solemn moment comes: the space between the windows is wiped down, the catches are raised, the outside window flung wide. Fresh spring air, wild and cool, fills the room, bringing with it the city's bright polyphony of voices, bells, and squealing wheels, mingling in a pleasant, uninterrupted hum, the pulse of the living town. The transfiguration is complete.

CHAPTER 8

ICE ON THE MOVE

WHEN I started telling my granddaughter about old Moscow, naturally enough she enjoyed the improbable scenes best, disassociated as they were from the life of the town in which her eight years had been spent. Moscow River in the thaw was a fine example. Nowadays the large ice-floes are intercepted and blown up by the military many miles above the town, and we see only the river's high waters, a dark, troubled brown, flowing freely between our banks. But forty years ago ice on the move was an unforgettable sight, even in the city confines.

Unlike my son, I didn't see it for the first time as a three-year-old child, but as a grown schoolboy. At his age, we lived a long way from the river, which didn't form part of our childhood walks, and it was only by chance, in my early teens, that I happened to find myself on the embankment. I was so struck by what I saw that from then on I made a long, intentional detour to the river on my way home from school. Our school stood at the beginning of the Povarskaya, nearly where it opens on to Arbat Square; going home, I used to follow Vozdvizhenskaya Street past the Kremlin, or cut through the Alexandrovsky Garden to reach the river. In summertime it dwindled to a shallow trickle, but in times of thaw and spate it was most threatening and enticing. The whole town talked of the ice-floes, and many gawpers lounged on the bridges and quays. They were a disreputable lot for the most part, whom the police moved on sharply, never allowing a crowd to collect by the railings.

In those days the section of the river between the Cathedral of Christ the Saviour and the Ustinsky Bridge flowed between steep brick walls; running alongside them new earthy slopes had appeared, whose combination of green undergrowth and red brick gave the river a natural frame. Moving outwards in each direction, from the Kamenny Bridge to Sparrow Hills, and from Krasnoholmsky Bridge beyond, the river flowed between its native banks, topped by an irregular wooden country fence. In the thaw, I used to go to Kamenny Bridge, and try to slip unobserved on to a little balcony above its main pier, where there was a protective stone parapet instead of an iron railing. Here I was less easily seen, and the view over the river, its ditches and backwaters, was magnificent. Beyond Babyegorodsky Dyke the river ran its full width through the wastes of the city outskirts, and I had an unbroken view of the distant countryside, so built up now that the open landscape seen from my vantage-point would be hard to imagine.

Here we are, then, on the bridge, the ice moving at full tilt. The water can hardly be seen, it is so crammed with a convulsively straining crowd of floes, hurrying as though late for something, overtaking where they can, mounting each other, smashing thunderously into the floes before them. The colossal force behind them is easily felt. Fleetingly it seems as though the water itself is elbowing the floes off, struggling to shrug free the lumbering ice packs scrambling over its surface.

The river bank, already bare of snow, is black with damp earth. Where last year's grass still clings it looks like a sodden sponge, olive-brown and lumpy. Its slopes are intermittently buried under huge ice-drifts, squeezed aside and levered ashore by the floes thronging alongside and behind. Massive as the shapeless hulks of sea-beasts, they crawl heavily out, to doze on their difficult journey. Suddenly, inexplicably, some inner perturbation troubles the herd (a bad dream, perhaps?) and the peace of the breeding ground is broken. In a body they slither back into the water, their onward rush culminating in back-flips and belly-flops. A second passes, and once again the earth is hidden from sight by a new pack, shouldered on to dry land by the leviathans behind them.

It is quite inconceivable where all that ice can come from! In the distance, it looks like a crisp, unbroken meniscus; as it comes nearer, its glaze reticulates with cracks, whose mosaic of clean blues and dirty browns becomes increasingly distinct. Some icebergs preserve the tracks of a former roadway, the marks of horse and sledge, the usual urinous stains of travelled snow. You can tell from forgotten relics which floes came from village river banks, as they carry past old buckets, a child's toboggan, logs dropped off a cart. Once I saw a heavily laden sledge, which had evidently been abandoned at the last minute, for horse and driver to save themselves. Another time there was a black dog, which had crawled up the ice to be carried whining to its death.

An even, thick rustling hangs steadily over the river. In the broad panorama, the speed of the ice driven from the distant horizon is hardly apparent: it looks as though it does not move at all. But as soon as some invisible line is crossed, details emerge and suddenly pick up momentum, just as you become aware of the surface energy. The whole white mass is *breathing*, fast and heavily, like an exhausted thing.

Bearing down on us with ever-increasing speed, the whole ice-field flings itself against the bridge's breakwater; black waters seethe with yellow froth round the pier below. The elemental forces of water and movement, obscured before by ice and its uniformity, are suddenly thrown into sharp relief. Here and there big whirlpools funnel down their glassy sides to vanish in the water's solid mass. It is simply terrifying to look under you: it seems the spate will sweep you to the river bottom. You struggle, but cannot tear your eyes away to rest on the calmer distances. Then the river-ice, with all its jetsam of garbage rushing to meet you, suddenly stops. A click, and the process is thrown into reverse. The bridge and its frail balcony leap forward into the patiently waiting expanse. Like the ram of an ice-breaker sailing at full steam, the bridge ploughs straight through the ice, clearing its prow, sharply nosing splayed crusts aside, biting deeper and deeper into the whiteness. It is all so clear, you almost feel the hot shudder of furnace and churning turbine beneath you . . .

Now the river's speed can really be appreciated. Like a ship, an ice-breaker, the bridge drives forward, not slackening a moment, as floe after floe is hurled against it: a dull crack like muffled cannon-shot, and they split to uncover the black waters below. But here comes one of such extraordinary size, surely no breakwater could have the force to smash it? Something new comes to pass. As we crane from above, our ship seems to dither and draw in its strength. Like a weight-lifter, it eases the iceberg upwards very slowly, to climb the breakwater's brick hump. The white underside protrudes higher and higher, displaying the full thickness the water had obscured. Imperturbably, interminably, it rises, with a splintering rasp drowning the river's roar; still heavier, still slower, it rears aloft, spreading vast and threatening wings. Its tail has long dipped below the waves. The water, rolling off its back, washes it clean. Its blue breast grates painfully against the brickwork . . . A sudden bomb-burst, and it is riven by its own weight, unnaturally craned for flight beyond its native element. Diving into the water with a loud splash, two new icebergs rise beyond the bridge, while we draw shaken breath once more, as though victorious ourselves in the barehanded grappling of ice and stone.

At last dusk falls. Yellow lamps wink. Reluctantly, I tear myself away from the white river and all its gleaming distances. Fog is falling, blotting out horizons, sky, and the dim town. It is time to go: the policeman comes up for the umpteenth time, stuffed with cold, hoarsely demanding the bridge to be cleared at once. It is strange to think that when all the onlookers have left, the same spectacle will go on, with never an eye to watch. Lingering, I look back for the last time, committing to the gods river and benighted bridge, and the poor, doomed river-monsters, ice-orcs, and seal-floes, white patches against the darkening banks. They all came to their eternal end, forty years ago . . .

CHAPTER 9

PALM SUNDAY

THE Great Fast! The severe-sounding words suited the festival of Lent, which was observed in serious quietness. Distinct as drops from a loosened tap, church bells tolled their slow funeral note, marking the fast's attenuated weeks and days. After Shrove Tuesday and its noisy gaiety, the long penance began. All entertainment was banned by the Church; the town's night-life shrank to the shelter of home, while yet another change was taking place. Deliberate, methodical, the calendar's great clock marked the numbered days as winter Moscow, retreating backward step by step, swept the way for spring.

Spring came, and on our March breakfast tables plaited pastry larks appeared, the currant-eyed, aromatic harbingers of the season. On the streets, squares, and alleyways, slow-footed figures passed, russet-stemmed willow branches in their outstretched hands. Drawing fresh bunches from the sacks and baskets at their backs as they walked, they would sell them to everyone, unasked and unanswered. Not a word was spoken in barter or in thanks. Red bilberry twigs with their firm, dark-green leaves were woven in with the softly budding pussy-willow. At home we put them in bottles of water. Gradually the willows aged; the stems darkened to cherry-black; the little pussies fell away. The bud-cases withered and dropped, revealing weakly shoots of coming green, while in the bottles a long beard of white roots shivered as if alive. Its first beauty lost, the willows' symbolic sense came to an end with Palm Sunday and the bazaar that took its name.*

The bazaar, too, had its own distinctive quality. On this unique and marvellous Sunday the city underwent a total transformation. For the grown-ups it brought the change from fast to normality, from short days to spring light and warmth, and, on this day alone, a brief release from the respectability society demands. Adults reverted to their rash youth; we children revelled in the cheerful town which seemed taken captive by

---

* In Russian, Palm Sunday is known as Willow Sunday.

squeaking, honking, clattering toys, mother-in-laws' tongues, inflated piglet squealers, whistles, rattles and the quieter attractions of shaggy monkeys and the monsters of the deep.

The modern child, growing up with his electric toys, might not appreciate our ugly simians, mistakenly preferring his automatic, mechanical models. But, for all their simple craftsmanship, those monkeys of ours were beloved objects of fantasy—no toy, perhaps, but the idea of a toy.

In essence, each monkey was just a length of thick peasant yarn, boldly dyed all sorts of unlikely colours, woven into a soft wiry body, which you could twist into any attitude you wanted. The wool was trimmed close like stubble or the thick shag of a little animal. Two bead eyes shone in the round head, knowing and quite unmonkeylike, and even the long, thin tail brought it no closer to the monkey world. The craftsmen turning them out played a double game, dressing them as dancers in tutus and ballet shoes, chimney-sweeps with ladder and brushes, chefs in white hats, fork or ladle in hand. There were firemen in brass helmets, policemen in black greatcoats, sailors in round sailor hats and striped vests, chemists in white gowns. What did they *not* think of? The variety was increased by the monkeys' poisonously bright bodies which were raspberry red, yellow and blue, regardless of rank or trade. You could scarcely find two alike. A clasp was run through their backs to pin them to your cap, coat or jacket, or the vendor's black placard. Arranged there, vivid, variously dressed, they looked like butterfly collections under glass, while the vendors, carrying their placards on long poles, turned into Roman legionaries bearing the glinting ensigns and symbols of their cohorts in the sun.

Does anyone now remember the monsters of the deep? Ingeniously twisted, fluttering, unexpectedly bouncing little devils blown of thin coloured glass? They swam in the pink or green waters of a special tiny retort. You warmed it in your hand to give your devil vital energy. When our son was about two years old, my wife brought home from the market the last little sea-devil I ever saw, swimming in a test-tube, not a retort. None ever surfaced again. They were probably banned on grounds of safety—what if the glass burst and the child cut his finger?—or, worse still, the liquid splashed in his eye! But in our childhood there were no such fears, and even in the crush of Red Square everyone carried a retort with its little, leaping glass figure, just as the young Virgin of Cimi da Conigliano climbs a steep stair, a candle burning in her hands.

But it was not the monkeys and monsters of the deep that gave Palm Sunday Bazaar its unique quality. After all, there were plenty of other fair and market days when everyone was on the streets, which were just as colourful. But they didn't unite absolutely everyone, young and old, in such a universal, unforgettable impulse—a sense of something snapping, and joy bounding free.

On that day alone, from earliest light, Moscow prepared itself. We bolted through our morning chores: washing, brushing teeth and hair, breakfast . . . even breakfast, so pleasantly delayed on ordinary holidays, when there was nothing to hurry for, seemed on this day deliberately dragged out, since all we wanted was to get outside.

But there! It's done! and I'm outside, quickly fastening the last buttons on my high-necked jacket, as I run down the Myasnitskaya, to join the crowds all moving together to Red Square.

Drawing closer to the Square as I cross the Vladimirsky Gate on to Nikolskaya Street, I dive into a yielding, transparent hubbub, softened by distance and the crowded air into an even hum. Such an atmosphere, vibrating with far-off turmoil, always evokes vivid memories of my earliest childhood by the Black Sea. Our dacha used to stand on a high cliff above the sea. In heavy storms, when the groaner sounded, and there was just such an overwhelming uproar, even the stillest new sounds seemed to make themselves heard, somehow balanced in the big sky. The benign bass of the sea increased as we climbed down the cliff. Yet even on a pebbly beach the sigh of the tide could still be heard, scrambling and thinning out over the sand. Rustling foam, beaten far up the beach, lay like whipped cream on the wet sand; pebbles rattled under the retreating waves with their unmistakable spurting suckle and indrawn gasp. Far out to sea, in the cannonade of great rollers and sliding mountain waves, the belligerent, hump-backed ocean thumped and boomed, its instrumentation diminished by distance to a rhythmic bass.

So the shouts and cries of the far-away crowd came to us, a soft foretaste of Red Square during Palm Sunday Bazaar.

On this day Red Square was unrecognizable. Naturally vast, it became tight and circumscribed; generally quiet, it whistled, roared, and squealed; normally respectable, it was overtaken by Bacchic revelry. People didn't walk, they were borne along. The current ran from the Iverskaya Chapel to the ancient place of execution, wheeling round and back to the Iverskaya again, each stream of people flowing in separate and opposite directions, although whirlpools, eddies, and backwaters were constantly forming. The square bubbled with inexhaustible celebration. Drifting with the crowd, iridescent balloons clustered above the press, shivering and swaying in the currents of air, suddenly blinding as they caught the sun. Now and then a single, small balloon would sail up into the blue, its bright disc sharply distinct as it rose, apparently slowing and growing smaller, driven at the wind's whim, to lose itself in the transparent sky.

Below, dark placards pinned with monkeys and paper flowers for future Easters crawled slowly over the crowd, black beetles clumsily resisting all efforts to turn them. Along the length of the Kremlin wall, refreshment stalls and booths were set out. A constant quadrille of visitors danced aside to knock back a glass poured from outsize jugs, and rejoin the crowd. And along the pavements of Torgovy Ryad quite another life was to be seen. Here mercantile, moneyed Moscow had cleared its own patch for the brag and strut of capital. There was an imitation quasi-European Corso here, a carnival procession of well-groomed horses, with expensive harnesses and spanking carriages. On the boxes, monumental coachmen sat enthroned: grave as grandees, cocky as Italian *condottieri*, barely stirring the reins in their gloved, meaty palms. Arrogant, fat-arsed, bolstered by coat and greatcoat, they easily outswanked their masters, slumped and bored in the carriages behind them.

High above the square, the upturned cup of the sky was bright and wet as rinsed crystal. Rare, light clouds intensified the blue by their blinding pallor. The sky's wide cupola rang from rim to rim with the peal of Moscow's forty times forty churches. Their chimes swung surging to a deep crescendo, till the song was a palpable tremor in the solid air . . . and died to a whisper of uncertain harmony. The climax came with the bottomless bass of the Kremlin's named and mighty bells—Great Ivan tumbling hand in hand with his little brother, Reut, a puny two-thousand pounder, in their thunderous cascade. Solemn and majestic, the massed choir rolled about the sky, engulfing and engrossing all that passed below. After the melancholy tolling of the single bell knelled through the great fast days, this joyful carillon was perhaps the supreme reason for the unique place Palm Sunday held in all the feast days of the Moscow calendar.

CHAPTER 10

MUSHROOM MARKET

FEW remember the Mushroom Market now. In my day it was as colourful as the food markets of Okhotny Ryad, once nicknamed Guzzlers' Way. But without a doubt even Okhotny Ryad will soon be forgotten; new generations of Muscovites know nothing of it—and where, indeed, could they get to hear of it? If anything, it will be remembered for its salesmen's second profession as the agents of the Union of Russian People, members of the notorious Black Hundred who rode out under the portrait of the Tsar, wielding knouts and whips against the defenceless workers and student demonstrators. *That* is what will be remembered.

The Mushroom Market was just as much a part of Moscow life as Shrove Tuesday, Palm Sunday, and Easter Week; it was the necessary precursor of the long Great Fast. Here we could stock up with the foods the Church permitted, while the sale of forbidden flesh was driven from the markets on to the open streets, and even there no one bothered with such godless stuff.

As everyone knew, the market was traditionally held on the right bank of the Moscow River, between the Ustinsky and Moskvoretsky bridges. They used to say that it sometimes spilt on to the river itself, but I doubt it: even the thickest ice could hardly have borne the large numbers visiting it all day. Since it lasted only a few days, it was held under the open sky. Everything was primitively displayed in open barrels, the frozen carcasses of great fish simply laid straight on the snow, yet its tradesmen were tidy and their food was impeccably clean and fresh. It was held in the centre of the city, the embankment being specially closed to traffic for the occasion. Hence, presumably, my vivid memory of the Mushroom Market in particular, distinguished as it was from other food markets by its brevity, ordered cleanliness, the high quality and beauty of its produce.

Drifting along the river bank on those few frosty days came the appetizing smell of pickled cabbage and soused apples, dried or salted mushrooms, and fish smoked an amber brown. Not only the food was first-class, so was the trading. Customers were not cheated, or wooed with sales talk. Pushing and shoving were surprisingly rare. It was typical of that market, too, that we took our purchases home, not in paper wrappings, but in bast punnets and lime-bark purses with their fresh, woody smell.

The market itself was strictly divided into different rows according to the wares. The mushrooms, though not the most memorable part of the whole, were excellent. Boletus caps of exclusive quality hung in plush, corpulent garlands. Their stems were sharply trimmed away—rejected in those days as a shoddy trifle, an insult to the vendor's professional pride. Nowadays, dried mushrooms, leg and all, are threaded in little pigtails, passing from the most insignificantly tiny (nothing more than the blackened twig of a crooked stem), to just one of more or less respectable middle size. In those days we never sank so low. If you sold mushrooms, you sold real ones. White-bellied caps were strung in an even chain, each matched to each. Of course inferior selections could be bought, but not at this market.

Pickled, soused, and salted products stood in ranks of big oak barrels. Brim-full, they stood—vats of bilberry, cranberry, cloudberry . . . The frost-bitten cranberries were a wonderful dark burgundy, glossy as a glass necklace on the Christmas tree, tight and plump and bursting with juice. In smaller tubs smooth Antonov apples gleamed a pallid gold, smooth and round as ivory billiard balls, breathing an exquisite fragrance, half winey, half suffused with secret herbs. In contrast, beside them gloomed the dark, tanned leather-brown of frozen apples, with their sour, persistent scent.

In other rows black and red caviare was for sale, pressed into broad slabs, or sold loose from tubs. It was not the high quality I found so amazing, but the extraordinary abundance that never seemed to diminish, however brisk the sales. Pelts of frozen fish lay almost under the crowd's feet in equally inexhaustible piles. It was fascinating to watch the boys at work, hacking chunks of frozen fish. Few of them had proper stalls. A graded set of lethally sharp knives hung from their belts, in leather sheaths. Before attacking the next fish, they would whet these knives, then cut so well that no makeweight slivers ever seemed called for. There must have been mistakes, but who was asking? When the spine was unusually tough or hard-frozen, the knife was changed for a hatchet and, with a significant exhalation (h-h-h-h-a!), the carcass split in two.

The stall-keepers' endurance always surprised me, although they wore white felt boots that were the envy of us schoolboys, smartly trimmed with brown leather and folded over at the knee. They had special thick leather soles, too. They wore fur hats and sheepskin coats under the white overalls with their conical black leather cuffs, but still the frosts were sharp, however much they slapped their arms and stamped. Fog-smoke settled down on the river; the plum-red sun, neither bright nor warm, glowered through the opaque air, the seeming source of cold. Like mystic, allegoric beasts, frosty-coated horses snorted steam. Thick fumes rose from the crowd, as though they were all just learning to smoke, uncontrollably streaming clouds from mouth and nose.

The main attraction for us idlers were the rows where permitted sweets were on sale—barley sugar, the sugar of the Great Fast, in plain blocks or twisted into fantastic shapes; every kind of ring-shaped bun, cracker and rusk; the dried fruits exclusively purveyed by Prokhorov, and Balabukha of Kiev, the Siamese twins of this industry. Since competition could no longer alter price, they vied instead over quality, each rival reaching ever more succulent perfection. Curiously, though, the then familiar 'pods' were in much greater demand. God knows what plant bore these violet-black pods, smooth and shiny as a grand piano, twice the size of acacia and the ordinary pea. It was a tough, sweet, woody substance that yielded reluctantly to persistent mastication, which everyone doggedly chewed as they walked, like Indians chewing betel. Their pretty, smooth surface, and the baby's rattle of their hard, oval beans, appealed to me more than their taste.

Among all the housewives, gourmets, and onlookers like myself with little more than five copecks to spend, there were *aficionados* of another trade, watching the absorbed, busy crowd with a sharp eye for their pockets and purses. Neither fish nor fair nor caviare diverted them from their single aim, to slip a hand—in pure friendliness, mind—into a stranger's pocket. Pleasantly drifting, in the midst of food, nearly everyone munched, and munching teased the appetites of the rest. There was a family atmosphere of common interest and domestic simplicity. I watched and wandered, not thinking of anything much, till the hard evening frost drove me home—one more cold-cheeked rider on the great merry-go-round that turned from dawn to dusk in those Muscovite days of early spring.

CHAPTER 11

SUMMER IN OBOLENSKOYE

THE summer of 1903 was memorable for a number of reasons, not the least being that it was our first holiday spent in the country below Moscow instead of Odessa. With the birth of a fourth child in the family, trips to the south ended. Counting our nanny, there were seven of us now, and long-distance travel became too cumbersome and tiring to be practical.

These long train journeys, repeated from year to year, settled deep in my memory. Suddenly waking in the night I would find myself not in the nursery at home, not in my familiar cot, but, as I gradually realized, in the compartment of a train. The train was waiting at some station—and there I was again, among customary and yet stirring sensations, the infinitely expressive world of sound alone. That world of secrets, gradually divulged! Different in timbre and volume came the cross hoots of shunting engines, the conductor's sharp whistle, and such a calm descending with the pointsman's bugle, way down the line! Pattering close from far away, the wheel-tapper's tocking tip-toes down the train. His long-handled hammer clacks against our wheels; his light abruptly bobs into our compartment, briefly catching my brother asleep in the opposite bunk. Intricate and incomprehensible, the night hubbub of voices on the platform drifts and then recedes. The water-carrier runs along the roof of the carriage: I can't see him, but I hear him drag his hose behind him, filling the tanks of our sink and lavatory, till they overflow in a loud cascade. The carriage has the unique smell of dusty moquette; seats and cushions in striped covers; fusty dark-brown curtains, with their two-headed eagle, and the linked monogram MKVZhD, the Moscow-Kiev-Voronezh Railway.

It was pretty exciting by day, as well. Everything seemed romantic: the shifting click of the wheels, half-forming some obsessive phrase like *what did you do? what did you do? what did you do?* interminably, on and on, till suddenly it began again: *not that! not that! not that!* And the landscapes: quite different from our Muscovite countryside, so rich in lime, birch, and pine. Vacant and unchanging, these plains stretched to the faint horizon, where the odd windmill wearily turned its heavy sails against a sky dirt-grey with heat and dust. They seemed to stay in the window for hours.

Eight years later, in 1911, I had to accompany my two younger sisters and our sadly ageing nanny down the same line, in the same fast train. In those few years much had changed, but the sounds and smells survived; only I, a grown adolescent, no longer took the old pleasure in them. When, many decades later, I was sent as an architect to blitzed Sebastopol, powerful diesels, even and unbreathing, still raced down the same route. But where were the seven or eight little rust-and-blue carriages of the past? Smokeless, steamless, scattering neither soot nor cinders, trains of inordinate length shot past even the larger stations, dropping short mechanical shrieks of warning, broken blocks of sound. In the timetables of my youth, such towns were marked with a knife and fork; the unhitched engine was refilled with water, while passengers scattered for snacks . . . Everything is different now, even the conductors and conductresses who took the place of our portly old chief guard and his underlings, in their accordion boots.

We spent the summer of 1903 not far from Moscow, on an estate set in hilly countryside of exceptional beauty and variety. Our stop (as it happened, on the Kiev-Voronezh once again) was the last before Maloyaroslavets—a little halt used only by holiday residents and goods trains. Larger trains scornfully snorted straight through, enveloping the platform in steam and dust.

On the estate, belonging to one of the Obolensky princes, there were only three chilly little wooden dachas to let. No country seat, no church services, no farmsteads, none of the normal life of a landlord and his peasantry had existed here for many years. The only vestigial sign of the estate was the halt's unofficial name, Obolenskoye (officially, it was the Hundredth Verst*). And yet, there was the estate, and its holiday houses. It rose on a fairly high promontory, jutting like a ship into the open water-meadows which stretched to the edge of the railway. Where a well-landscaped park had once been laid out, the hill was overgrown with pines, forcing out the old limes' alien beauty and taking the dry ground into their own possession. With unsuitable grandeur, this small

---

* A verst is roughly two-thirds of a mile or half a kilometre.

expanse of overgrown park consequently came to be known as the Obolensky Forest.

None the less, when winds strolled through the pines, the deep sighs of this miniature forest sounded like the high seas, and we could hear sloops and brigs, the hiss of rigging, squeak of mast and smacking sail. On peaceful days in the sun it also had the trappings of a full-grown forest: slippery pine-needles overlaid the ground in a bouncy mattress; everywhere rusty-needled, conical anthills shivered their sliding scree; colonies of squirrels high in the pines boldly scattered us with a sharp chatter of recrimination, seed husks, and tattered pine-cones when we passed.

The forest and the three dachas on its edge stood almost at the crest of the hill; to the left, a narrow, fast, and beautifully clear river (oddly known as the Puddle) appeared round the corner of the hill and flowed on into the distance. The railway-line crossed it by a little iron bridge on high brick piers. Beyond the railway a village or two, some larger houses, and parkland could be seen.*

The whole area was remote and underpopulated. The local train used to set down one or two passengers at most, and often none at all. The dacha we first hired was directly opposite the bridge: our veranda had a wide view over the river-flats and the forest brushing the skyline. The sun rose behind the bridge, and set at our backs, so that the panorama below varied with the light. It was most beautiful steeped in the red wash of evening, while on moonlit nights it was easy to imagine its winter face, as mists rose from the river and chill drifts collected in the basin below.

For some time my father had been planning a genre-painting of horses being driven to their night grazing. But this typical country sight, which my father had often seen, was evidently envisaged by him in much larger, epic terms, like the gallop of Scythian hordes. The subject first struck him when he saw a reckless cavalcade of peasant girls, riding bareback on a herd of unbroken horses. My father had done his national service in the artillery, and knew quite well what dangers lay in this unreined mass gallop over rough ground.

Every day in the neighbouring village these Valkyries could be seen herding their horses for the night. Boris and I were suitably envious. The whole scene blazed. Young Amazons on shying, liquid horses, their

* This precise setting, and a fatal accident witnessed by the family, which delayed the five o'clock express for many hours, were later transferred to the suicide described in the first chapter of *Doctor Zhivago*.

richly dyed jackets, skirts and scarves smouldering in the setting sun, the incandescent spirit of the coming gallop over the wild—it could only be called a poem in fire.

The three of us often used to wait at the village outskirts where the girls gathered—my father with his inevitable sketch-book, my brother and I as onlookers at first, then porters for his easel, folding stool, and other necessaries. Young, coquettish, and cheeky, the girls soon lost their shyness, but although they still couldn't understand what the old buffer was up to (who could make out those city types! Wasn't he taking notes or something?), they ceased to pay us much attention. Sorting the horses in preparation for the ride, they would exchange incomprehensible jokes, at which one or another would blush and draw her kerchief end across her mouth to the loud guffaws of all the rest. Lightly casting lithe bodies astride, they lingered, chatting, legs a-dangle, the horses shifting uncertainly from hoof to hoof.

It was wonderful, how casually they sat astride, without saddle or stirrup, with such easy certainty that even at full gallop they could still shout remarks to each other, loudly laughing. Their red, blue, and bright yellow kerchiefs were swept back and off their heads; their long plaited hair flew up in gorgonesque coils; their full skirts beat into a bubble with the wind; everything billowed and blazed in the sun, sinking behind our forest mound. The last light died. Crimson clouds still burned above; below, all dimmed in smoke-blue shadow.

My father had already progressed from pencil to coloured sketch. Everything promised a major new departure: with the picture's completion he knew that he would take an important step in an unprecedented direction and revitalize his art. For the first and main compositional plane he chose a beautiful bay. Its mistress, nicknamed 'The Sneck' (she had fine chiselled nostrils), had even started posing at the dacha—to my father's irritable disappointment, since she lost all her former fire seated astride a studio chair. 'A mannequin! A doll! I'd have done better with a real doll!' he used to grumble after she had left. The walls of his room were already papered with coloured sketches. Everything was moving swiftly and smoothly, not without the necessary tension, to the final stage, the picture's transference on to canvas. Parts of the composition were already marked in charcoal, and notes of colour like little buoys had been chalked in here and there.

As a large orchestra, tuning up only a minute before, suddenly falls still, waiting for the conductor's baton to set it free, so my father had everything ready. All he needed was the conductor's command to bring out easel, stretcher, chair, and oils, for his orchestra to sound in colour on the canvas . . . But neither then, as I anxiously waited, nor ever did the baton drop. And not a word was said. Everything was broken off, at a blow. My father never returned to the abandoned canvas: he even went out of his way to avoid it. Was there a reason for this unexpected conclusion? There was.

From his childhood my brother was distinguished by an inordinate passion to accomplish things patently beyond his powers, ludicrously inappropriate to his character and cast of mind. The same thing happened here. Watching the cavalcade ride out every day, he longed to test himself by the same standard. No persuasion could shift him. He bored everyone so much with his arguments that in the end they simply shrugged and let him have his head.

In spite of opposition, the day came when he managed to talk one of the girls into lending him her horse, apparently weaker and more tractable than the rest. It all began quietly. Glowing with pride, he sat astride among the motionless herd. In unison they moved off, the girls evidently restraining their horses' yearning for speed. Naturally, though, Boris's mount promptly sensed its alien rider; none too pleased, its ears began to twitch.

Calamity always comes when it is least expected.

My father took up his normal vantage point; I unfolded the easel and set it up in its habitual, marked position. We watched the accelerating cavalcade, expecting it to gallop past. This time, however, it was led not by our Valkyrie's bay, but by a black stallion whose rider chose to change the usual course. As the herd swept up to the river, the shrill neigh of a strange horse started up. Wheeling sharply behind their leader, the horses wildly flung themselves after the summons. We clearly saw Boris, bewildered and out of control, carried past on his panicking filly, which started to buck. Disconcerted by this on top of everything else, Boris began to lose his balance, failed to right himself, and dropped sideways out of sight beneath the rest of the herd that kept thundering past. Silence fell.

Everything seemed to vanish. We were at a loss what to do. Should we run up? Would we find him alive?

Running got difficult. The meadow was tussocky, the grass un-scythed, and it was getting dark. I ran on ahead. Boris was alive and conscious; in a state of shock, he could feel no pain. I raced back, leaving my father with him. Fortunately a friend and neighbour of ours, a doctor, had called at home, and other people were there. Instead of a stretcher, they took a light wicker garden couch, and snatched anything that might do for bandages. With great difficulty we carried my brother home. He seemed unnaturally heavy. The doctor set his leg; the next morning my father left for Maloyaroslavets to fetch a surgeon and a nurse. That one shock would have been enough but, at the same time, graver misfortunes outside our family occurred.* Together they put an end to the ill-fated picture, to which my father never returned.

For him it was an irreparable loss, which I can only begin to comprehend today. After all, the whole of my father's subsequent creative course might have had a different cast. A new style, a change of outlook, an artistic rebirth—none of them took place. There is no question that Boris also understood this. The irredeemable nature of my father's loss was too evident.

In the Twenties, we discovered a large, half ripped, half rotten, cherry-brown blind, which my father used to cover the southern window of his studio on the Myasnitskaya. Along with a mass of other old stuff, we had transported it from his studio to our new flat on the Volkhonka, back in 1911. When he was preparing sketches for this picture, it had evidently served him for a canvas. Over the blind's dark ground he had blocked in the coloured patches of the entire composition. The figures were nearly life-size: there was our Amazon in her bright red jacket; her sunburnt knee; her bay at full tilt . . . Those two were almost complete; other bareback riders were suggested, the blotches of glowing pink clouds. We knew nothing of this large study at the time of its composition. When we found it, it was still fresh, its colours bright and interesting, but it lay on floppy flannelette instead of canvas, badly

---

* 'I have no intention of describing in detail . . . how at Obolenskoye in 1903, with the Scriabins as neighbours, a ward of some acquaintances living on the other side of the river Protva fell into it. How a student lost his life by jumping in to save her, and how later, after having tried to commit suicide a number of times over the same cliff, she went out of her mind. How later, when I broke my leg, in one evening evading two wars, and lay pinned to my bed in plaster, the house of those acquaintances across the river caught fire, and how ridiculously the feeble village fire-bell shook and strained itself . . .

How, riding post-haste home from Maloyaroslavets with the doctor, my father caught sight of that billowing glare rising in a cloud and giving him the idea that the woman he loved, and with her his two children and a three hundredweight mass of plaster which nobody could have moved for fear of ruining it for ever, were in flames.'

Boris Pasternak, *Safe Conduct*, p. 169.
See also the same incident described in *An Essay in Autobiography*, p. 45.

stretched and loose to the touch. The pastels in which my father was working are not a long-lived medium at any time; on such a feeble base they were bound to perish fast. So they did. However carefully we protected the study from disturbance, its days were numbered.

Remembering that frail study today, after more than fifty years, I find it hurtful to reflect how slight a shock can leave a masterpiece still-born. In those years many people saw the coloured study in the flat my brother and I shared. We talked and argued about it at home. (Comparisons were drawn with Malyavin and Zorn, but in reality no such parallel could be made. All three painters were too different as people and as artists. They did not sneak sidelong glances at each others' easels, or look over each others' shoulders, but worked in isolation, absorbed by their own creative problems.) It is still deeply hurtful that my father's major work should have been cut short by external accidents unconnected with his art. It is even harder to accept that gratuitous chance should have had the force to deter him definitively. Then time, all-annihilating time, erased the last traces of that unfinished masterpiece.

Almost from the start of our stay at the dacha, my brother and I made fresh discoveries daily. It was Boris's school task for the holidays to collect a herbarium, which he did punctually and methodically, setting it out in attractive order. In pure mimicry, I made my own much less professional collection of flowers and grasses. Our pursuit often took us far afield. Then we felt like redskin braves, Leatherleg or Bearbeater, emulating their example in our camouflaged and imperceptible progress, although it was ridiculous to conceal ourselves when we knew quite well that there wasn't a soul for miles around.

If it was very hot we stayed in the forest's fresh shadows. Here grass-collecting gave way to the more absorbing study of woodland life, and our Red Indian antics acquired some justification. Prowling in a new direction through the undergrowth one day, on the trail of nothing in particular, the silence only intensified by squirrel clatter and the rare chirp of a bird, we suddenly heard a snatch of piano-playing far away. Tracking it down became the immediate object of our Red Indian skills, and we wriggled towards it with hardly a sound. At the forest crest our way was barred by an abandoned shrubbery, impenetrably overgrown; in a sunlit grassy plot beyond stood a dacha like our own.

The music came from this dacha. It sounded like somebody practising, but with a difference—there were no hesitations here, no sticking at

Musicians at the piano: drawings by Leonid Pasternak.

Scriabin. Moscow, 1909.   Rachmaninov. Moscow, 1916.

Busoni. Moscow, 1912.

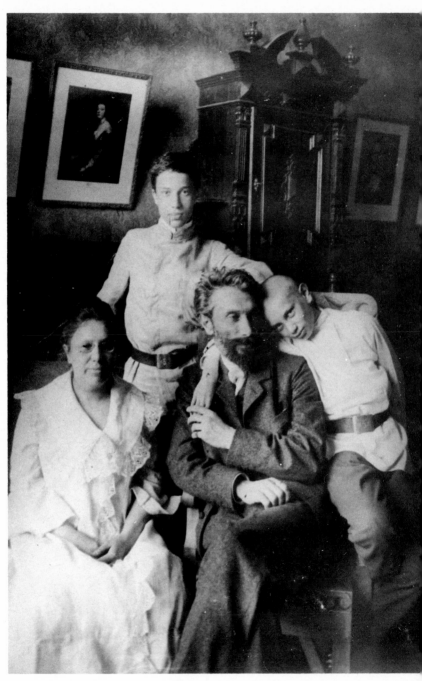

Rosa, Boris, Leonid and Alexander in the dining-room of the Myasnitskaya flat. Moscow, 1905.

difficult bits. At some bar the music would unexpectedly break off; an indistinct muttering was heard, one or two notes were repeated, as though the player were about to take a run at his piece, just as a piano-tuner tries separate keys several times over, testing himself, it seems, as well as the instrument. Then the interrupted phrase began again, played with its former unfaltering speed and accuracy, and carried a long way further on, till the grumbling mutter and tuner's repetitive check shifted to a more distant point. Between these interruptions the music ran steadily forward. Boris, understanding more than I, said that the player wasn't practising or sight-reading, but *composing* for sure.

From that day we made ourselves a perfect hide, where we could listen without fear of discovery, since there were no dogs at the dacha. The first law of the redskin is to hear and see. By the same token, prying and eavesdropping are outlawed by paleface custom. We knew all this perfectly well, but in the present case neither contradictory law affected us. Music was our only imperative, forcing us to lie low, and listen. Music, after all, had walked beside us from the day of our birth; it had taught us to come to its call, as faithful proselyte and tenderfoot disciple.

Every day my father used to go for a long walk down the Kaluga Highway, a beautiful and generally deserted road. One afternoon he came home in high good humour, and told us, laughing, that he had met a crank coming down the hill. The other fellow, though, wasn't just walking, he was bounding down, flapping his arms like a vulture or eagle trying to take off. If it hadn't been for the rigidly straight course he followed, you'd have thought he was drunk, his gesticulations were so peculiar. But it was quite obvious from his face and dress that he was stone-cold sober—probably he was just a bit touched in the head.

They often met after that. The stranger stayed true to his oddities; although his sobriety was now assured, so was his eccentricity. Finally, they started up a conversation, but even then his bounding gait and arm-waving continued undiminished. It emerged from their first exchange that he was a holiday visitor like my father, that their dacha was way over there, on the crest of that wood (and my father pointed directly to our hide), that he was a Muscovite too, called Scriabin, a musician and composer, busy this summer composing his third symphony, which he referred to in conversation as his *Divine Poem*—not as a descriptive adjective, but as its title. From that moment our father, and later our mother as well, made friends with the Scriabin family, and our secret, stolen intimacy with his music came to an end. Thirty years later my brother described it in *Safe Conduct*: in the Fifties he told it for the second time in *An Essay in Autobiography*.* Like a sculptor chipping away the finest final layer of stone, my brother laconically delineated that overwhelming music in its most concentrated form. I have no desire to water his distillation down. There only remain some sequels to that summer for me to tell.

After both families returned to town, the friendship flourished. Even in Obolenskoye I grew intensely devoted to Vera Ivanovna, Scriabin's wife. She was a most gentle, somehow special person, the embodiment of spiritual tenderness, and I loved her with the deep secret passion of a ten-year-old. In Moscow my chivalric ardour increased. In their family conflicts, whose complexity I partly understood, I naturally took Vera Ivanovna's side, without losing my enraptured admiration for Scriabin's work. When she talked to my mother about hurtful home affairs, she heroically managed to avoid giving my mother grounds for compassion towards her; on the contrary, in these conversations it seemed that Vera

---

* 'In the spring of 1903 Father rented a dacha in the country near to Maloyaroslavets on the Bryansk railway (now known as the Kiev Line). It turned out that Scriabin was our neighbour. We had not been on visiting terms with him until then.

The two houses stood at some distance from each other, beside a forest clearing on a hill. We arrived, as usually happens, early in the morning. The sun filtered into the rooms through the low branches which overhung our roof. Inside, bundles wrapped in sacking were cut open, and food, bed linen, frying-pans and pails unpacked. I escaped into the wood.

God Almighty, what that morning wood was filled with! The sunlight pierced it through and through from every side. Its moving shadows tilted its cap this way and that; and from its rising and falling branches came that always unexpected, always unfamiliar chirruping of birds which starts with loud, abrupt calls and, gradually dying down, repeats in its warm quick urgency the alternating lights and shadows of the trees running into the distance. And in exactly the same way as lights and shadows alternated and birds sang and fluttered from branch to branch, so fragments of the Third Symphony or *Divine Poem*, composed upon the piano in the neighbouring house, carried and resounded through the wood. . . .

[Scriabin] and my father would often go for walks along the Warsaw Highway which cut across the countryside not far from our house. Sometimes I accompanied them. Scriabin liked to take a run and then to go on skipping along the road like a stone skimming the water, as if at any moment he might leave the ground and glide on air. In general, he had trained himself in various kinds of sublime lightness and unburdened movement verging on flight. Among such expressions of his character were his well-bred charm and his worldly manner of putting on a superficial air and avoiding serious subjects in society. All the more astonishing were his paradoxes in the course of these country walks.

He argued with my father about good and evil and life and art, he attacked Tolstoy and preached Nietzsche's superman and amoralism. They agreed only in their conception of the essence and problems of craftsmanship, in everything else they differed.'

Boris Pasternak, *An Essay in Autobiography*, pp. 42–4.

Ivanovna was expressing pity for my mother, as though not she, but my mother, was the injured party.

In the Scriabin household I sensed then, and understood for ever after, the bitterness of division between two people who love each other, yet set their artistic vocations higher than the quiet of domestic happiness.

Such childish observations were later often confirmed.

The blow falling on an ordinary couple when they separate is severe enough. Its force is felt even more deeply in a partnership where both members are distinguished by their artistic gifts.*

At first the Scriabins visited us together, informally, sometimes accompanied by their children. As friction grew they called separately with increasing frequency. When they finally split up, Scriabin went abroad for a long time, as though to free everyone by his exile. Vera Ivanovna stayed in Moscow as before, giving many successful concerts in which she gradually restricted her repertoire exclusively to Scriabin. She was a fine musician, and since she had spent much of her life in the orbit of her husband's playing, composition, and conversation, she was unquestionably the ideal interpreter of his work. Consequently, perhaps, she was the only Moscow pianist to play his music, and to play it in his own style, while he was abroad. Of course, I can only report my own impressions, which are inevitably open to question, but in those days I heard the same opinion expressed by others who knew the playing of both intimately. I can only add that pianists who specialized in Scriabin's work, such as Konstantin Nikolayevich Igumnov, not to mention my own mother, took Vera Ivanovna as their declared model.

Our entire family spent 1906 in Germany. During that time my parents' friendship with Vera Ivanovna waned, in spite of a correspondence between them; on our return to Moscow a year later the intimacy appeared at first to pick up again, but it faltered and finally petered out altogether. After an absence of several years, Scriabin also returned to Moscow. He seemed to my parents, and indeed to Boris and myself, changed in some way—apparently renewed by theosophic theories of philosophy and art acquired abroad, and by an unprecedented, expansive view of future art, and the clear conception of his own projected compositions. As my brother wrote, 'he arrived, and rehearsals for *Extase* began straight away'.

---

* This may be an oblique reference to Boris Pasternak and his first wife, Evgenya Lourié, who was a talented artist.

Poème de l'Extase was written abroad. The Third Symphony, whose birth we had witnessed in the bushes of Obolenskoye, was first performed in Russia in the winter of 1906, when we were in Berlin. Its first conductor was Emil Kuper, who was also the first to conduct *Extase*. A few years later Koussevitsky also tried his hand at it, with less success. It is almost certain that Kuper, uniquely, studied it under Scriabin's guidance; the interpretation of such novel music must originally have depended on the composer's explanatory commentary. And of course such authorial assistance could only enhance the conductor's reputation.

From the very first my mother took me to all the rehearsals of *Extase*; Boris often accompanied us. They were held in the large auditorium of the Conservatoire, which was vast and gloomy in its unfamiliar daylight desolation. I felt shy in that resonant half-light: the lightest rustle seemed ready to set off an avalanche. No lamps were lit, and on the oval portraits opposite sunlight lay in bright, vaulted patches, creeping slowly from face to face. Aslant the hall, hewn beams of shimmering air stretched from window to wall; within their shafts bright motes danced like midges, their perpetual play of light a part of the music we heard.

First rehearsals are often most interesting for their interruptions. At the dry tap of the conductor's baton an abrupt silence falls, and a man's weak voice succeeds the full-throated orchestra, authoritatively explaining how that last phrase should be played. A new bar-line is picked, and the orchestra begins again, till the next irritable baton rap. In that alternation of sound, silence, and the single voice, the idea of the music seems to grow. Everything finds its beginnings, its bifurcations, ramifications, and final resolutions; independent threads are gathered up and led to a single conclusion. In this case the conclusion was ecstasy—a title which later appeared pretentious to my brother, but which, at that time, expressed for everyone the ecstasy demanded by the music itself. When I heard the first rehearsals (as indeed when I heard the first piano snatches of the Third Symphony), admittedly there seemed to be only the chaotic clatter and dust of a building in collapse. But the dust settled; the air cleared, and from tumbled disorder each element moved to its proper place till to our delight the music built up into a single, coherent edifice. The more we were absorbed by its destruction and restoration, the more rarely the baton tap interrupted the periodic resurgence of chaos for the broken to be made whole, the more clearly we understood the strength and originality of Scriabin's symphonic poem.

I was fifteen at that time; I loved music and listened to it constantly. But did I understand it? On the other hand, what does it matter which pictures were awakened in the mind of a fifth-former, listening over-whelmed to rehearsals of *Extase*? I saw the deluge consuming a con-demned earth; I saw the playful Creator in turbulent radiance bellowing 'I am'. In the peremptory trombones, cutting short all that went before, solid structures and intertwining ornamentations rose before me; the French horns, raised in unison towards the end, sang like a clear female choir; and in the final bars the full orchestra set sail like a clipper in full rig, triumphantly driving through wave and storm. The first chime of a bell rang out, rose and rolled over orchestra and auditorium, a flood of thanksgiving drenched in might and joy and love of life.

However often I heard that music, knowing in advance what instru-ment entered next and how each phrase would unfold, I still reached the finale shaking, bathed in a cleansing sweat as of glad and heavy labour. After Kuper and Koussevitsky, subsequent interpretations, bit by bit, diverged from the original tones which had derived in all probability from the composer himself. Now the bell is replaced by a metal tube; the French horns no longer sing out with a woman's voice, and, alas, no clipper gallantly sets sail through wave and storm . . .

In those years I took particular pleasure in music, studied the violin to little effect, attended nearly all the concerts of the time, and heard excellent music constantly at home. I had the good fortune to hear performances by three outstanding pianists: Rachmaninov, Busoni, and Scriabin. All three differed in every way, from character, behaviour, and manner of interpretation, to choice of programme. Their styles of playing confirmed these differences, yet left them on the same lofty plane of achievement.

Rachmaninov was always stern and unsmiling, his movements simple and spare. He played his own and others' compositions equally well, as though fulfilling a religious duty; the idea of service properly conveys the ascetic seriousness of his attitude. Every aspect of his personality, as composer, pianist, conductor, and individual of great gentleness and spiritual strength, was expressed in the sobriety and scrupulous simplic-ity of his performance. He usually appeared not in the conventional coat and tails, but classic frock-coat (the conductor Nikisch did the same). His playing always impressed by its masculinity: it was succulent as well as dry, somehow heavily dropping. Everyone knew his wide range, which was the envy of other musicians. He had least success with Chopin, in my view, although few must be granted the skill to play Chopin in Chopin's own manner. (And who actually knows how Chopin played?)

A performer's character is usually betrayed by the way he sits at his instrument. Rachmaninov sat at the piano as prosaically as at his desk or dinner table, a bowl of soup before him, quite forgetting the many eyes fixed on him. That's how I remember him: straight back, lightly inclined head, motionless torso, all the force of impact concentrated in his fingers, his back evidently lending no force to that inimitable fortissimo.

Busoni was the exact opposite. At the piano he struck me as a maniac enraptured by the music he transmitted, not controlling, but controlled by it, utterly in its sway. I don't know how he appeared off the concert platform, but I cannot believe that he could ever be free of music, even in his dreams. When he sat at the piano—lay on it, rather—he was drawn deep into a world of sound, till neither hall, public, or he himself appeared to exist. Deaf and oblivious himself, his insouciance infected the audience, which registered his supplementary mumbling hum, and forgave it. He was forgiven, too, his apparent indifference to the effect of his performance, bolting off-stage, barely acknowledging the ovations of the auditorium with a curt nod of the head. As this habit became known, his delighted admirers gave up clustering beside the stage, clapping and clamouring for an encore.

Busoni excelled at Bach. The distinct notes and rich timbre extracted by him suggested an organ tone. Playing more slowly than is usual for Bach, he gave the impression of improvising, lost in some distant mood of his own.

And Scriabin?

Before describing Scriabin as a performer, let me digress into history. It is easy to imagine that a musician plays like Rachmaninov, for instance, although he will never reach the quality of Rachmaninov's playing, or like Egon Petri, or Busoni. People played 'like' Medtner. That 'like' was tagged to many idols, none of whom reached the perfection of their originals. I remember, for instance, how Josef Hofmann played; he reigned supreme as the acknowledged interpreter of Chopin. Everyone imitated him. Unfortunately, it is quite impossible to listen to the recordings of those times; Grieg plays like a three-year-old; Hofmann, who seemed at the time to unite everything Chopin stood for, is insufferable now, he is musically so helpless. It is better not even to think about Ravel's recordings. Yet in talking about them we can imagine some approximation of how they might have played.

To play 'like' Scriabin, though, was a total impossibility. He was unique, in the sense that in his case even the idea of 'playing the piano' defied imitation. This was no ordinary playing, whose sounds, tones, strengths or weaknesses could be reproduced. Of course Scriabin had all that, but it receded to a secondary plane. In the foreground was his utterly idiosyncratic attitude to his instrument, and *this* was the unrepeatable secret known only to Scriabin.

It is strange: I have no memory of Scriabin on the concert platform, although I often heard his public performances. But I remember perfectly how he played in the sitting-room at home. It was here that I was struck by the persistent something, which was always the same, regardless of what pieces he chose and what mood he was in—precisely that quality which I have never experienced in anyone else's playing, before or since.

It is difficult to explain exactly. But as soon as the piano sounded, even if I sat with my eyes shut, I instantly knew that his fingers elicited the music not by dropping down on the keys and striking them (which was, of course, the factual reality), but by lightly plucking his fingers free of the keyboard. You had the complete illusion that he was drawing out of the piano a sequence of sounds constant in their light, curt force. His critics said that this was not piano-playing at all, but cats mewing and birds twittering. And yet, for all his lightness of touch, Scriabin's forte was twice as strong as that of the ordinary pianist, although it lacked the mannerisms traditionally proclaiming a 'difficult' passage—undue crashing down on the keys, emphatic pumping at the pedals and so on. His Scriabinesque forte was achieved by the contrast between it and his normal, chiming tone, and yet within the spectrum of his own sound such contrasts were great enough to achieve the right effect.

The spiritual lightness so characteristic of everything he did was reflected in his playing, as in his way of walking, gesticulating, and tossing his head in conversation. It was natural and instinctive to him, not a theatrical affectation. On the contrary, his whole appearance, the suits he wore, the way he presented himself, were all directed to the least artistic effect possible. At the piano he always sat further than usual from the keyboard, leaning with his head tilted back. Hence the impression that his fingers did not drop on to the notes, but fluttered above them.

Everything together created that light sound which was the chief beauty of his playing.

Although many first-class pianists performed his music well (for instance, Sofronitsky and Neuhaus), their playing could not and did not give the same light, fluttering impression I remember so well. But in some pieces, like the fourth and seventh sonatas, *Vers la flamme*, and *Fragilité*, Stanislav Neuhaus almost achieved that 'uncoordinated' and nervous playing so characteristic of Scriabin.

In conclusion I would like to return to a last, apparently trivial detail from the summer of 1903.

Some way from the Scriabin household, the last of the three dachas on the Obolenskoye estate had been rented out to a group of students, either from an orphanage or an old-fashioned seminary. They were sometimes to be seen, dressed in their summer uniform of dark-grey, high-necked jackets, with brass-buckled, black leather belts like the ones we wore at school, lugubriously herding like cattle down to the river for a swim. They were a beefy, inoffensive lot, evidently members of the school church choir, and were accompanied by their supervisor, a precentor and a servant. Often as I eavesdropped on Scriabin's gradually unfolding *Divine Poem*, transported from our hide in Obolenskoye into the world of my dreams, I was nearly shaken out of the bushes by the bovine bellow of a Helicon-brass breaking the summer peace, backed by a clatter of cymbals and a bass drum—the orchestra of lunkheads beyond the trees.

The piano-playing would break off at once. The orchestra's enthusiasm died as abruptly as it had been born. Complete silence fell. A bird cheeped, and the *Divine Poem* would begin again. Under such apparently insufferable conditions an entirely new music came into being.

Ever since, listening to the *Divine Poem* in its completed, orchestral form, I find myself starting at the affirmative 'I am' of the familiar, exulting brass trumpet, rising clear above the orchestra. Involuntarily, I find myself again in the bushes on those bright, clear mornings; the sound of piano-playing is broken off by that sudden, all-engulfing brass bray . . . and a blasphemous thought occurs to me. That deep trumpet-call, gloomy as an echo of the Last Trump, is extended and lightened in its development, recurring in the passages proclaiming the joy of struggle and conquest, the Bacchic revels, and the final strains, bringing blessed rest after glad labour. Is it not some kind of comment, the transfiguration of the pointless lowing of the bass tuba in the woods behind the dacha, the transformation of bovine force into the celebration of mind and will? It is not for me to say. But it is surely conceivable that such a nothing should have its undisputed right of place in the music of a creative genius.

CHAPTER 12

I'M A SCHOOLBOY

M.5.G. Three white flourishes, garlanded with oak: the grammar-school boy's cockade. The same three characters stamped in the metal clasp of his belt. Each school had its own number. M.5.G.—The Moscow Fifth School—was further distinguished by the word 'classical', meaning that Greek was taught here from the third form. This is where I went to school.

My début took place on 16 August 1903, among rows of new boys like myself. The whole school collected in the assembly hall. Everybody was dressed in the uniform of officers' grey broadcloth. The boys' heads were shaven close. Everyone stood to attention. At first I didn't know what to do with my hands, which dangled futilely by my side. Remembering the soldiers' order, '*attention!*' I convulsively clapped them to my legs.

So the first of my eight school assemblies passed. Eight times I stood beneath my number at the beginning of eight academic years. And yet, during that time, my home life remained pre-eminent. The hours spent in class were a transitory absence; coming home was still the happy return to my own world.

Our school stood on the corner of Povarskaya Street and the Great Molchanovka, in a detached Empire building belonging to the Count Golytsin family. Some old lime trees fringed the school's fenced façade, running down the Povarskaya. The yard behind looked on to the brick walls of the seventeenth-century Church of St Simeon Stylites. A number of other classic buildings of Empire design lined the street to its opening on to the square at Arbat Gates. Today not a trace remains of school, houses, or their quiet yards and gardens. All were demolished to make way for a screaming urban highway that bit straight through them. As for the square at the Arbat Gates, in its present state it is nothing more than a cartographic identification, surviving in name alone. Its architectural essence, the city square, began to be eroded many years ago.

Nowadays we are accustomed to, or have been schooled to accept, any shapeless expanse of waste land as the norm for a city square: its futile dimensions no longer distress us. But there was a time when such squares could not lack a function. Summoned to life by life itself, they were born with the strength of necessity, and emerged in harmony with the city's needs.

How, in fact, did a square grow up at the Arbat Gates?

By the fourteenth century the mercantile quarters surrounding the Kremlin had grown into suburbs of considerable size. To protect the inhabitants from the constant attacks of outside raiders, they were ringed by a dyke and battlemented ramparts, set with strongly fortified towers —and *gates*—for the trade routes to enter the city. Two such roads, from Smolensk and Novgorod, converging on each other just below Moscow, entered the city through the gates named from the suburb, the Arbat, through which they passed.

After a long and difficult journey, often threatened by the bandits common to those days, the merchant caravans and wagon trains passed through the Arbat Gates and came to rest at last within the shelter of the city walls. Naturally, night camps were pitched near the protective fortifications, the gates, and the road itself. This logical choice was consolidated by time. The horses were unharnessed at last; they were tethered, fed, and watered; wagons, and in winter sleighs, were drawn up in strict rows like a village street. Hawkers of food and drink appeared; hammering and blacksmiths' clatter started up. For the travellers, a half-settled life began. Goods were bartered, loads shifted, whole wagon trains thoroughly overhauled. All this required storage space, so sheds, barns, and warehouses appeared. New taverns and eating-houses provided food and accommodation. Life will not stand still! The former waste was now a busy, functional city square demanding a church to hallow its concerns. Three in all were summoned into being, and funds and worshippers sufficed for them all. So, 'spontaneously' (in the scornful term of modern theorists of city planning) the square at the Arbat Gates was born, to flourish for four hundred years. It seemed nothing could threaten its long and prosperous life.

But everything comes to its allotted end. Internecine warfare and the Tartar raids died out; the country entered a long period of peace, and the once vital defensive city walls lost their function. After long and faithful service they turned into an unexpected hindrance to the city's development. In the fourteenth century they had been zealously set up;

in the eighteenth they were demolished at the Tsar's decree, and the boulevard ring (surviving to this day) was built in their place. By a different royal charter the open areas, created by intersections and squares interrupting the boulevard ring, were to be emphasized by framing sets of similar, two-storeyed hotels, as planned by the architect Stasov. Thus the concept of a complete boulevard ring circling the city was brought into being—and here the problems began for the square at the Arbat Gates. In defiance of the Tsar's orders, someone took it into his head to have an imposing city theatre, instead of the standard two-storey hotels, erected on the ring's intersection with the nearby Prechistenka. The task was entrusted to the architect Carlo Rossi, who approached it with a generous flourish better suited to St Petersburg than Moscow. Before his large, fine theatre (according to eye-witness reports), he set a formal square of severe dimensions alien to the Muscovite spirit and quite out of harmony with its neighbour, the ancient square at the Arbat Gates, which was smaller, more intimate, and residential in character.

The theatre survived a mere five years, burning to the ground in the Napoleonic fires of 1812. It was never rebuilt, and soon forgotten, while its widowed square continued to drag out a futile existence no architect found means to justify. Distinct yet linked, the two squares, set side by side, led the uncomfortable existence of Siamese twins.

At first they were distinguished by name, one known as the square at the Arbat Gates, the other as Arbat Square; I used to cross both daily on my journeys to and from school. All efforts to unite them, and equally, to part them definitively, ended in failure. Matters grew worse when the new trend for urban development led to the square's clearance (for by this time the two were seen as one shapeless whole). First the Church of Boris and Gleb, fronting the square at the end of Vozdvizhenskaya Street, was pulled down. I remember the corner well: the horse-drawn tram taking me to school used to turn sharply off the street into a narrow alleyway skirting the church. With the speed of modern traffic such a narrow corridor was, of course, indefensible: the church fell, leaving a small vacant plot. The beginning was hardest: after that, everything went swimmingly. A large three-storeyed building ending the Nikitsky Boulevard was removed, to open up a perspective no one wanted. It was worse when the old Empire house containing the Zalessky Store (known to every schoolboy; we bought all our school materials there) was also destroyed. It stood on the corner of the square at the beginning of

Vozdvizhenskaya Street, and with its demise the square's consolidating corner was lost. As house after house was bulldozed into oblivion, the square's clear confines ebbed further and further, while new patches of uncovered waste intensified its amoeboid shapelessness. The end came when a new avenue was driven into it, and an underpass dug at right angles beneath it, to accommodate a complex knot of traffic in the intestinal convolutions of overpass, underpass, and pedestrian subway. Thus ended the history of Arbat Square and the square at the Arbat Gates, their combined fate originating in an error never completely understood. Had the line of the boulevard simply been continued till it crossed the square at the Arbat Gates, and the architectural system conceived by Tsar Paul I been correctly maintained, it might have survived to the present day.

Scarcely half of my first year at school had passed before our cruiser *Varyag* sank in Chemulpo in February 1904, triggering off the Russo-Japanese war that had long been rumoured as a possibility. And yet, in spite of prognostications, we were unprepared. The immediate flood of boastful posters and jingoistic journalism didn't stop even us first-formers seeing that the war was being conducted with colossal incompetence. The unfortunate soldiers suffered from the enemy Japanese and their own superiors alike. Everything slipping through the censor spoke of the high command's stupidity, while the official dispatches drivelled improbable adulatory eulogies of valiant Cossacks and dauntless Russian derring-do. Everything was stilted and idiotic, not least the officers' identical telegrams from the front, repeating each other word for word: 'Having swept across the Urals, we send our relatives and friends . . .' and so on. These stereotyped messages were to be read in the papers daily, as though the most important achievement in the war was to cross the Urals. It was so ludicrous that in the school corridors we used to shout to one another, 'Having swept across the Urals, we're going on an outing today!', or 'Having swept across the Urals, I got a gamma for maths!'

The war was distant and well-nigh inaccessible. Moscow hardly felt it at all: it impinged on us first-years personally only once, when we saw our form-master off to the front.

Teaching us was probably Nikolai Nilovich Filatov's first job after university; he gave every sign of being a quivering novice. I speak of course with hindsight; at the time, his youth was an attractive contrast to his hardened, hoary colleagues. Everything he did proclaimed his nervous inexperience: his flight through the classroom to the haven of the teacher's rostrum, miraculously failing to trip over the dais every time; the way he grabbed the saving text-book for the first lesson of the day. At first he wore a half-unbuttoned black civilian frock-coat that flapped with every convulsive swivel and turn. He was very popular then: right from the start, his callowness inhibited our usual bent for mischief. In appearance, too, he was a welcome change from the usual old school walrus. He had a prominent red beard, which he would suddenly jut out with a jerk of his head at the end of a sentence, amiably smiling, as though to say, 'There! fooled you, didn't I?' Gradually, however, this lovable trait began to irritate us, and while his endearing shyness died away with time, that mannerism stuck till the end of his short school career.

When Nikolai Nilovich came into the classroom as an ensign in the reserves, he changed in nothing but his warlike exterior, which now matched that of every Russian officer of the time—wide, black, red-piped breeches ballooning to the top of crumpled boots; a dark-green regimental jacket with a collar so tight it looked as if it was forged of iron; stiff cuffs, embroidered with little golden railway sleepers, like a roman II. But although he was now the ensign-bearer of officerdom, the uniform led an independent existence from him, and instead of moving in a military manner, Nikolai Nilovich continued to jerk, stutter, and jut his beard in the most unregimental way. Until recently I managed to preserve a photograph taken just before his departure to the front—an amateur snap which unfortunately faded, and finally crumbled away. Out in the school yard, the whole class is collected round Nikolai Nilovich, fixed in the traditional pose. In spite of the cold, he sits without his overcoat. His cap, peak to the fore, rests on his knees. His hands grip the sabre planted between his legs . . .

On his departure, our class decided to give him an image of his patron saint—a customary gift at that time. To his surprise, almost the entire class appeared at the station with the offering. It was evening.

Seeing people off is always painful, not merely because parting is sad. The very length of the process is dispiriting. Everything has already been said; enough wet eyes have been rubbed dry; ever heavier silences damp the jolly cries of safe journeys and happy returns, and still the train, almost out of spite, refuses to move. My own natural feelings at such station partings vanished quite quickly—not because I was more unfeeling than the rest, but because I soon lost myself in the more vital, real world surrounding the silent gathering at the carriage doors. So it was then. At first this leave-taking with a real soldier on his way to war absorbed me. I noticed, to my surprise and sorrow, that no one apart from us schoolboys, neither family nor friends, was there to see him off. It was nice how touched he seemed to be by our modest present. He kissed the medallion and ran straight off into his compartment. Our two representatives followed him, while the rest of us loitered behind, rather bored. Quite different farewells were being exchanged in the neighbouring carriage, with loud tears and lamentations, shrieks and embraces. Grieving faces mingled with the ring of spurs, dry crack of heels, snatches of command and snake's hiss of flaring station lamps. In the darkness far down the tracks, sad engines hooted and the pointsman's bugle was melodically calling. Absorbed in these familiar sounds, I hardly registered the train's first tug free of the crowded platform, jolting and squeaking on cold springs. Hand to his breast on the carriage step, Nikolai Nilovich was slowly drawing away from us into the mist and dusk. At the turn of the tracks his train disappeared, its red tail-light winking a final farewell. Free of the anchor of timetables, it travelled on at speed through the night, and while we descended the station steps, the passengers had already begun their new life. Changed into comfortable travelling clothes, one makes up his bunk, swaying to the beat of the train; another steps into the corridor, to lean by the window and smoke; a third, undecided, yawns in uniform still . . .

How many of them returned from the front? Why, this was the Russo-Japanese war!—the first of four wars in my lifetime, inglorious and most ignominious at its end.

What impression did it make on me then? It is hard to isolate in their purity the feelings of a first-former from the later, fused layers of accumulated opinion about that notorious war. At home we cannot have talked much about the war itself, more about the reaction to it—the conduct of the high command, the responsibility to the people, the possible consequences, the certain expectation of revolution as the price to be paid. All this I heard and remember. Similar conversations would have flourished at school, if the sleepless eye of authority had not withered them at a glance. Yet what were the lavatories for, if not for the anxious exchange, here at least, of rumour and surmise?

In town everything kept step with the strut of the two-headed Imperial eagle. The nation may have seethed secretly, but the surface was calm;

like a pond smothered in duckweed, it was plastered over with posters in whose potency the state had infinite faith. Those ubiquitous, monstrous posters! Who could ever have thought them up, and for what? I can swear with absolute certainty that they never fulfilled their intended aims. Oh, but they did achieve the reverse effects, as often as you could wish.

People of my generation will probably remember those wartime posters. They were meant to suggest the cheap prints of popular literature, with their bright, improbable colours, and strong salt of folk humour. Alas, the posters achieved neither the one nor the other; they were distinguished only by their counterproductive passion to persuade. The Japanese were uniformly portrayed as knock-kneed weaklings, slant-eyed, yellow-skinned, and, for some reason, shaggy-haired—a puny kind of monkey, invariably dubbed 'Japs' and 'macaques'. Opposing them were the legendary heroes of our army, Russian stalwarts and the Manchurian Cossacks (distinguished by their yellow, rather than red, braided trousers). One poster, for instance, displayed a swarm of spider-like Japs, faces twisted with fear, vainly trying to struggle out from under a huge Caucasian fur hat. The caption ran, 'Catch them by the capful!' On another, an Olympian hand squeezed a fistful of macaques, legs and arms writhing in their last agony. The *chef d'œuvre*, I remember, was a Cossack, riding at the trot with lance aslant his shoulder, a clutch of Japs skewered on it like rats on a spit, while another, in flight, was about to be transfixed. We knew the reality well enough! We knew that the Japanese won not by heroism, but by their swiftness and skill in manoeuvre, their excellent new arms, and above all, their use of camouflage. The whole army was dressed in khaki, the colour of the scrub where the battles took place. No wonder that after this war khaki became the standard battledress of the English army, and then of all the world. Yet our Russian soldiers still wore their old-fashioned tropical uniform of white shirts and jackets. Together with the multicoloured insignias of the different regiments, they made a perfect target for the enemy, who could map their disposition and movement from a great distance. The Japanese, furthermore, relied principally on the machine-gun, a weapon we lacked altogether at the beginning of the war. No wonder the posters lacked popular impact. In response to the slogan, 'Catch them by the capful!', people used to say sourly, 'Better shell them!', or 'Only idiots fight with their caps nowadays!'

Naturally the general war-spirit found its way into our daily play. The toys and table games sold in the shops were adapted to it, with the intention of inculcating patriotism, veneration for Tsar and fatherland, and faith in the might of Russian arms. I cannot tell whether they succeeded in general, but they certainly had no such effect in our home, although we too had games like these.

I remember one in particular, because either Boris, or one of his friends, Shura Shtikh or Misha Romm, turned it into a version of chess. Originally it was a game of chance, of the usual Snakes and Ladders type, called 'War at Sea'. There was a board, marked with the conventional squares of triumph and disaster, a roulette wheel, and four tin battleships, Russian and Japanese, for the four players. In its new form the game had different rules, governing the destroyers' various moves, artillery loads, and vulnerability to attack. We made up a large new fleet out of my father's modelling clay, using the four tin ships as models, and drew a comprehensive map of the sea, marked with the Russian and Japanese coastlines, gulfs, bays, reefs, shoals, islands, and coastal forts. It must have been made up of several sheets of paper stuck together; it was so big that the table couldn't accommodate it, and it had to be spread out on the floor.

Boris probably invented the game, but its *juridical* side, as they called it, was the work of Misha Romm. He was a morose, gawky teenager, a little older than Boris, with a sharp tongue and unquestionably sharp wit. A good-humoured smile perpetually played about his mouth, while his grey eyes stayed imperturbably serious. Boris and Misha were leaders in the game; I was only enlisted out of necessity, to serve as the fourth player. When one of the older boys, absorbed by his opponent's Machiavellian strategies, gloomed over the map for hours, pondering a complex countermove, I used to get fed up and fidgety, and wander off unnoticed.

One day Boris was caught out by a decisive ambush into which Misha's flotilla had enticed him. It was a catastrophic defeat: Boris's fleet was blown to bits. Pale and silent, he got up off the floor without a word, and walked straight out of the room. Poor Misha, the triumphant victor, looked aghast. Such dire occurrences were quite common with Boris. (They were a trait to which I will return in more detail later.) We all knew that it would be crazy to go after him, ask him what was wrong, try to talk him round, or, worst of all, to show any sympathy. From that day, I never saw the game again. I have no idea where it was hidden. It never surfaced in any of the great tidying sessions and redecorations that regularly took place in our flat. Perhaps one of the others took it off home with him, to spare Boris the memory of his fleet's humiliation and categoric destruction.

Meanwhile the war, the real war, continued miserably. The laconic formula, 'so-and-so died a warrior's death', recurred with increasing frequency in dispatches and newspaper reports—as though that were the ultimate absolution from all sins, the final consolation for bereaved and deceased alike. The destruction of a great battleship, with her cargo of a thousand lives in the waters of Port Arthur, one April night, was more than that; it was a heavy blow to the country, to Russia itself.

Everyone, including the Admiral, died on the *Petropavlovsk*. Admiral Makarov was a great innovator and reformer of Russian marine power, in whom all the sailors of the new type had high hopes, although the entire naval and non-naval supreme command was ranked against him. His death was an irreparable loss for the Russian navy. The death of the artist and war correspondent, Vereshchagin, was an equivalent cultural loss for the nation. Vereshchagin sailed out of harbour with the rest of the *Petropavlovsk*'s crew, to record his impressions of the sailors' lives; he died with them in the first minutes of its journey.

Vereshchagin's work, which is sufficiently well known and widely hung in our galleries and museums, has been accounted, perhaps justly, as outmoded in manner and subject: it was a typical product of the Wanderers school. Yet in his own time he was an important military artist. Granted his work held no interest for a new generation. Granted his large, laboured canvases with their harsh images of war, pyramids of skulls, and bones scattered about the desert sands, were not transcriptions of reality, but cool concoctions of the studio—a combination of sketches, memory, and posed models. Granted all that! Those canvases in their heavy frames may long have ceased to breathe living breath for us, yet they are the work of a formidable artist who knew, for instance, how to dispose an exhausted soldier in flight across an enormous canvas; how to drive the dead-beat through the infernal blaze of midday, and yet not let him drop, all the balance of the dying man captured in his last steps. He knew exactly how the southern sun in a naked sky consumes all colours away, not intensifying them to the rich brightness we expect. He did not paint his Turkish and Asian skies a glaring ultramarine; he was not shy of the misty ash of heat-haze, the light grey-blue of cobalt.

He was invited to become a war correspondent once again, and he agreed, wishing to cast off age and his old devotion to the Wanderers.

Who knows? Maybe, when he agreed to join the battleship and its crew, he dreamt of an artistic rejuvenation in the new study of sailor life? Who dare say that his hopes might not have been fulfilled?

How merciless fate is! At night, when spirits were high, the absurdity of chance suddenly overturned all hopes. A tinpot brickbat beat the giant, a pebble from a popgun, more devastating than all its opponent's sophisticated accoutrements, its officers, sailors, soldiers, armour-plating and arms. With unslackened speed, the dead destroyer sank through the waves, waterspouts bursting into each watertight compartment, crammed with its living dead.

Peace to the men of the *Petropavlovsk*!—and peace to you, Vereshchagin!

The other master who evoked in us an even greater longing for friendship and intimacy than Nikolai Nilovich Filatov was our young teacher of geography and natural history, Alexander Sergeyevich Barkov. An enthusiastic and gifted naturalist, he later became a university professor and member of the Academy. We were proud that he treated us like the older boys, setting us interesting homework, and in class teaching us by dialogue, rather than rote, as the other masters did. In our final year, six or seven out of the class of ten (strange now to think that there were never more than fifteen of us!) studied biology with him. Each of us had a proper microscope, with three adjustable lenses and an attractive pale wooden case; young as we were, we studied with careful absorption, and enjoyed making sections, staining and sealing them with balsam.

From the start, whatever we learnt in theory during the winter was shown to us in nature rambles that began with the earliest warm spring days. Those excursions! There we really drew close to Alexander Sergeyevich, sensing in him an older brother, rather than a stiff-collared, dress-suited master. From him we learnt a love of all country things. Together we admired a dragonfly which, after long quivering, settled at last on a stem with still trembling, transparently netted wings; or a tiny frog, no bigger than a sequin, flipping across our path . . .

We prepared for his excursions carefully, leaving home with specimen box, net, and black oilskin with its curious smell rolled into a tight bolster and slung, as a cadet or policeman might, by a strap across the shoulder. At school we were arranged in a crocodile with Alexander Sergeyevich at the head, and Vasily, the school cleaner and caretaker, bringing up the rear. He was an old friend of ours whom I remember perfectly, with his faded old uniform buttoned up to the throat.

We marched past our form master, who taught us gym and drill, out of the school yard and on to the Povarskaya, keeping rank till he was out of sight. By the time we got to the first stop of the horse-drawn country tram, our crocodile had degenerated into a tangle of happy children, clustered round Barkov and Vasily, our companions now. The best trips were to the steep banks of the Moscow River, where Alexander Sergeyevich led us into the strange new land of palaeontology. On those sunny banks all school laws were forgotten. Chucking down jackets and caps in a heap for Vasily to watch, we clambered over the escarpments, grubbing for ammonites, nut-shaped belemnites, and devil's fingers. Offering up our finds for Barkov's praise and blessing, ears hot from happy excitement, we would stow them in our cases, wrapped in soft tissue and cotton wool. And some of those rare ammonites really were beautiful. In the moist black crumble and grey sliding dust something would suddenly glint in the sun. Carefully scraping the earth aside with fingers or a little scoop, you uncovered a tiny medallion of gold. Cupping it in your palm, you blew it clean, tenderly so as not to damage the delicate fossil that had lain in the earth thousands of years, just for you to find it. There was a reason for red ears! When you had blown away the dirt, and dusted it with a little brush, the sunlight set it burning in deep rainbow tones over its clear gold base. With words of praise, Alexander Sergeyevich would carry you away with wonderful hypotheses of what might have been here, below this river bank, so many aeons ago . . .

I used to come home happy and tired, with grubby clothes and dusty hair. Proudly, I would unpack my find to the family's exclamations, and Boris would carry it off, to add to our joint collection. The new addition would be scrupulously cleaned of dust and cotton-wool wisps; a shellac solution was shaken up in surgical spirits, and with a squirrel-hair brush Boris would paint the fossil with preservative varnish. Under that shining film the spiralled coils of its surface looked like the work of a master goldsmith, a treasure that should be laid on the bilberry-black velvet of Mamma's jewel boxes—with the rest of her *bijoux*, as she called them.

The year before I started school I had already begun a botanical collection in imitation of my older brother. Then, of course, I could not hope to emulate his exquisite displays. Now we too learnt from Alexander Sergeyevich, as Boris had done before us, all the secret skills of a herbarium; now my folders were no worse than those which had aroused my timid rapture the summer before, in Obolenskoye.

Once when I was telling my granddaughter about the paraffin lighting in our first flat, my wife asked me whether we too had a magic lantern in our childhood, as she had?

Of course, of course we did!

And everything—lantern, pictures, and all—was identical, down to the smallest detail. I cannot remember now when that wonderful thing appeared in our household: most probably in our earliest years, because I remember Mamma being in charge of it, whereas later, in the new flat on the Myasnitskaya, Boris demonstrated it to our younger sisters, soon handing that task on to me.

'Children, the magic lantern is on the table!' our mother calls from the drawing-room, which looks quite different from usual. The chairs are set out in a tidy row across the middle of the room, and in front of them a sheet has been stretched over the wall. The small, heavy, carved table has been brought out of Papa's room: on it stands the familiar wooden box, covered with glazed paper, green with irregular black splodges like a large frog's back. Our mother takes up her post beside it, like a ship's captain about to give orders, but all she says is 'Sit down, now!' to my brother, myself, and our friends. We watch anxiously for her to throw back the catches and open the box. Inside lies a black, smooth something, reflecting the light of her candle. This is it, the magic lantern! A short, squat cylinder of black enamelled tin is slid out of the box's grooves and set on the table. It is firmly attached to a base of two thin boards, which in turn are fitted into the runners of the lantern's wooden pedestal. All these wooden parts are painted a vile matt red. A kerosene lamp is put on the stand, so that its glass funnel fits inside the lantern's black cylinder, which has two apertures at back and front.

To tell the truth, it wasn't the subject and quality of the pictures that counted; although we knew them inside out, we still met them like new acquaintances. No, the charm evidently lay in the adjustment of the *focus*—magic word, which in Mamma's presentation became a kind of conjuror's *hocus-pocus*! With that, the little pictures would suddenly loom to almost human size on the screen, and their watery blur contract to a crisp outline. After a time, the room filled with a warm, pleasant smell, as it did on winter evenings round the Christmas tree. Then it was the scent of resin, pine needles, and melted candle wax; now the smell of burning kerosene and the lantern's hot black lacquer. There was, too, the room's unusual gloom, intensified by two sole patches of light, on ceiling and screen—a special darkness, where no one slept, and everyone was enjoying themselves. Everything added to the secret wonders of the magic lantern, as I knew it in my earliest days.

By the time I was a schoolboy, however, the secret wonders had faded. The red mount fell to bits, and the last vestige of mystery was lost when the window-glass dropped out. Boris, who had taken over from our mother by this time, decided to extend the old stock of pictures by painting new ones on tracing paper begged from our father. But he didn't foresee that all their sense would be lost when they were magnified many times their size. Our disappointed younger sisters clamoured for the old originals, which Boris slotted into the projector, jiggling it about so that everything on the screen began to move, like the shipwrecks and earthquakes of the early cinema. The spirit of the new century was partially reflected in Boris's innovation; there was already an impulse to animation in the air. We first met it in a curious novelty sent to us by our uncle in Vienna . . .

This was a set of attractive albums with what looked like ordinary snapshots, stuck on to thick paper and stoutly bound. But neither albums nor photographs were ordinary at all: when you turned the pages over, quickly and smoothly, the dead pictures suddenly came to life. Under your very eyes!

Each album had its own theme and its own characteristic movement. One was given over to so-called *concours hippiques*—a horse and rider leapt at full tilt over a series of obstacles. Another album had soldiers exercising on the parade-ground. Judging by their uniform of sporting kepi and long trousers (worn outside the boots) they were Austrians who drilled so energetically: 'Attention', 'Shoulder arms', 'At ease', and so on. The third album showed you the chaotic movement of traffic and pedestrians on a crowded, possibly Parisian street. The great difficulty was to keep up the rhythm as you leafed through. Boris became such an expert that his horse sailed over fence and ditch without perceptible hesitations. The rider beat its neck as it raced over the ground; when it was airborne, he seemed bodily to heave himself over the fence, dragging the horse behind him, rising in his stirrups and leaning forward well beyond his mount. Boris managed it all perfectly. But my little soldiers only jolted about in the most curious way; their exercises disintegrated into jerky, broken episodes, as my butterfingers let too many pages past at once. And sometimes we purposely broke the rhythm for grotesque comic effects.

Boris was determined to master the secret of the albums. We used to study individual photographs for hours, particularly amazed by the incredible pictures taken in mid-action. That horse, for instance, nose practically burrowed into the ground, braced on its front legs, while the back ones dangled in the air. Could a horse really stand like that? We tried to put ourselves in the same positions, and fell every time. Then again, how was it possible that a horse should hang suspended like a bird over the fence, without impaling itself? But when we leafed through quickly enough, it simply made its leap and landed, without a hint of catastrophe—just as we could jump a rope without dropping in mid-air. Gradually we worked out that each photograph differed from the next in some imperceptible detail, and that if you skipped several pages the difference became obvious. In the end we came to the conclusion that everything in nature acted in the same way as we saw here; there was an uninterrupted chain of infinitesimal movements, a small number of which had been caught by the camera. Boris made this discovery, which had a truly overwhelming effect on us both. Later, it also helped us to imitate the early films we saw, for our younger sisters' entertainment: we too made those odd, jerky motions that drew us away from the action of nature, to its unnatural image on the screen.

Erman's Emporium, the pharmacy I have referred to more than once, had a special attraction for me, because the owner recognized us as regular customers, and used to give us little presents as a reward for our purchases. At first these used to be curious glossy white postcards, with 'surprises' which you could discover on your return home by rubbing the card with a ten-copeck piece. Black patches would gradually coalesce into a picture—usually, to my disgust, that of the same soldier of some alien fleet, tediously caught in mid-trot across a bowsprit, gaily waving, a heavy kitbag slung from his shoulder. Later, another sign appeared alongside that of the Emporium, advertising a new 'cinematograph' (with the accent on the second 'a'), for which Erman's began to issue free entrance tickets. Evidently it was an arrangement of mutual advantage to both concerns.

In spite of its imposing name, 'The Cinematograph of the Brothers Pathé' would have appalled any fireman chancing to glance inside. Fortunately for the proprietors, I never saw anyone there except hot, excited children, and the rare adult, curious to know what the 'cinematograph' was and who these brothers with the strange name might be.

Everything from projector to auditorium was ludicrously home-made and primitive. Quite obviously an ordinary, rather low-ceilinged first-floor apartment had been gutted to create a little hall, reached directly from the main house-stair. Perhaps as a precaution against fire, the door had been lifted off its hinges and replaced by a heavy red-plush curtain, which was drawn tight during performances, to block out the light from the stairwell. Ordinary Viennese chairs were set out in two or three rows, and, in contradistinction to all later cinemas, the Pathé projector, with its trademark of the cockerel 'who sees and knows all things', stood in *front* of the audience, reminding me of the old magic-lantern shows at home. It was set up on a primitive trestle stand, and in front of it hung the screen—if not a sheet like ours, then some equally makeshift substitute, which used to billow in mid-performance.

The projectionist cum proprietor, usher, cashier, and cleaner all in one, announced the film's subject and extinguished the overhead light, leaving a single small lamp glowing by the entrance. The sessions were short, not because the films were, but because his projector quickly overheated and there was a danger of the film catching fire. During the fifteen or twenty minutes of the film's duration we would sit motionless, transported far from our daily Moscow life by the new world on the screen, where everything seemed magic, not least because ordinary photographs sprang into motion, figures waved hands and legs, eyes blinked, and mouths stretched wide in laughter.

Of course I can remember little of the repertoire. Often we were shown newsreels taken by the French on the battlefields of the Russo-Japanese war—Liaoyang, Mukden, and the banks of the Shakhé river. There we saw with our own eyes the attacks of the Siberian Cossacks, the movement of armies, and scenes of battle on our own front line. We were well aware that the men we saw fell not at a photographer's whim, but in earnest . . .

What if everything twitched and jerked? It was still the movement of the immovable, and we accepted it as such; not as a travesty of that smooth, uninterrupted flow that is nature itself, but as its documentary proof and evident confirmation. Grateful and reverent, we left the little hall with a wonderful feeling of having participated in a world of visible miracles, a sensation so strong that this is what I remember now, while the pictures which summoned it to life have been utterly forgotten.

CHAPTER 13

SAFONTYEVO

FOR a long time Papa had dreamed of a trip abroad, to see the museums in Holland, Belgium, and Spain. At home we knew how vital this was for him, but our habitual financial difficulties made it impossible—a situation not unique to our family, incidentally, but common to all the intelligentsia.

Consequently, when he came running home one day with a big, yellow envelope in his hands, the stamp of the German state resplendent in its left-hand corner, we were delighted. We knew that boldly stylized single-headed eagle from our German stamp collection—everything in it stressed the bird's predatory qualities, its braced talons, crooked beak, flattened head, its malignant angularity. By comparison, our Imperial two-headed eagle looked more like a placid farmyard fowl, a straddle-legged pullet bedecked with iron frills and furbelows, the orb and sceptre in each claw robbing them of their malevolent sharpness; the crowns on its two heads like tin dowager mob-caps.

In the envelope was a sheet of glossy paper with the same awe-inspiring eagle embossed on the letterhead, fiercely guarding its con-tents—a functionally brief invitation to take part in the international art exhibition at Düsseldorf, and the added request that my father should organize the section devoted to contemporary Russian painting and sculpture.

The exhibition was due to open in the May of that year, 1904. The invitation was attractive for two reasons. After Munich, Düsseldorf was the centre of the newest trends in German art; it was here that the Secessionists (a splinter group breaking away from the academic school) were established. French Impressionist originals were to form the basis of the exhibition; they were going to be shown in Germany for the first time. Equally, the Russian artists invited to participate would be introducing the Germans to the most recent Russian art. But the invitation to organize the Russian section had one even more important aspect: my father would be taking upon himself not only all the donkey-work, but the selection and arrangement of the exhibition as well. At the same time, the offer resolved all his difficulties about a trip abroad. Small wonder that we were proud and happy for him. Fortunately, he foresaw many problems of selection, and on my mother's advice asked some colleagues from the Union of Russian Artists to work with him. They were, I think, Korovin, Arkhipov, and, possibly, but my memory is uncertain, Pereplechikov. Serov he decided to leave unmolested, consulting with him informally, as was habitual to them both in other matters.

The process of selection turned out to be a tiresome and unpleasant task. At first the troika (or perhaps it was a four-in-hand) ran side by side with unanimity and enthusiasm. But the first impetus failed, and differences began to emerge. They were slight enough at first, but soon swelled to graver divergencies in taste and evaluation—'particular attitudes' which were natural enough, but complicated everything. Maybe politics muddled matters even further. Increasingly, the final decisions unanimously agreed on during one session were subjected to new doubts and discussions at the next. This uncertainty of opinion, not based on any fixed principles, worried my father intensely, all the more because his deadlines were approaching. The Exhibition Committee, not understanding the reasons for the delay, bombarded him with letters, at first in the form of polite queries, then reminders, and finally urgent demands for the immediate dispatch of his list for inclusion in the general catalogue. When the Committee had him by the throat, he finally asked my mother to help. She took upon herself her habitual role of personal secretary, and matters improved. But when the all-powerful voice of the Transport Office joined the impatient chorus, they began to move at full speed. The company of Gerhard and Gey, well known to the entire artistic world, had been chartered to transport the pictures to Germany. Their long, dark-red van, big as a one-storey barracks, appeared in our courtyard as it had often done before, by the shed where the pictures for exhibition were stored; it was loaded, and set off without a hitch on its long journey.

Now, at last, my father could also prepare for departure. All the nervous anxiety of the last three weeks was dispatched with Gerhard and Gey's van, and we were left in peace. When the pictures arrived safely, he set off himself, tired but with a quiet conscience, for three months abroad. My mother began looking for somewhere to spend the summer; for the first time in our lives, we would go to the country without my father. But since he always left holiday arrangements to his wife, she knew just what to do. On a friend's recommendation she chose a small house 'somewhere on the Istra', which a Moscow landowner and notary was letting for the entire summer. In his office on the Iversky Gates, my mother and I were shown a photograph of a small 'manor house', as he styled the stone building, deep in the stormy green of an 'ancient park'. The estate's neglect appealed to my mother at once. She travelled down with the proprietor to look it over, and shook hands with him on the spot. Our summer was decided—but our school year still had to drag to an end, its last days passing in a flat that had become unusually stuffy. The school doors finally closed behind us. Then our dear, kind Kuzma, the library watchman and habitual aide in all such domestic affairs, appeared in our flat at first light, Ivan Kotov close behind him. Ivan was an interesting type—a frequent model in my father's life classes, a muscular fellow like a blacksmith, who always used to refer to my father, with his quick, stumbling mispronunciation, as 'Lenyosipich'—a kind of shorthand for Leonid Osipovich.

Kuzma, the more 'belicate' of the two, packed up china and glass in sweet-smelling hay, meticulously stowing away lamps and other break- ables in huge crates. The herculean Kotov sewed up beds, mattresses, and other indispensable 'nurniture' in fresh bast matting, and corded up massive chests, bales, and hampers. We kept out of the way. They knew what had to be done. They came with the exact number of squat, pressed hay bales, tightly belted with thin iron strips; they hired carts and brought them into the yard at the correct moment; they and the carters loaded them and covered them with tarpaulin, securing it tightly. Then—the final act in our drama—our chambermaid and cook were settled in some comfortable cranny. Caps in outstretched hands, the carriers punctiliously crossed themselves, gathered up the reins, and seated themselves on the side of the carts. With a threatening bass bellow 'Giddee up!', the journey began.

Year after year I was surprised how they found their way unerringly to a completely unfamiliar destination, arriving, on time, at the precise spot—a little jolly, perhaps, but with their animate and inanimate cargoes intact.

Safontyevo! The name suggests nothing to you, or any other Russian. But for the whole of our family it became the sound and synonym, the very symbol of the most pitiable poverty imaginable, and an even acuter poverty of spirit. Here we spent two consecutive summers, not at all badly, a mere sixty versts from the capital.

Yet I only need to remember the roads from the nearest railway station, New Jerusalem, or the more distant market town, Voskresensk, to give up expectations and astonishment alike. What could the peasants do? The distance from those centres of cultural life were negligible enough: a good fifteen versts, according to the local carters; in actual fact rather less. But even on horseback you would squander three hours and more on those few versts, and it was much quicker to go on foot. More than once we savoured the special delights of that journey in some unsprung gig or antediluvian droshky that still ran on rubberless, iron-bound wheels. The first time, my mother was seriously frightened. The river had to be forded; half way across it came well over the gig's sides, forcing us to lift our legs nearly as high as the driver's box. For all his assurances that it never reached the seats, it was pretty uncomfortable sitting there with the water flowing swiftly and freely beneath us. It didn't last long; the little horse, phlegmatic as its driver, slowly drew us out of the deepest part, and we settled ourselves in a more human fashion once more, swinging our legs down on to floorboards wet and gleaming in the sun.

But after that! At a certain point the dusty, beaten-up cart-track took a turn through a bog—a runny dough whenever it rained, sucking up gig and droshky to the wheel-hubs. Drivers preferred to make a long detour through virgin land to one side, inevitably turning it into the same impassable swamp. (The sight is a familiar one on our country roads even now.) And even when the cart-track was dry, no one drove down it anyway; everyone preferred to dismount beside the lurching *tarataika*, hopping beside it from one rut to the next.

But there, everything is behind us now! The village can already be heard in the distance; a dog's barking comes from far away; cocks are crowing. The road rises up a gentle incline. The driver takes a right turn, leaving the village to our left behind us. Passing between two crumbling obelisk gateposts, we drive down a well-made road through the seigneurial part of the estate. The horse puts on a final spurt; the driver, cheered by the prospect of a vodka, livens up as well, and we roll jauntily up to a stone house, the goal of our difficult journey.

I didn't like going to the village, which lay to one side of our usual walks, and even avoided glancing into it. But I had to go there, all the same,

when I helped my father in his work, carrying his easel and umbrella for
him, or whatever got in the way of his quick sketching. And I had to go
there with my mother, on excursions for milk and curd cheese. Walking
with manly stride behind her, I carried back earthenware jugs of warm
milk, and baskets of transparent, freshly laid eggs. Here I first had the
chance to see decayed Russian peasantry in all its ugly destitution. And
yet the sight evoked neither pity nor sympathy. On the contrary, I was,
quite simply, angry at what I saw. The villagers' passive submissiveness,
their total indifference to filth and poverty, seemed to me a denial of
their humanity.

The inhabitants can never have washed at all. Washing—and with
soap, what's more!—was evidently a luxury reserved for the gentry. And
the gentry? The gentry were anyone beyond the village, the other side of
the road. No one in Safontyevo would have dreamed of talking about the
romance of country life! Smoky and soot-encrusted huts, with stoves but
no chimneys, were the norm; the two or three houses with a chimney
were an aberration disturbing the settled dictates of antiquity. With
chimney or without, all were thatched. I never saw a shingle roof, and
iron sheeting must have been well beyond their means. Wind-tossed
and rain-washed for decades, the straw on every hovel was uniformly
grey; some roofs were long past repair, and the old straw, rotted through
and black in patches, looked as though it had been gutted by fire. Since
the huts were without foundations, each had its own particular tilt, some
nuzzling so deep into the ground that their windows could hardly be
seen. Yet they all followed a single pattern: three small windows at the
front; a fenced yard with warped wooden gates opening on to the street.
Even on the hottest midsummer noon those small squares of yard open
to the sky were a depressing sight, perpetually awash with wet muck that
no one bothered to clear away.

The barefoot aborigines slopped ankle-deep through a warm, stink-
ing swill. My mother tiptoed with skirts lifted high, but the dung still
clung dreadfully to everything it touched. Nor did the bog end with the
threshold; it came inside, to join (at the very least) a cock, a hen, and the
ever desirable calf, still unsteady on splayed legs, lowing behind the
stove or curtain where it had been hurriedly thrust from sight.

No runners or Negro slaves went before us, no gongs were rung or
trumpets blown to herald our approach—and yet they always knew and
waited with evident panic. As we entered, children hid behind their
mothers' skirts, chickens clucked and clapped their dusty wings, and the

calf, frightened by all the clamour, would add its plaintive lowing to the confusion.

By the end of the summer, they got used to us and knew we meant them no harm. The women often turned to my mother for medicines and advice, and some of the older children forgot their fear. But even now, I cannot forget those eyes—the eyes of six- and seven-year-old girls which saw not us, but terrifying aliens. In the early mornings the girls came with kerchief-bound bowls of wild strawberries; nervously scratching one leg against the other, they snatched their five copecks, and scarpered barefoot through the scrub, their naked legs a lightning flash in the sunlight.

The neglected community of ancient limes, young hazels, maple-clusters, and pines on the forest's edge, and its tangled undergrowth of nettles, elders, wild raspberry canes and giant ferns, was known as 'the manor park'. For the villagers it was forbidden ground. But apart from this 'park' there was nothing to the estate. Its manor house remained a mystery. Boris and I climbed every tree that could be climbed, and yet, in the course of two summers, we found nothing, not even traces of its foundations. The stone building, of which we rented a part, could hardly be called manorial: it was, rather, servants' quarters, a service wing to the non-existent 'manor'. From the wide veranda added to its façade long ago there was a pleasant view over a semicircle of open ground, and down the straight line of a once-broad lime avenue, now half overgrown with grass. At the avenue's end, the scattered ruins of a summer-house marked out its circular base. What counted, though, was not the summer-house, but its completely unexpected, breathtaking view over the open landscape below. The surprise was easily explained. All the length of that dreadful road from the railway station to the summer-house at the very end of the lime avenue, the ground sloped imperceptibly upwards, growing slightly steeper in the last stages of the journey from Safontyevo to our estate. The mild and regular incline ended at this point in a high, precipitous cliff. Almost at your feet, the river Istra ran below, curving round the base of the promontory, bending once more, and vanishing from sight. As was common in the countryside around Moscow, on the river's other bank lay water-meadows and wide pastures, ending, far away, in a soft blue forest seam stitched along the horizon.

On sultry days I loved this place best of all. In that cool, silent undergrowth, no longer woodland or cultivated chase, the forest spoke to me in all its tense and sounding quietness. And though I soon knew it well, that sudden shift from half-dark to blinding light, from my high shelter to the naked river and undressed plains below filled me with exultation. Criss-crossed and crevassed, the bluff presented a difficult climb. But from my vantage point I could sit on a fallen tree for hours, thinking of nothing, and living in my dreams. Bright-green water-meadows, crossed by a wavering line of deserted road, trembled and streamed in the hot air. On early mornings a great herd of cattle, large even for those times, was driven past the river: cows, sheep and horses slowly moving, as if deep in thought, often drifting to a halt, their heads hung low to pasture.

Occasionally, a spurt of dust would rise from the road. Seconds later, a sharp click, like gunfire, would reach my ears: one of the herdsmen had cracked his long whip to distract a dawdling cow on the river bank, absorbed by the gaze of another cow hanging upside-down beneath her . . .

Everything lay in the flat of my hand—those two cows, muzzle to inverted muzzle; the dark patches of cloud racing over the meadow from far away. As if in play, the shadows skim the grass, swing effortlessly on to the cattle's backs as they chew their cud unperturbed, and leap-frog off again to scamper down to the river. The river cannot stop them; turned suddenly transparent, they swim across to scramble on to my bank and slither smoothly up the difficult climb, vanishing among the pines behind my back . . .

And that river! Concussed by the sun, it lies between the banks, reflecting the swimming clouds, inverted fisherman, boat, and line. Abruptly piercing the water's self-sealing skin, a fish will leap and flop, its ripple a long thread paid out by the current to lose itself downstream. Suddenly shivered by a light breeze, the mirror darkens to a leaden dullness in which nothing can be seen.

Pensive and at peace, I loll in the park's liberal shade, while the heat-haze drones in the heavy air over the meadow-furnace below, like the thin, even whine of a distant electric saw, like a scythe that sings in the mower's hand as he lays each swathe with even stroke. Chance currents of air bring an acrid whiff of hot earth, of wormwood and the river's dripping weeds. Half-heard, sometimes, my mother's playing carries from the dacha beyond the trees.

People often ask me about the role our father played in our childhood. I find such questions difficult to answer, mainly because our relationship was constantly changing. In the winter, while half our day was spent at school, my father led his absorbing life in his studio. As we came home in the afternoons to do our prep, he left for his life classes in the Art School, and stayed there till early evening, returning home quite worn out, just in time for supper. Under such circumstances, how could he take part in our lives? Yet you need only leaf through his sketch-books, mainly filled with drawings of us children, to see that there was no alienation. We realized clearly enough how busy his life was, and the bond between us was manifested instead in a real, friendly affection which we tried to confirm in practical terms, by keeping out of his way—though when I look back, I can see how often I must have been a burden to him. Our mother decided all family matters; my father kept out of domestic trivia, and so a matriarchal spirit was permanently established in our household. But it never occurred to any of us to think that this was caused by a sense of superiority on his part. There never was a man of more simple and genuine delight in other people. It was just a matter of time and opportunity, and these came only with the summer.

For the three months of the summer vacation my father belonged to his family. He went on our short walks, he joined in our far-flung picnics, he played our games and forgot his age. It transpired that his childhood had been exactly what we were threatened with as the epitome of total degradation and family disaster. By his own account, he had grown up in the gutters from which he had later, with difficulty, extricated himself: he had been the street urchin we were never allowed to be. Many of his talents—for instance, his ear-splitting, ruffianly two-fingered whistle—came from that background. He offered to pass these skills on to us, but in vain; evidently the social transformation of his children was so decisive that our jaws, or our fingers, were deformed. Whistle we absolutely could not.

He took part in everything—croquet, boating, tick-tack-toe, giant's strides . . . He loved cutting the grass in front of the house, even though he tired quickly. But the mowers praised him, and that was good enough for him! One summer years later, not in Safontyevo, I remember, he either bought or made a bow as big as I was, and we shot long, feathered arrows at a respectably distant target. Neither Boris nor I could beat him. When summer ended, so, it seemed, did our friendly closeness. But this was a separation in externals only, as each of us withdrew to his winter corner.

*

Giant's Strides. From left to right: Josephine, Lydia,
Boris (and Alexander out of sight). Raiki, 1908.

Family group on the dacha veranda. Back row, from right to left: Boris, Dr Lev
Levin (the family doctor and friend), Alexander, Leonid, and the Pasternaks'
German Fräulein. Front row, from right to left: Olga Bari (a pupil of Leonid
Pasternak), Pavel Ettinger (art critic and family friend), Lydia, Rosa, Josephine,
and Olga Bari's sister (?). Raiki, 1907. See Introduction, p. xxii.

Akulina Gavrilovna, the children's nanny,
knitting. Undated sketch by Leonid Pasternak.

Rosa at the piano, accompanied by Jacob Romm, Boris listening.
Drawing by Leonid Pasternak. Moscow 1905.

Lydia and Josephine with their father on the dacha steps. Raiki, 1908.

МОСКВА в баррикадах и развалинах. Баррик. на Долгоруков. уг. Садовой. | barricad et ruines a Rue Dolgoroukovskaya. MOSCC

Moscow barricades. Postcard, 1905.

Hôtel Fürst Bismarck, am
Besitzer: Hermann Brüchner
Telephon: Charlottenburg 632

The Pasternaks' first hotel in Berlin. Postcard, 1906.

As the day for my father's return from Germany came closer, my mother decided she would go back home to meet him, taking Boris and myself with her to help on the journey. We squeezed heroically into tight sailor suits and heavy black boots—city habits forgotten in our carefree summer months—and set off on 15 June 1904. I can fix the date exactly, because of what happened when we got home the following day.

In Moscow we were knocked flat by the stifling, almost palpable stuffiness of our overheated apartment, which had been shut up since spring. We began throwing windows open at once, hoping to set up a draught. But everything seemed inert, waiting for the release of a thunderstorm that wouldn't come. Our father's train was due at four in the afternoon. Mamma was busy in the kitchen preparing a celebratory meal. The heat grew. I thought regretfully of my breezy, open bluff and the forest coolness.

Meanwhile the thunder performed those interminable preludes that precede every storm. The scorched air thickened till there seemed nothing to breathe. The sparrows on the window-sills grew quiet. The pigeons had already made off somewhere, probably gathering to roost on our back stair for the night, although it was hardly lunchtime. Every natural sound in street and yard grew still, as though blotted out by cotton wool. It began to get dark.

I can still remember how doomsday broke at two o'clock. Night fell. Lamps had to be lit. The windows drummed with rain and hail. Later, people swore there were stones as big as hens' eggs; certainly the ones lodged in our window-sills were the size of walnuts. Since her childhood Mamma had always suffered in thunderstorms. Now her palpitations began; her head ached as she lay prostrate, the curtains drawn and a candle burning on her bedside table. Comforting her as best we could with medicines, damp towels, and kind words, Boris and I kept running into the other rooms to see what was happening outside. Something quite indescribable was going on out there. It sounded like a typhoon; it was, in fact, the famous hurricane that hit Moscow on 16 June 1904.

What we saw beyond our windows was no tame illustration of Victor Hugo's *Travailleurs de la mer*, but an entirely new and dramatic text—an extraordinary gala performance played with incredible force and speed. From the bedroom windows overlooking the Myasnitskaya we saw oceanic waterspouts knocked sideways by the whistling squall, flying in horizontal sheets down the street, buckling under the waves of pursuing wet. The speed of whirlwind and water was such that the window-panes dried in a moment, leaving us free to stare at the street below, now a torrent ridged with foam, roaring down to the Lubyanka. The courtyard of the main Post Office was a lake: whirlpools swirled by the gates and slapped at the waves flung back by the office walls. A master-chef's hand was beating the trees, lilac bushes, and iron fencing into a brisk, brown froth, and salting the mixture with handfuls of hail. In the corners of the yard whipped white drifts promptly sank under swamping foam.

Broken branches flew past the windows, straining to God knows what goal, alighting on roofs for a moment's rest before spinning up and away. It was as though two fashionable modern fans were at work together, one at the Red Gates pumping air out, the other at the Lubyanka sucking it in. The Myasnitskaya was like a ventilator-shaft between them, shot by lightning-flash and gloom, by thunderclaps half-heard in the frenzied clatter of rain and hail.

In the dining-room, the huge pane of clear glass habitually framing the cathedral dome had turned into a frosted lavatory window. A cataract clouded the cathedral contours; glaucoma blurred the view. It was somehow sickening to look in this direction, and even the sustained virtuoso drumming of the elements was frankly tedious to listen to. Chance thoughts started across my mind: what if the hail grew worse, what if it really did get as big as hens' eggs? . . . Heavens above, would the windows hold out? What would become of the dining-room, when branches big as rafts rammed into its doors? How long would we be able to fight off the waves, barricaded in our nursery?

Lightning followed on lightning so fast that the thunder rolled without pause. Through our front windows we could see dirty waves washing everything off the glass roof of the Exhibition Hall opposite. Branches, splintered planks, and broken tiles all poured down the steep roof to plunge headlong into the enclosed cube of yard below. It filled with flotsam, hailstones, water, lightning, and the shriek of storm, like a narrow well-shaft into which some lunatic fireman forces great waterjets of freezing foam.

Although we could feel the strength of the hurricane, we had no factual concept of its force. Later we found out that our region lay on its periphery; the centre hit Sokolniki, from the Annenhof Grove down to the Rogozhskaya. In this park everything that the tornado could rip out of the earth was uprooted, and tossed aside. It made a clean sweep of Annenhof Grove, which keeled over like a nursery of little saplings. Giant trees were floored; massive trunks were snapped and twitched aside. The ten famous clearings in the Sokolniki plantation were joined by yet another swathe, more spacious than the rest put together.

But what of our father all this time? Prostrated by the storm, our mother could barely express her anxiety, which we shared acutely enough. We talked of other things, trying to encourage hopeless optimism in each other, but all three of us could easily imagine every kind of catastrophe. He should have got home, or phoned, long ago, and in his silence we could only assume the worst. Fortunately, at such times, cold reason deserts you—with reason! With the returning calm that evening, as the rivers subsided and pavements dared show themselves once more, when the Post Office came down to earth and the garden settled back in its lap, a postman crossed over with a badly delayed telegram. Our father wrote from Germany, joyfully informing us that on the 16th, thank God, he'd be leaving Berlin. Even Mamma, already eased by the storm's retreat, came to life again with the good news. Only on the next day did we read in the papers that heavy goods trains in the storm's path had been flicked aside like so many empty matchboxes . . .

In due course our father made his own way to the dacha, and we ventured on no further expeditions to meet him. Little changed in the last weeks of vacation, except that studio smells mingled with those of the dacha and hot summer days. Time drew us on to 16 August, to work, school, and life in boxed-in rooms.

CHAPTER 14

WAR AND REVOLUTION

As usual, the first days after our return were spent reacquiring forgotten city ways. The last year had not only given me added maturity, but also widened my intellectual grazing-ground, sharpening my interest in the newspapers and war I had hardly noticed in the past. School, which was already subsidiary, now moved into the background altogether. By our second year we knew perfectly well whom to fear and whom to avoid, when to duck and where to steer clear. Nothing worried us any more, but neither did it interest us; there wasn't even anything new to look forward to, like the Latin we would begin in our third year, or the Greek in our fourth. For this reason, I suppose, the masters and boys with whom, willy-nilly, I spent every day of that second school year have left little trace.

Naturally the war filling the newspapers became a more disturbing element in my life. I began to understand something of our ignoble military ventures, the many attacks of ours, even those with the most promising beginnings, which ended, alas, in panic, flight, or retreat 'to previously prepared positions'. Wasn't that phrase in itself an a priori acceptance of defeat? Everything spoke of the factions, incompetence, and corruption undermining the supreme command. Our maps were so bad they led the commanding officers into catastrophic miscalculations. Our old-fashioned army was ill-equipped for the unexpected mountain terrain; instead of the essential pack-horses, our transport consisted of wagons whose wheels broke constantly, making it impossible for our troops to manoeuvre quickly. Could it really be true that a second-year schoolboy knew more than the high command? Even our Japanese enemies recognized how heroically the ordinary Russian soldier paid for his commanders' errors with his own blood.

Running ahead, I must say that all the battles, from the very first on the Yalu River, to Motienling, Liaoyang, Shakhé, Sandep, Mukden, and Tiurenchen, all told the same story—they began in cheers, and ended in tears. And the shameful loss of Port Arthur, which everyone knew was the stout outpost of the Liaotung Peninsula? When it was besieged it still held back the huge army led by General Nogi for a considerable time. And then what? As soon as the leading spirit of our defence, General Kondratenko, was killed, General Stessel promptly surrendered the fortress to the Japanese! What was that, if not treachery? And yet his authorization came from St Petersburg. What of the catastrophes in the Tsushima Straits? What did they prove? Our slow-moving, outmoded vessels ('self-sinkers', the sailors scornfully called them) were pitted against the heavily armoured Japanese dreadnoughts. With their first shot, those aptly named floating fortresses scored a direct hit on our ships' bridges, carrying off the controls and turning them into wash-tubs crammed with helpless men. Was it mere technical deficiency that led our squadron of ships, dutifully following in each other's wake in a column of parade-ground punctiliousness, to present a beautifully clear target, turned in profile, to the two Japanese flanks which neatly nipped them in? With futile heroism we spattered their armour-plating with our weak shot, hardly tickling the hide of those thick-skinned hippos.

And after all that, a shameful peace, in which the Japanese confessed to being on the brink of utter collapse, they were so weakened and exhausted by their own victories!

Of course repercussions were bound to follow on such a disgraceful war. Life at home was inevitably coloured by the indignation felt at the front. Looking back today, the panorama of those days seems clear to the merest child. But we, the children of the time, couldn't grasp it all. Missing the nuances, we nevertheless sensed that something was distinctly wrong. From our childhood we knew how the doctor visiting us when we were ill would ask us questions to find out the cause of the disease, before he attempted to cure it. Here, instead of the cause, the results were roughly remedied, and the strikes of a still obedient nation were put down by force of arms.

All that autumn and early winter the strikes grew from the little and local to the large-scale and threatening. The measures regularly taken against them—the threat of whips and rifles—soon failed. The official tactic of metaphorically dousing down fire with paraffin reached tragic proportions on Sunday, 9 January 1905*—a day on which even the most right-thinking traditionalists joined the ranks of the outraged protesters.

And so they should have done! A large, peaceful, and sincere crowd of

* Old style. Russia did not change from the Julian to the Gregorian Calendar until 1918. In the twentieth century Old Style lagged behind New Style dates by thirteen days.

workers, with their wives and even their babies, gathered with icons and religious banners and a single aim—to go to the Tsar their father, the patriarch of an Orthodox nation, to confide in him the suffering and distress of his people. Singing holy psalms, they went, led by Gapon, the Tsar's secret agent and *agent provocateur*, as it later turned out. They trusted him to lead them to the Tsar, and bring everything to a happy conclusion.

The happy conclusion was a highway sown with dead and wounded. Soldiers and police shot them down indiscriminately, and the official strength, that had failed so lamentably to put the Japanese to flight, now glowed in its dispersal of a defenceless crowd.

The ninth of January! That unhappy Sunday was a more potent piece of propaganda than the most inflammatory exhortations of pamphlet and proclamation, more incandescent than the hot words of assemblies and impromptu meetings. That Sunday opened many eyes to things that still lay half-hidden. The ninth of January began collecting the drops that gathered into the fatal ninth wave* which engulfed Moscow in December that year, beginning with a nationwide general strike, and ending with the armed uprising of soldiers and workers.

Naturally I had only the most superficial understanding of the conflicting currents of the day. And yet, like all my classmates, I was a wholehearted revolutionary. It was, for instance, quite natural that when a friend and I were strolling down Clear Ponds Boulevard one day, he should shout out, provocatively and quite irrelevantly, 'We're Social Democrats!'—making all the passers-by cautiously turn their heads. It was obviously just a bit of schoolboy nonsense, and yet I remember the scene because it typified our attitude at the time.

After breakfast one frosty February morning, I was standing by the big dining-room window with my father, looking out at the exquisite oval of the Polish Cathedral, its ribbed dome kindling with rosy sparks in the rising winter sun. We were deep in conversation about the perfect forms of nature, and lines of beauty in art, when suddenly a baffling, ponderous detonation punctured the air. According to my father, well versed in the sounds of artillery, it was no cannon shot, which would have discharged more than once, but some kind of an explosion, and a powerful one at that. Nothing else happened. Everything grew still again; the dome glowed on, and we resumed our conversation almost as before.

* According to Russian superstition, the 'ninth wave' was fatal to sailors.

Within a few hours we heard that a bomb had been thrown into the carriage of the Grand Duke Sergey Alexandrovich. He was a trustee of the School of Art and we had often seen him in the classrooms on the eve of various exhibitions. For that reason, perhaps, of all 'those' people he was, for our family, not a faceless name but a real man, alive in his crisp regimentals, dress sword, Hessian boots and ringing spurs. Tall, dry, upright, rigid as a steel ruler—so my father had caricatured him on one of his visits to the School.*

He was killed instantly as he drove into the Kremlin through the Nikolsky Gates. A modest memorial was later set up for him behind a wooden fence. When I passed the Kremlin wall, in even the worst weather, I could see the flame that permanently burnt beside his wooden cross.

An uneasy period began. Serious, extended strikes grew more frequent and widespread, as did the repression that triggered off yet more strikes—in Warsaw, Białystok, Riga, Viborg, Ivanov, St Petersburg, and Moscow. All the boys at school were in turmoil. Involuntarily and however insignificantly, I too found myself drawn into the revolution underground.

One of my mother's old friends, whom my father nicknamed 'the suffragette' because of her independent, masculine air, turned out to be a Social Democrat whose job was to distribute pamphlets among the students and workers. To avoid the risk of discovery she had turned from commercial printers to her least suspect acquaintances, enlisting them to copy the texts by hand. Among others, she asked my mother whether I could help, since my childish script, and our flat (which adjoined the Director's, and, like it, was State owned) were least likely to come under suspicion. All that winter I played the proud conspirator, copying treasonable documents in secret from everyone except my parents. In order that I might lie more tranquilly, if the need arose, my suffragette paid me a nominal fee per sheet, and clutching my coppers, I used to run off to the stationers on the Myasnitskaya to buy new stamps for my collection. Like Erman's, P. Samsonov and Sons, and the other

---

* 'The spirit of pomp and ceremony was inseparable from the College which was under the ægis of the Ministry of the Imperial Court. The Grand Duke Sergey Alexandrovich was its patron and he came regularly to its exhibitions and its speech days. The Grand Duke was thin and lanky. Shielding their sketch-books with their hats, Serov and my father drew caricatures of him at the receptions which he attended at the Golitsins' and Yakunchikovs'.'

Boris Pasternak, *An Essay in Autobiography*, p. 33.

shops I had visited with my mother from my earliest childhood, Polygraph was for me no mere shop name, the label of a commercial concern, but a living person. It signified, quite simply, the benevolent proprietor, a roly-poly German who used to shove his spectacles on to his forehead to look down at me. When I visited Polygraph's shop now, a grown schoolboy who could almost decline Greek (though we hadn't started it yet, Boris passed a modicum down to me), he used to dignify me with the grand title, 'Mr Schoolboy' (and I was only eleven years old!).

The copying didn't go all that smoothly. At first, not understanding everything I wrote, I made endless mistakes. But the uniformity of theme was reflected in its monotonous vocabulary, which soon acquired a kind of generalized sense. SRs, SDs, Smenovekhovtsy, Bundovtsy, the Bund, despotism, deposition, people's government and so on, novelties at that time to our milieu, became recurrent and familiar. Certain formulae solidified in mistaken configurations at first sight, and somehow persisted even when I knew their sense and spelling perfectly well. I remember, for instance, that the slogan *zemlya i volya* ('land and liberty'), which the suffragette rattled off so quickly, ran together into the idiotic *zemlya Ivolya*—Ivol's Ground. Of course I knew no such landowner existed, but somehow my hand transcribed the mistake time after time. Just as moronic was my involuntary insertion of a superfluous 's' in 'vlast' (power), and that silly 'vslast'* made everyone laugh at me.

The poor suffragette got caught in the end: she was decoyed, arrested, and exiled. No enquiries, though, were made about my activities. Shortly before her arrest she gave me an ultra-primitive ur-Remington typewriter—not quite full grown to the real thing, nor yet a child's toy. It turned on the axis of a metal disc, whose outside edge was fringed with keys embossed with the letters of the alphabet, painted in black enamel. Beneath it was a similar rubber disc with the same embossed letters, which you had to coat with purple printer's ink. Rotating the upper disc and pressing the required keys, I could type out a whole word, letter by purple letter. I can't remember how you got a sentence—whether paper or disc slid sideways, but in any case the whole process was far slower than writing by hand. I kept it, and showed off with it for a long time, before my mother, in natural anxiety at the

---

* Colloquial: 'to his heart's content'.

possible consequences, hid the dangerous revolutionary weapon. It vanished for good, and later even she couldn't remember what she had done with it.

Meanwhile the ragged, often interrupted academic year came to an end. One sunny day, the wonderful smell of fresh hay and damp bast matting filled the flat once again, and once again Kuzma and his assistant, 'Lenyosipich' Kotov, packed up our household things for transport to Safontyevo. Once again all the rituals of departure were repeated in their minutest particulars, and every peripeteia of the journey met us in its proper and familiar place.

On the veranda our trunks and bundles were waiting for us. Doors and windows were unbarred; winter stuffiness was engulfed in spring smells. Even this had all happened before.

And yet, something was concealed deep in the most familiar things, waiting for its time to come. Even that is nothing new! Sunlight need only splash a room from an unfamiliar corner, a drab day unexpectedly clear, for the whole world to step out in a new light. Such is life: the permanent succession of change, a perpetual revelation of the new in the old.

This summer we found the lawyer-proprietor and his family at Safontyevo in full force. He was nervous, he explained, of leaving his wife alone with their daughters. He didn't trust the villagers, and rated his own protective capabilities pretty high—pointing to the two rifles hanging on the wall, and a revolver in the table-drawer. Such remarks, and other even more obvious precautions against a confrontation with the peasantry, caught my parents unawares. In Moscow they hadn't dreamt of such things. Even proprietorial cares didn't lead them to the same conclusions. It was natural for us to deal simply and amicably with anyone we met, assuming an equal friendliness on their part. So Mamma went on calling in the village for this and that, doing the peasants no harm, and sometimes helping them.

And yet the proprietor's talk made us uneasy. After a short holiday, he left with the rest of his family for the city, keeping my father for an hour in his study before they went. As the dust of two carriages settled behind them, my father told us that the lawyer had tried to talk him into accepting the firearms, and, in the end, overriding all my father's protests, had forced the revolver and a stock of cartridges on him.

A guilty atmosphere lingered after their departure: the first few days on our own we all felt uncomfortable, as though we had been caught out in something shameful. Gradually the ordinary pattern of life re-established itself, and we forgot about 'red cockerels'* and other horrors. Ammunition and revolver slept peaceably in their drawer, till my father's old military skills awoke, and he decided to play with the toy that had been lent to him.

The three of us used to go together to the most distant and unfrequented end of the park, where we had found a suitable clearing and nailed up a home-made target high on a tree. My father shot accurately, with an experienced and steady hand that neither Boris nor I could hope to emulate. He demonstrated again and again, even guiding my hand, but it always jerked as I pulled the trigger, and the bullet flew wide.

One day, however, such peaceful, innocuous pastimes were ended once and for all, and the revolver was returned to its drawer. We arrived at the clearing to find that our supply of cartridges was low. Boris was sent back for more, while my father and I waited. At this moment an ill-fated crow chose to settle, cawing, on the branch of a tree nearby. On an impulse, my father decided to try himself out on a moving target, and, without stopping to think, startled it out of the tree. As soon as it lifted, flapping heavily, he aimed and fired. With a somehow distorted wing-beat it tumbled, twisting and scrabbling clumsily at the branches as it fell. I distinctly saw its malevolent eye and convulsively gaping beak as it dragged itself into the undergrowth, croaking and trailing its wing behind it.

A heaviness settled upon us. Boris came up with the cartridges, saw our guilty faces, and without a word we turned for home. I had never been much of a sportsman, and the memory of that evil eye and ill-boding caw quenched the last spark of the huntsman in me.

It was the last event of the summer. Lassitude and a persistent, melancholy drizzle set in. Our gloom was intensified by the few newspapers reaching us. The return home grew tempting. On a dreary day of thin mists and fine drenching rain, we let ourselves into the warm rooms of our Moscow flat.

Rumour of the latest summer's disasters—squadrons slaughtered at the front, strikes in the rear at Riga and Ivanov, barricades at Łódź—had

---

* Fires were very common in the Russian countryside: whole villages of wooden thatched huts would burn down. But 'red cockerels' implies acts of arson when peasants burnt down the landowners' properties, attacked the gentry and killed their cattle.

drifted down to us, hazy and distorted, even at Safontyevo. But when we came back to town we were struck by a blast of gossip, guesswork, and hot, open declarations. The volcano, whose grumblings had been only distantly audible a few months back, was fully awake. Restlessly stirring, it yawned and cracked, each subterranean shock perceptible on the most insignificant street corner. 'If you can't fight a war properly, chuck it in,' the people were sneering, openly now; 'you've made asses enough of yourselves as it is', they said. And so the ignominious war dragged on to its long-predicted conclusion—a shameful peace—while many considered the unspoken question, whether the monarchy should be allowed to survive.

Even we schoolboys came back no lambs, but seasoned old-timers, independent-minded third-years, indoctrinated by life itself to take our own way, not to sit in obedient rows reciting lessons and getting marks out of ten. Nor were we the exception. Every school in the country was in uproar, as the official proclamation, closing all the schools down for an indefinite period, 'owing to the great unrest among the pupils', publicly admitted.

Those were the kaleidoscopically fast-moving days of early September 1905. If you had asked me then what single word characterized the time, I would have replied, promptly and unexpectedly, but accurately, 'Browning'. Yes, that alien, un-Russian word captured it all. For me it meant my Browning automatic, chipped out of a block of wood and painted black, which I, like every boy of my age, kept permanently in my pocket. Of course there were the last vestiges of childishness in this, and yet it also carried different overtones: a sense of loyalty to the real revolutionaries, the older students who kept their flat, frightening, loaded automatics hidden in their pockets. They walked side by side with us. They were ordinary students in the technological and medical institutes, among them boys from the older classes of my father's School of Art, aspiring architects and artists whom we knew by sight and often met, sometimes specifically to run errands (a job in which I took a particular pride). These were no bandannaed bandits, no cuirass-brandishing brigands, but nice lads in the familiar belted, high-necked blouses that were the usual uniform of the time. And yet they were the dread vigilantes, the real revolutionaries who would fight on the barricades. Those were no games they played with their automatics. They used to go off somewhere, and be gone for a long time, either to vanish altogether, or to return, serious and secretive, to hang about the Art

School corridors once more. We knew that they were taking lessons in small-arms fire and the manufacture of other, even more dreadful toys than the Browning—but what, where, and how, no one said, and no one asked.

We knew, too, that the students of the Fiedler Technological Institute wore the same uniform—high-necked blouses, buttoned, belted jackets and all. (Much later we were to stand by the Institute's charred remains, on Clear Ponds Boulevard, after the Tsar's artillery had bombarded it, and burnt it to the ground.) We took no offence when these young, unshaven and intense revolutionaries, whom we knew well, would look us deep in the eyes and send us home without a word of explanation. Later, they were joined by booted workers in grubby jackets—and later still by soldiers, their arms laid aside, who arrived for revolutionary meetings in our School of Art, where there was no room for us yet. Boris and I would go up to our third-floor flat, keeping everything we knew to ourselves, as though fulfilling a mission. 'The actor, waving his paper sword', I once recited to myself, and realized that Camoens's line applied to me, and to the wooden Browning automatic in my pocket.

Now, here and there, single shots sounded out, and scattering volleys, like the rattle of dried peas. September drew to an end. Fresh news came from Sebastopol, Kiev, Kharkov ... Something hung over us and everyone was preparing himself.

17 October brought the Supreme Manifesto—contradictions riddling it from beginning to end. On the one hand, the worn, stereotyped phrases from 'We, Nicholas II, Tsar' of this and that and so on and so forth, to the final, formulaic 'written and signed by the hand of His Imperial Highness'; on the other, promises of light and hope, were you only to read it without scepticism. All lingering doubts of its absolute sincerity were dispelled less than twenty-four hours later, when a student of the Technological Institute, epauletted, high-collared, and jacketed like the rest, was shot dead at a meeting devoted to reading the Manifesto.

All Moscow mourned Bauman on 30 October. I have never forgotten his funeral. All our family, except my young sisters, stood with the rest of the Art School staff between its massive balcony pillars, like extras in some classic tragedy—the fall of Oedipus or the epic end of a noble Empire family and all its wide estates. Mute and motionless, we watched the broad black band of mourners pass below. Row upon monotonous row of ten or more, steady, silent, subdued, hour after hour after hour, they filled the broad Myasnitskaya down to Lubyanskaya Square. The silence of that moving mass was most menacing; it was so heavy you wanted to scream, till it was broken by voices singing the requiescat, or the valedictory hymn of the time, 'You fell as victims in the fight . . .'. Then silence fell once more. The rhythmical ranks paced on below. Rank upon rank upon rank, hour after hour after hour.

I remember the head of that procession most vividly. As usual with funerals, the line of mourners was led by the hearse, not horse-drawn in this case, but carried on the shoulders of six pall-bearers. Before them came a light, one-horse carriage filled with fir branches that were strewn, regularly and sparsely, beneath the mourners' feet. That was traditional. What was unique was the procession's absolute head, which preceded carriage, catafalque and cortège with their scent of trampled pine: not an icon borne by hand, not a priest, but a man in black with a palm branch in his hand. He swung it from side to side, in time with his steps and those of the crowds behind him, unifying the mass as a conductor leads his choir. It was lofty, ceremonious, unheard-of; I have never seen its like again.

The behaviour of the procession was perfect. The same measured severity of tone was sustained, whoever met it, joined it, or silently drew aside to let it pass on its way to the cemetery. But on the return journey the crowd dispersed in tired clusters, and fell into the hands of reactionary forces who beat them down and shot at them. Those going past the Riding School walked straight into the abattoir of the Black Hundred, their numbers swollen by police, dragoons, door-keepers, and other disreputable riff-raff, who had found themselves inhibited by the united strength of the outgoing procession, and only now dared let themselves go. There, we were told later, the valour of these bastions of the State, armed with sticks, whips, and guns, was at its height. Their violent dispersal of an unarmed crowd demonstrated the veracity of those paragraphs from the Supreme Manifesto which promised us the liberties of speech and individual conscience.

The Director of the Art School decided to set up a barricade in the main entrance hall, well aware that a pogrom was likely in this haven of students with revolutionary sympathies. A high wall of oak timbers was set up, fortified on the inside by buttresses and struts, and punctured by a single postern, only wide enough to admit one person at a time. Here our bearded old door-keeper, Anton, took up his post in complete security. The barricade caused a lot of trouble for our director, Prince

Lvov, from the powers-that-be. Preserving his good relations with
them, he laughed it off, and on our return from Germany a year later, I
found the barricade intact.*

October passed. With November came fresh signs of impending
revolution. Open preparations were being made for an armed confrontation with the Tsarist forces. The Ochakov uprising, the imprison-
ment of Lieutenant Schmidt, Meller-Zakomelsk's punitive expedition,
new general strikes, and the arming of the people followed quickly on
each other. The tide was rising, and everyone was waiting, some in
impatient expectation of success, some in dismay and secret loathing, for
the fatal ninth wave to break. Still it hung back, while the groundswell
grew.

Winter came with premature frosts and a heavy fall of early snow. I
still remember those vacant November dusks, the Myasnitskaya hushed
and the Post Office courtyard deserted. By day it looked like a vignette of
winter country life: plush snow concealing the street, plump, pillowy
pavements and unpeopled silence, the disjointed tracks of a single,
startled pedestrian picking his way, like a crow, across the road and
stealing out of sight.

Unexpectedly the expected came to pass. One night I was suddenly
jolted awake as though I had been shaken. In my dazed state, it seemed
that our entire quarter had been invaded by an army of carpenters busily
at work. Someone somewhere was indefatigably hammering nails into
thick planks; with the even, regular whoop of a hatchet splitting billets,
they were chopping logs here and there; tin-tacks clicked and axes rang.
With a great rumbling some round object rolled off a trestle-table and
plummeted dully to the ground.

---

* 'In answer to the student demonstrations which followed the Manifesto of 17th
October, the rabble of Okhotny Ryad looted the University and the Higher Technical
Schools. The College was also threatened. By the Director's orders, piles of stones were
kept on the landings of the main staircase and lengths of hose connected with the taps for
use against possible raiders.

Every now and then, a crowd marching down our street turned aside and entered the
building. Classrooms were occupied, meetings were held in the Assembly Hall, and from
the balcony speakers addressed those who had remained in the street below. The College
students formed their own militant organisations and our own home guard was on duty at
night.

Among my father's papers is a drawing of a girl speaking from the balcony; she is
wounded and supporting herself against a pillar; dragoons are charging the crowd and
shooting at her.'

Boris Pasternak, *An Essay in Autobiography*, pp. 52–3.

We were already acclimatized to rifles, revolvers, and rare machine-gun fire, but on that night the carpenters hammered away with greater regularity, so that I could sleepily detect a dotted rhythm—a sustained staccato toccata, syncopated and counterpointed by acciaccatura and trill. I woke Boris and we listened for some time, commenting on the errors in tempo as new instruments joined in. I can't say for certain whether this was the beginning of the December Revolution or one of its many rehearsals. But from that time night firing became the norm, an apparent pastime of night-watchmen vainly trying to keep themselves warm in those hard early frosts. We, however, suffered from a chill beyond that of the time of year.

As a precautionary measure, the Art School stokers had decided to put out the boilers and shut off the water when they went off to one of their revolutionary meetings. Unfortunately, they neglected to close the pipe heating our flat, which was now the only inhabited quarter in the entire building, since the Director's flat had been vacated long before. The pipe froze and then burst. Our flat turned into an extension of the street, a corridor of cold with constant sub-zero temperatures. Just at this point, my three-year-old sister Lydia fell seriously ill. As always in such moments of stress and uncertainty, the least deviation from the norm seemed a divine punishment. We shrank like troglodytes to a cave existence, huddled round my sister's bedside and the table next to it, where a large kerosene lamp, a 'Lightning', was kept permanently burning.

But where was Boris? Where had he gone, without a word of explanation, when the streets were in disorder and people leaving our yard found themselves under fire, beneath the hoofs of the cavalry, or, at the very best, under the knotted whips of the Cossacks?

Boris had disappeared. He stayed away for so long that even I became uneasy. He was, after all, only a headstrong fifteen-year-old, with, thank the Lord, the personality of an adult. To the accompaniment of moans from my baby sister and my mother, who was beside herself, my father paced from window to door and door to window, pretending a calm he couldn't feel. On the beat past me he dropped in a casual undertone, 'I'm going to look for him', and paced on with his wide stride to the window; on the return journey he muttered again, 'Look after your mother', and made to go. At that moment, to our delight, the front door slammed and Boris appeared—but in what shape! His hat was crumpled, jacket torn, one button hanging on a tattered snatch of cloth,

half-belt dangling, and Boris himself beaming, simply beaming. Gradually we made out from his disjointed explanations that he had walked
some of the way down the Myasnitskaya towards the Lubyanka, when he
ran into a cluster of people running away from a mounted patrol. The
women among them caught him up in their panic when the dragoons
overtook them and let fly with their whips. The crowd tried in vain to
squeeze through the railings into the Post Office courtyard. Someone
jammed Boris against the fence, taking the main force of the blows on
himself, while Boris struggled to join the fray. Even so, he was hit hard
enough on his head and shoulders, a mild taste of the then common lot
which he felt he had to share. The dragoons cantered off, leaving a few
bodies on the road, and someone from the School, recognizing Boris,
dragged him home.

The December Revolution began, as everyone knows, on the eighth of
the month. For Boris and myself it began much earlier, in the classrooms of the Art School, long closed to its students and yet teeming
with an unofficial life that had nothing to do with Painting, Architecture,
and Sculpture. More and more, soldiers' greatcoats could be glimpsed
on unfamiliar backs; the habitual tobacco smells were overpowered by
the reek of cheap shag and military boot-black. Suspicious glances were
cast at us, fidgeting nearby, as a crowd of these unknowns would lock
themselves into a classroom, while the School students cooled their
heels in the corridor outside. It seemed to us, too, that the Revolution
had already begun, because of nightly artillery fire, the utterly altered
face of Moscow life, the deserted streets and rumours of barricades. In
the nearby Fiedler Institute the increasing meetings were crowded with
workers and armed vigilantes. Yet the Revolution had not actually
broken out when our pipe burst and the flat was turned into an ice-
box.

   It may well be that the fall in temperature contributed to Lydia's
illness, which would have been grave enough in normal circumstances.
It was acutely aggravated by the uncertainties of the time, with normal
communications disrupted, telephones cut off, and all the concomitant
imponderables—whether the chemists were functioning; whether, indeed, it would be possible to go out at all. Paralysed, lethargic, half
stunned by the cold, our horror intensified as the disease took its course.
Before our eyes, the child burned in the freezing room. All my parents'

earlier discussions—whether to scrape enough money together to go abroad now the School was closed and my father free to do his own work—were abruptly cut off by sickness and the general rail strike. The terrifying diagnosis, 'double pneumonia', mesmerized them. With the all-engulfing addition, 'complicated by croup', my mother could only wring her hands and burrow into her pillows, soaking them with her tears.

Our family doctor visited us daily, till, luckily, our area was cut off from the Tverskaya Street where he lived, and he was stranded in our flat. Knowing the illness's probable course, he advised us on what stocks of medicine to lay in, recommending, incidentally, that we should put aside a bottle of dry champagne. So our lives dwindled to a single tremulous point. The flat was desolate. A sense of emptiness oppressed us. We shuffled on tip-toe in felt boots and fur slippers (without which our feet would have frozen) and huddled without speaking (for there was nothing to talk about) round the bedside of the child who had once filled the rooms with happy, noisy life.

Great events filled the days outside. Indoors, we huddled like cavemen, intent on keeping alight the lamp on its table and the life in the cot. We thought of nothing beyond our walls. The doctor, for all his knowledge and skill, could not predict the course of the illness. Its outcome and our fears could only be resolved on the ninth day, when the crisis was expected, and she would recover—or die.

The ninth day, the ninth wave . . . How inexplicable nature is! Day follows day in even flow, altering nothing, allaying nothing. Nothing that we can see differs in those eight days: temperatures are taken, compresses changed . . . And what if nothing changes inside her? The eighth day ends; the ninth dawn breaks—and if there is no miracle, must she die? Who decides down which road the little body must go, to left or right?

As on every previous day, the doctor sat on Lydia's bed, mechanically drawing his golden watch from his waistcoat pocket with the improbably beautiful gesture of an actor; automatically taking her limp wrist. Suddenly, unpredictably, he jumps up and sponges down the suddenly drenched body. 'Champagne!' he says, knowing that he need only reach behind him for it to be put in his hand. He spoons the startling, tingly drink through tight lips, spilling it down her cheeks, past her ears, on to the pillow. A little trickles into her mouth. There is a weak, almost inaudible breath, and another . . . Bewildered, cloudy eyes open, still heavy with sleep, and close again, as though yearning to doze just a little longer. And they open again.

What else is there to tell? Everything becomes ordinary and predictable: in one corner my parents are crying in each others' arms; the doctor, no less delighted than we, busies himself about the cot. Our old nanny comes up, crossing herself and carrying something white in her arms. No longer scared of disturbing us, Dasha the servant walks boldly in with a tray of sandwiches and hot tea—and, suddenly, we all feel hungry.

Now too, equally abruptly, we remembered that about five days earlier, when everything had seemed dreadful beyond bearing, we found we were wrong. The Governor-General delivered an ultimatum to the Director of the Art School, informing him that if the premises were not cleared of all rebel elements by a particular time, they would be bombarded by the artillery. We knew what that meant from the charred remains of the Fiedler Institute, which had been cleared and obliterated in some thirty decisive minutes. Ultimatum in hand, Prince Lvov had consulted with my father about the best solution. Since all the residential staff of the School had already left, only we had stayed on in our habitual and now dangerous place, immobilized by my sister's illness. Day wasted into day with nothing decided and no move taken. Where could we go, with a dying child on our hands? The deadline crawled up—and, as unpredictably as a storm first breaks and then disperses, it passed by. Discovering that their whereabouts were already known, the revolutionary band vanished overnight. They left, silently, comprehensively, as a man might leave the room for a moment—and never return. This was no night flit, but an orderly departure, with the rooms swept clean. The ultimatum was lifted and no second Fiedler Institute took place.

A week later Lydia was fully recovered. We started talking about a trip abroad in more practical terms: applications, preparations and packing followed, as the projected gradually became real. Beyond our walls Moscow suffered bloody reprisals: the wolf-hunt was on. White-belted, nattily uniformed and heavily armed Tsarist forces drew the noose tight around the town. When it was all over, there was nothing for it but to thaw out the railways' frozen lines and start up the cold engines. Moscow life returned to normal. As a flooded river, retreating, leaves traces of its destructive force, so the revolution left detritus as it ebbed away.

The frosts intensified. The day came at last when we were told that the carriage was at the door. With these words our journey into a new unknown began, our only certainty, that within an hour we were to leave for Germany and Berlin.

CHAPTER 15

A YEAR IN BERLIN

(i) *In the Old Coriander Shop*

IN the appalling frosts at the end of December 1905, the whole of our family set off abroad. Verzhbolovo was the last station on Russian soil; beyond it lay the invisible barrier between our country and 'theirs': the alien, un-Russian Germany. We had hardly eaten our bortsch, cutlets, and buckwheat *kasha*, the traditional meal for station buffets, before our parents finished with the passports and customs, and fetched us on to the German train.

It stood by the platform, in freezing mist and clouds of steam, quite different from our trains with their brightly lacquered green, orange, and blue carriages. It was a boring, depressed dark brown, each carriage indistinguishable from the last, except for the number over its door. 'Here', said our porter, stopping by one of them, and with a broad sweep of his sleeve wiping away the sweat that was out of place in that cold.

The German conductor checked our tickets in silence. Everything about him was different too—the imposing way he held himself, his natty uniform, above all the ladylike little patent-leather handbag he wore on a shiny red strap. Stepping to one side he growled 'Bitte' quite distinctly, and let us into the carriage. With that 'Bitte' we began our acquaintance with the unknown Germany where we were to stay till the autumn of 1906. We arrived in Berlin in January of the new year, in frosts that boldly refuted the Russian monopoly on intense cold.

In the train we were struck by a number of novelties, not the least being that everyone, from the solid chief guard to the meanest newspaper boys and cleaners, spoke perfectly fluently, without stuttering or hesitation, in a language that we had to be taught specially. Boris and I kept exchanging incredulous glances, as though they were making fools of us by purposely talking German, instead of Russian, as they ought. And weren't those little cupboards in the lavatories marvellous, with their neatly piled towels and cakes of soap, which you could plunder endlessly (no one checked), and then chuck away, after using them only once! Yet no one took more than they needed, or pocketed a few extras for themselves! We honestly envied the waiters' agility, as they carried trays of full coffee-cups down the exact middle of the corridor carpet without spilling a drop. And the train ran so inconceivably fast that we could hardly take a step without being flung from side to side. When it took a curve we were positively squeezed into the carriage walls.

The windows inside the train were obscured by frost, so we saw nothing of our several days' journey, and as we drew into the suburbs of Berlin, failed to notice how we gradually climbed on to the viaduct that carried us past third-floor windows, elevated minor halts and major stations, till we reached our stop, Berlin Am Zoo, where we left the train.

Having begun my first impressions of Germany, I found myself wondering how they might strike someone like my son. Wouldn't he be surprised by the kind of things catching the attention of a twelve-year-old, and, judging me by his own standards, wouldn't he find it hard to suppress a condescending smile? And, indeed, wouldn't he be right?

It was quite true that when we found ourselves in this foreign world, we kept colliding with mysteries which took us totally by surprise, most of all when they lurked in the minor details of ordinary life. We remembered these best because they delighted our boys' imaginations more than the predictable attractions of a new town, its sights, streets, and squares. And here, alas, I must add that Berlin was not a city whose every corner afforded new architectural masterpieces, whereas, in contrast with the Moscow we had just abandoned, the commonplace minutiae of life seemed miracles to us.

Let me explain. The childhood of my generation coincided with the transition from the era of steam and kerosene to that of electricity. That tired phrase actually obscures a vivid reality. Like all my contemporaries, I spent my first decade serenely by the light of a paraffin lamp. I remember the different phases of its existence perfectly. For instance: the grown-ups would suddenly break off their work with cries of 'hey, it's smoking!', and busily trim the rebellious orange flames that shot up, trailing a dusky veil. And then they came to put it out for the night. Sweetly, intimately tutting to itself, it made its idiosyncratic farewells, flaring up (is it for the last time?), running a quick necklace of dim blue flames round the rim of the burner, and finally dying away with a deep, dull sigh . . . In the first years of my life it didn't even occur to me that the paraffin lamp hadn't been created with the sun and moon on the first day. I was quite disconcerted to find out that, in the past, people lit their houses, and even their palaces, with candles, while cottagers made do with rush lights. And then electricity appeared! Good God, how everything changed! How could we have survived in the backward days of semi-darkness?

The gradual arrival of electricity flung me into a sense of flustered hurry and rapturous confusion. First came a light without match or flame; much later, the black tube you talked through, with people you couldn't see, at the other end of town. But that was after our return from Germany. Before that time we were innocent of lifts and electrical appliances; no cars drove down our Moscow streets. But already we had stopped filling our lamps with blue paraffin; wick and burner were replaced by plug and socket, into which you screwed a little, pear-shaped glass balloon with a thin bent hair trembling inside it. There! —someone clicked something on the wall, and, wonder of wonders, the looped hair promptly blushed, brightened to a hard, white incandescence, and the room made itself even lighter, perhaps, than it had done in the days of kerosene. They called the bulb a 'pear' in those days. A pear of eight or ten candlepower was quite enough for us to do our homework by. When my parents had guests, both leaves of the dining-room table were pulled out; the adapted skeleton of the oil-lamp hanging above it was fitted with a twenty-five candlepower bulb, and the room seemed bright as day. Aren't such figures—eight, ten, twenty-five—laughable now?

By the time my son was born, oil-lamps were long forgotten; their electrified remains had vanished. Everything was properly settled in its place. At four years he would boldly seize the telephone and chatter into it without a tremor. It was hardly worth mentioning! All sorts of electrical fixtures were at his service. Nothing new in the long chain of progress surprised him. It was all natural and ordinary; for him, it was merely the next word in a simple sentence begun long ago.

But when we arrived in Berlin we were dumbfounded by novelties of every kind from the grandiose to the trivial, even, for example, the street vending-machines that ministered to the Berliners' minor needs and advertised the goods of a company called Stollwerk. In exchange for our ten-pfennig pieces, the machine, bells sweetly ringing, would spill out a small packet of sugared almonds, or a miniature bar of chocolate, on to its little tray. The same machine provided other customers with cigarettes, matches, a cigar, and even scent. With equal excitement we spent hours watching the six red or blue carriages of the underground thundering out of the earth and ripping headlong up the rising incline of its ramp. Tunnel and ramp were surrounded by a grassy square securely shut off from the pedestrian by a high stone parapet, where someone like us always dawdled, admiring the wonders of the new technology.* And yet my son is right—where are my memories of the town, its edifices, avenues, and squares? Surely it didn't all pass us by? Oh no, certainly not! I remember those big crossroads where a policeman, in a black uniform (proper long trousers! and gold-spiked helmet, just like Bismarck!) conducted the traffic with the faintest waft of a wrist. He was so different from Russian policemen, with their ballooning breeches crookedly crammed into their boots, their scruffy brass number-plates and swords loosely dangling by a shoulder-strap, that we quite forgot this transfigured Zeus was a representative of the most highly developed police state in the world. We were entranced, not by a policeman on point duty, but by a monument come to life—by the beauty of its movements and its superb measured calm.

With strident icy wheels, like some dragon, a Fafner of Wagnerian opera breathing clouds of steam, smoke, and freezing mist, our hot-bellied, frost-whitened train crawled slowly under the vast glass roof of the station. It was already getting dark. Lamps were coming on, and their deathly yellowish-green light seemed to make the icy air even colder.

Climbing out, snug in our warm hats and boots, we looked eagerly about us. We had hardly left the train when an unexpected chime rang out nearby, and part of the asphalt platform suddenly split in two, like the

---

* '1906. For the first time in my life I was abroad. Everything was unusual, different from what it was at home. It was less like living than like dreaming, or like taking part in some improvisation on the stage, some entertainment without rules, which no one had a duty to take part in or attend. There was nobody you knew, nobody to lay down the law to you—doors flapping open and shut in an endless row along the lane of carriages—each compartment with its separate door. Four tracks curving along a circular viaduct overlooking the gigantic city, high above its streets, canals, racing stables and back yards. Trains chasing and overtaking one another, running side by side and separating. Street lights dividing, intersecting under railway bridges; lights in first and second storey windows, level with the tracks; jewelled clusters of pin-point illumination on slot machines in station restaurants (the slot machines threw out cigars, chocolates and sugared almonds). I was soon familiar with Berlin, loafing about in its countless streets and in its endless park, breathing its mixture of gas, train smoke and beer fumes, talking German with a fake *Berliner* accent and listening to Wagner.'

Boris Pasternak, *An Essay in Autobiography*, pp. 59–60.

familiar trap-doors of our country cellars. Bells still ringing, the two flaps somehow began heaving themselves up, as though someone had knocked them apart and was pushing from below. From this ever-widening crack two arches gradually emerged, separating the cellar hatches till they stood vertically, leaning against the fully extended arches, straddled on their tubular iron supports. A lift floor eased out of the hole, and as it drew level with the platform a laden trolley was quickly rolled off it on to solid ground. The lift promptly sank again, dragging after it arches and trap-door, till everything returned to its original place, and the bells fell silent, their admonitory function fulfilled.

Who would be surprised by a lift nowadays? And yet the sight first meeting our eyes on Berlin station naturally evoked our wild delight! Every time the familiar melodic ringing sounded, we turned to watch the unfolding spectacle once again.

At last our parents finished their affairs and took us down the wide stairs to the street below. Here a one-horse Berlin carriage was waiting for us. It, too, was different, with curving shafts like ours but no arched shaft-bow over the horse's neck. As though to spite us, here again the windows were frosted over, and we travelled blindly along the miracu-lous smoothness of an asphalted road, till we arrived somewhere, were put on a pavement, and found ourselves at the doors of a hotel proudly calling itself 'Fürst von Bismarck', with the addition beneath, 'am Knie'. This, we already knew, was the name of the road junction fanning out from the corner-plot taken up by our hotel.

We had a set of three communicating rooms on an upper floor, where it was so cold that even we northerners were discomfited. The boys attending us (lanky lads called 'piccoli' by the hotel staff) promised that supplementary stoves would be brought. That surprised us. How could a stove be installed without a chimney? Much that we encountered, like the eiderdowns instead of blankets and mattresses, or the ledged wooden trays on legs instead of beds, were familiar enough from stories and cartoons in my father's German periodicals, and didn't surprise us in the least. At that time, though, we were quite unprepared for the widespread use of gas lighting. Consequently we both cried out together, incredulously, 'Call that a stove?' when the promised 'stove' was brought in. It was attached to the gas-pipe, lit with a match, and a pale blue tongue of fire, somehow catching its breath, snakily slithered up between some sort of little pipes. The two 'piccoli', grinning and exchanging glances, ran out of the room.

The smell of lighted gas! How much it tells me, even now, of the distant past! From my very birth smells have constantly pursued me, their visible counterparts lagging behind them as consequence, not cause. First, the queasy, sickly smell of gas; then the spurt of flame. Finally, the brass chains under the lamp, hanging from something like the crossbar of a scales. The chains end in flat brass rings, punched with the letters A and Z, like the alpha and omega of existence. Pull A and in a second the gas lights of its own accord, without a match; pull Z* and it all goes out again. So it has always been: first a smell caught my attention, and only later did the sight explain.

For me, the stay in Berlin was much more than life in the unfamiliar conditions of a foreign country. It marked a new phase in my life—a different relationship with my brother. There had been times when his three years' superiority (which he never abused) was completely obliter-ated, and our common friends and games, and above all the uniform attitude to us both, made us equals. In Berlin, for the first time, Boris became distinctly older than me—not in terms of time, but by virtue of a kind of moral co-ordination which was a measure of his maturity. How it happened I don't know, but one day it did. In the train bringing us to Berlin, in the Hotel Bismarck, he was still my equal. Perhaps it was his studying music once again, with an adult seriousness he hadn't had in Moscow. To my great misery, I saw that there would be no end to this new period of 'older' and 'younger', and the days would never return when the three-year gap was wiped away.

I don't remember how long the frosts continued, nor how they ended. I don't remember how long we stayed in the hotel, nor how, when, and why we transferred to a boarding-house run by a kindly woman called Fräulein Gebhardie. It was a small, many-roomed apartment inhabited by a number of short-term business visitors of various nationalities, most of whom spoke fluent German, the usual language at meal-times. However, the three rooms we took here were beyond my father's means, and on Fräulein Gebhardie's advice a small ground-floor room was taken for us boys in a fruit-shop round the corner. The proprietor, Frau Witwe, supplemented her scant takings by renting out one of the two back rooms where my brother and I spent the rest of our time in Berlin.

In memory of Dickens we used to call it the Old Coriander Shop. Like the Old Curiosity Shop it too united poverty with honesty and excep-

---

* 'Auf' and 'Zu': on and off.

tional cleanliness, while in the background there hung a perpetual light aroma of cinnamon, coriander and cloves, vanilla and pepper, dates, pears, grapes and even pineapples. In this dear shop we began our paradisal, independent existence—a life in Eden. 'Obst und Südfrüchte', the laconic shop-sign proclaimed, and its southern fruits were the source of our Eden in the Kurfürstenstrasse. Here lay huge, hairy coconuts and smooth, bald nuts the size of a baby's head. Golden bananas curved in heavy clusters. The packing cases exhaled vanilla, cinnamon, coffee, and everywhere figs breathed their sweet, winey fragrance. It was the first, and, it is now clear, the last time that we should live so close to the gifts of the East.

Certainly we had encountered oranges, mandarins, and even pineapples in Moscow. Pineapples could be seen in the Eliseyev shop-windows on Tverskaya Street. Oranges and mandarins were the food of festivals, which the middle-class intelligentsia couldn't otherwise normally afford. Eliseyev was not our Court caterer, and we visited it rarely—to buy, for instance, those outlandish nuts (which you can no longer find in Moscow) for our Christmas tree, wrapping them in gold-foil for decoration. Mangoes, with which our Muscovites are sometimes now regaled, were familiar to us from literature alone. Naturally, then, the days we spent in the midst of the tangible Orient made an impression on me. Everything I had once avidly read about lay to hand, in wall-cupboards and chests, beneath the counter and in the windows. The silence of desert islands hung in the unfrequented shop; the solitary window filtered a dim half-light, as of virgin forests overgrown with creeper and liana, lotus, ailantus and orchid.

The vision didn't fade. It was as though a breakwater stood against the stormy rhythm of Berlin streets, with all their nervous hurry and commotion. When the weak doorbell rang, the newcomer found himself bathed in amplitude of spirit, the optimistic, calming aura of an ideal world. We soon saw that the shop's customers were as constant as its scents and silence. In our imagination, the regulars became living accessories to the southern fruits, familiar natives of our paradise, just as they grew to know 'those Russian kids' quite well. Among the inhabitants of our Eden were Frau Witwe, a woman of powerful and sentimental calm, and her two adored daughters.

My brother hadn't touched a piano for some time. One day he was delighted to hear Frau Witwe's fifteen-year-old daughter playing on the other side of the partition. He offered her free music theory lessons, in exchange for the right to play himself; her mother agreed, and a wonderful life began. Boris initiated his pupil into the secrets of music, setting her, as he used to say, 'easy teasers'. The jaded, out-of-tune piano was set right, and when it was his turn, Boris came into his own. One might have expected that the combination of music and youth, the intimacy of study and equality of age, would foster some romantic idyll, but neither teacher nor pupil had time for such things. Meanwhile, I had my own preoccupations. I had to keep up my Latin and maths, and a Russian *émigré* student with black hair, black whiskers, and the appropriately ferocious name of Maybardyuk was invited to take charge of them. The lessons went badly. My other chore of serving occasionally behind the counter was infinitely preferable. The disappointingly small number of clients didn't disturb me, and the slight complications of sale presented no difficulties. Perched behind the counter, inhaling the aromas of the East, I dreamt my time away or devoured the Russian books that fell into my hands.

My brother's Berlin period was dominated by Wagner, whose work had appealed to him before our departure. Ever since it became clear that Boris had a musical future, friends had given him music. His cupboard at home displayed the scores of several Wagnerian operas, in beautiful editions with crimson and gold bindings. Yet it was my mother, rather than Boris, who used to play long extracts from them, so that much of Wagner's work became familiar to me. Boris preferred to improvise, particularly when no one was listening, seeing himself as a future composer, not a performer. For this reason he avoided the exercises he detested, and had no technical skill whatever, as he admits in *Safe Conduct*. A couple of years earlier he had started taking serious lessons in theory and harmony from the well-known Moscow music-critic, theoretician and composer, Y. D. Engel.

Here I must venture into the very region described in my brother's *Essay in Autobiography*. Boris, however, said nothing about his musical life in Berlin, probably because he wrote as an established poet, having broken his ties with music long ago, and ceased therefore to give it any serious weight. I shall try to reconstruct what he has omitted.

Engel was a gentle man, yet, as a teacher, he was captious, harsh, and miserly in his praise, which was all the more precious for its rarity. He regarded lessons, whoever the pupil, in terms of selfless labour and the joy of fulfilment. They never sank to the level of dilettantism, but demanded sweat and energy. And this was exactly what Boris felt, too. I often found him poring over a criss-crossed manuscript sheet in excited irritation. Although the room we shared in our Moscow flat was more than big enough for the two of us, it could barely hold him on his own at such times. He would fill it, running from corner to corner, humming, conducting something, settling for a minute, then irritably jumping up again, not speaking to me—as though I weren't in the room at all. How wonderful it was for us both when he came back from a lesson with Engel in a good mood, boasting that he had managed to compose such a fugue, even Y.D. didn't scribble over it with his red pencil! That was more than praise. Then I first heard of Riemann, the German musical theoretician whose fat blockbuster Boris used to lug home from his lessons. When Engel learnt we were going to Germany, he insisted that Boris should buy his own copy there, and continue his lessons by post. Boris bought his Riemann in Berlin, began to study it methodically, and was soon under way. New, not quite comprehensible words began to be heard in his conversation, such as 'tonic', 'dominant', 'counterpoint', the even more trenchant 'figured bass', and the strange slip of a word 'continuo', that seemed to have slid from the organ of St Cecilia herself. With that 'continuo' my brother reduced me to total annihilation.

He tried out all his new theories on his poor pupil—an exercise that was of more use to himself than her. When he had utterly confounded her with his easy teasers, he promptly resolved them himself, often with a complicating flourish, predicting in whose style he would round off the music—and lo and behold, it really did sound exactly like Bach or Beethoven, Chopin or Liszt.

So Boris became my unquestioned older brother. Music elevated him to an adult level. In the Old Coriander Shop he became a kind of guardian for me, delicately carrying out an imperceptible tutelage. Our interests began to diverge. I saw him press far ahead, and understood that the time had come for me to stretch after him, not for him, condescending, to stoop down to me. Not always successfully, not always apropos, I tried to solve this most difficult of problems. An indefinable rift between childhood and not-childhood opened at this time, and in this shop.

In Berlin Boris began frequenting the concert halls regularly and seriously. For some reason he was coolly disposed to strings, in solo performance and in chamber music, considering them to be no more than a necessary component of the full orchestra. The piano he only recognized in its pure form, as a solo instrument, or with an orchestral accompaniment in piano concertos, and in general the instrumental combinations of sonatas, trios, and even quartets left him cold. The concerts he attended were therefore generally symphonic ones, to which he used to take his pupil or myself for 'musical development'. I went willingly. I loved music, and, I think, understood it in my own way; I liked listening to it with my brother, who often explained passing details to me. Usually we went to the cheap morning concerts given by the Philharmonia. These were no different from the evening performances as far as the quality of soloists and conductors or the seriousness of programme was concerned. If anything, the distinction lay in the audience; the morning concerts attracted the young, whose sensitive, serious attitude to the music infected us all, whereas the conceited, moneyed social cream attended in the evenings.

We were lucky enough to witness performances by many great musicians in their prime, and, better still, to hear the rising younger generation. The most frequent appearances among the conductors were made by Nikisch, Mengelberg, the young Furtwängler, and Walter. We heard Godowsky and Schnabel. Once Ysaÿe made a guest appearance. The programmes included symphonies and concertos by Beethoven and Brahms, frequent Wagnerian overtures, and the symphonic poems of Richard Strauss. Everything was first class, which is why a trivial aspect of these morning concerts at first seemed such a profanation.

A small buffet opened on to the auditorium, where you could buy a glass of beer and hot sausages. Little tables for four were arranged in this recess, at which people usually sat in twos, in order to see the stage, simultaneously listening and gluttonizing shamelessly, to our intense disgust. Yet the music was not disturbed. The quiet waiters walked neatly over the thick carpet, as artistically as if they were themselves a part of the music. They asked no questions, looking attentively into their customers' eyes, and perfectly divining what was required. The orders were set down so gently, the marble table-tops seemed turned to down; the china plates and thick glass beer-mugs became soft as cotton wool. No one talked or joked. They ate with unconsciously expressed concentration—a raised eyebrow, an unexpected jerk of the hand—to which the incidental gulp of beer made little difference. Observing them, we realized that this was no matter of irreverent familiarity, but an honest intimacy in which music itself seemed to participate, winking at their modest breakfast, nodding *bon appetit* and passing on its way. Our original distress at the apparent incompatibility faded, and in the end we too sat at our table, sipping and listening with undiminished absorption and exact aesthetic delight.

I heard much that was new to me. Naturally my brother had a great influence over my responses, introducing me to contemporary music with the natural simplicity of an old *habitué*, protecting my shyness before his oldest friends. The only composer we didn't hear them play was Bach.

My childhood sensations had begun with his music. Just as air was instinctively drawn into my still weak lungs, oxygenating the body without my conscious participation, so Bach in my mother's interpretation permeated my unformed consciousness from my earliest days. But while I heard him in a solo piano arrangement, I could not understand his music properly. Now, on Berlin Sundays, Boris began taking me to the nearby Gedächtniskirche—no architectural masterpiece, certainly, but its acoustics, organ, and organist were excellent. Once we knew the church routine sufficiently well we used to call on weekdays to listen to the organist practising, and trying out different interpretations of Bach's melodies. Usually he played best at the end of the service, as the congregation dispersed. Heated by his appeal to the Almighty, Bach seemed to cry out, obstinate and insistent, thrusting aside the walls as a deep breath distends the rib-cage. Sound intensified on sound, supercharging the atmosphere, till we lost all bodily sense. Everything, it seemed, was lost in a vast universe—and yet we were held tight in a powerful grasp, the deep supporting boom of the bass. The last, superhuman chords sounded. The organ fell silent, attentive to the answering echo cast by the church's newly resurrected windows, walls, and vaults. Drained of sensation, and wondering that the streets and houses should still be standing, we were the last to leave, silently, for home.

'*Besser wie du!*' A laconic, scathing phrase. To our ears, that 'Better than you' sounded wrong, somehow; we would have said, 'Besser, als du', losing its quick sting. It rang out more than sixty years ago, and I can still hear it today. The incident that gave rise to it was trivial, the response significant. To understand them properly, I must return to our early childhood.

Even then, my brother often baffled me. The grown-ups couldn't understand him either, and there was talk about his wildness and extravagance, his quirks and crankiness. In any game, he absolutely had to be leader. There was nothing peculiar in that. *Cosi fan tutti*—all children naturally try to outdo each other, though my brother was distinguished by the ease with which he generally succeeded. He just seemed to carry off everything with a confoundedly light touch. What was exceptional was his terrifying reaction to occasional defeat. If someone else came out on top instead of him, he didn't burst into a predictable storm of indignant rage, but withdrew immediately into a deep, gloomy silence, vanishing without a word. This alarmed the grown-ups. I, understanding nothing, pitied him. In retrospect, I think he wished to hide his emotional turmoil from others.

My brother's habitual luck confirmed his self-confident faith in fate. Hence his devastated discomfiture in the face of defeat. He himself (already a successful poet) admitted in his *Essay in Autobiography* that 'from my childhood I had a penchant for mysticism and superstition . . . the providential attracted me'; that 'oblique reasons, guesswork founded on chance, and the expectation of signs and commands from above' were, as he thought, to blame for his disasters. Merely because he did not have perfect pitch, he gave up music—seeing this defect as 'proof that my music was unacceptable to Fate and the stars'. Phrases like these are perfectly applicable to the fiascos of his earliest years. Even then, he saw his childish failures as no chance occurrences, but celestial signs of his own inadequacy, and his dismay can only be explained in terms of a painful sense of such divine 'unacceptability'. His faith in himself was rattled, his illusory strength undermined—and the fates were to blame.

I dare say he had a subconscious need to test himself, and that such self-validation played a large part in the behaviour attracting our parents' disapproval. The most cogent example was his inexplicable insistence that he should be allowed to take part in the 1903 bareback cavalcade to the night grazing, which ended so disastrously. It was also typical that after such a débâcle the favourite pastime was abandoned, decisively and absolutely; he never returned to it, 'tearing it out of himself as a man parts with what is dearest to him'. In the same way he abandoned a stamp-collection in which he felt his weakness had been detected. And he gave up one of his favourite games, the naval battle based on the Russo-Japanese War, whose premium in ingenuity and cunning had attracted him. After his rout, the game vanished for ever—a typically abrupt and decisive rupture.

Even in the early days of our stay at Fräulein Gebhardie's, Boris was aware of slips in intonation and construction which betrayed the foreigner in him, however fluent his German. He smarted at the misguided certainty that people were treating him with indulgent patience, as a half-witted foreigner, one of those Muscovites, practically a Baltic yokel, who couldn't hope to master the German tongue. For this reason he went all out to make himself indistinguishable from the real Germans, especially the local Teutons with their Berlin slang. It wasn't for us to judge the similarity; he seemed to do so well, we stopped noticing the difference. After his and my transfer to the Old Coriander Shop, and our closer intimacy with simple Berliners, matters progressed even more satisfactorily.

One fine, early spring morning, we went out in excellent spirits for our usual walk together. The streets were deserted and swept clean, the air warm and bright. Like a dull moire ribbon laid across glossy chain-mail, the asphalt path lay between fan-tailed cobbles buffed bright by passing feet. A boy appeared in the distance, whistling cheerfully, like us enjoying the morning. As he came up to us, Boris complimented him with an unthinking, older-brotherly condescension, perhaps, and in the Berlin jargon, of course. What he said escapes me; something like, 'Don't you whistle well!' But the boy must have sensed his patronizing tone, as well as his failure to imitate the Berlin accent quite accurately, and his evident desire to do so. 'Besser wie du!' rang out, curt and provocative in the silence, and before Boris could collect himself, the victor had run on.

A total eclipse would have seemed brighter than the gloom overcasting my brother's sunny morning. He fell silent and paced on. Faint-hearted and tongue-tied, I followed. All purpose to our stroll was lost. We moved our legs mechanically, without thinking why or where we were going, till tiredness drove us home.

The old pattern repeated itself. From that morning Boris stopped Berlinizing. He no longer casually tossed cant terms through closed teeth; no longer distorted his natural intonation with a guttural gurgle, as though someone had gripped him by the throat. He gave up the local affectation of quickly snatching his cap off his head. It all vanished as though it had never been.

In spite of our difference in age, I always tried to read the books my brother was engrossed in. It did me no harm, and little good. I can't say for certain when I read Hamsun for the first time, but it made a great

Leonid and Alexander preparing for the Union of Russian Artists' spring exhibition. Alexander is hanging his father's study of Tolstoy on his death-bed, made a few months earlier. Moscow, 1911.

Details taken from an undated group photograph. Moscow, c.1910.

Scriabin and his second wife, Tatyana
Feodorovna.

The conductor Nikisch, and Chaliapin
behind him.

Koussevitsky and his wife.

Josef Hofmann at the piano. Drawing by Leonid
Pasternak. Bad Kissingen, 1912.

Nikisch conducting. Sketch by Leonid Pasternak.
Moscow, c.1910.

Vladimir Mayakovsky after he left school, *c.*1910.

impression on me and Boris and I talked about it a lot. This is of interest only in the light it throws on my brother.

Boris dates his reading of Hamsun, Bely, and Przybyszewski to 1903, saying, in his *Essay in Autobiography*, 'when I was a schoolboy in my third or fourth year I was intoxicated by the most recent literature—I raved about Andrey Bely, Hamsun and Przybyszewski . . .' This reference is related to the Christmas holidays he spent in Petersburg. However, that 'or' is incorrect. In the Christmas of his fourth year my brother's leg was in plaster, or only just out of it, and it is unlikely anyone would have allowed him to travel to Petersburg alone in such a state. His fascination for Komisarzhevskaya's Theatre* could only have taken place in his third, not fourth year—that is, the winter of 1902–3, not 1903–4. At that time I was only nine years old. It is hard to believe that I could read Hamsun at that age, or exchange my views with my brother. Such doubts would have little interest were they not connected with the important question, when my brother really was in Petersburg, and when he first started reading and raving about the latest literature. Let us suppose for a moment that he was more accurate in his reminiscences than I . . .

In the Old Coriander Shop we were given a small room which had no furniture except two beds, a small table, a large chest of drawers filled with Frau Witwe's things, a wash-stand, and, in the corner, a large round stove (an Utermark) reaching almost to the ceiling. There was no room for anything else. Above the chest of drawers (which we didn't use) hung a small bookshelf. All the furniture we used was in the open; there were no secret places in which we might hide anything, and neither of us made a secret of what we were doing.

That is why I can state categorically that the new passion which was to win my brother away from music and so change all his future life did not begin in this place, in 1906. Only the very first seeds of the new enthusiasm may have been sown here, but if so, then only towards the spring, at the very end of our stay in Berlin. Yet they manifested themselves so randomly and indistinctly, that they did not attract my attention. In these last weeks, however, the cheap pocket editions, and uniform brick-brown jackets of the Universal-Verlag type, began to appear on our bookshelf. I saw that my brother had begun to enjoy reading German classics, especially the poetry. I don't know where he got the contemporary Russian poets from. I didn't notice any sign of his

---

* The New Drama Theatre, in Petersburg, founded by the actress Komisarzhevskaya.

writing poetry, as I certainly would have done, had that been the case. No. He only wrote music at this time—exercises, and his own compositions. The chief judge is of course Boris himself, and in both his *Safe Conduct* and *An Essay in Autobiography* he says nothing about the birth of new artistic interests, although he speaks quite openly of his début in the musical arena, his 'strumming'.

In retrospect it is easy to postulate that this turning point in his interests did indeed take place in the shop. Yet in the days we spent there together nothing suggested it to me, not even the appearance of those Universal-Verlag pocket editions. I suspected nothing!

The fate of those books was typical. Boris used to buy them, read them, finish them and lay them aside. Somehow the number of books on the shelf didn't grow; the old ones vanished without his grumbling or even noticing. Maybe he gave them to his student, and saved himself the bother of transporting crate-loads back to Moscow, since he was never a collector and the acquisition of a library was quite contrary to his nature. The only fleeting exception to this was his accumulation of a herbarium and a palaeontological collection. Here you could indeed detect some of the true collector's proper characteristics. The file, filled with big sheets of filter paper and exquisitely laid-out specimens of flowers and shrubs, named in the correct manner, was beautifully methodical, as was the collection of palaeontological specimens brought back from the school expeditions to the Moscow River banks. These apart, he was a downright enemy of the collecting instinct. Even in his youth his room was strikingly simple and austere: a table, chair, a bookshelf; no pictures, no decorations. It remained a constant in all the different periods of his life, and I never knew him otherwise.

As Berlin grew warmer, we used to spend whole days in the Tiergarten nearby. This wonderful great green island in the midst of a noisy city became our spring refuge, reminding us of the Sokolniki park in Moscow, since in both you lost all sense of the town surrounding you. We avoided the wide avenues, the gardeners' show-pieces, where everything was neatly swept and garnished, where nannies and governesses promenaded with their charges and their uniformed or bowler-hatted admirers. We retired to the solitary, secluded wilderness, where leaping squirrels ignored us and sparrows collected in their hundreds.

Sitting on a bench, my brother would pull the latest Universal-Verlag out of his pocket. I knew it was prose he was enjoying—Hoffmann, or Jean-Paul, a particular favourite of his. He said he had read nothing to equal the *Travel Notes of Dr Katzenberger*. On our return home he managed to buy an expensive edition of this work from Lang's shop on the Petrovka, and gave it to me—in memory, perhaps, of our walks in the Tiergarten. He also got hold of several volumes of Hoffmann's tales in German, which he so delighted in that his own first novellas— 'Appelles' Mark', and 'The Tale of a Carp' (which was lost in manuscript and never rewritten)—were composed in the perpetually restless style of pure German Romanticism. Characteristically, my brother later repudiated the style completely, as though it had never influenced him at all.

(ii) *Rügen Island*

As summer approached my parents received advice from every side about the best places for a seaside holiday. How were they to decide, though, between Rügen Island, on the Baltic, and a similar place on the North Sea? The euphony of a Rügen Island resort—Goehren auf Rügen—was decisive, and we soon found ourselves on a fast train to Stralsund.

Boris and I were puzzled by the promise of the brightly illustrated prospectus that our train would be transported by ferry to the island. How could they waft those four big Pullman carriages from dry land on to the ferry's bobbing deck? We spent the journey inventing solutions, and missing the obvious one. Our carriages were simply driven, like a coach and pair, on to the ferry, which turned out to be a specially constructed broad-beamed vessel, an extension of the railway line. It was a short and simple operation. An engine cautiously nosed us forward; the carriages jolted heavily as they crossed the tracks from land to deck. Out of the train windows we saw the usual unhealthy grasses and greasy clinkered track shift abruptly to narrow, close-fitting planks, scrubbed and whitewashed, gleaming in the sun. The brown carriages, ponderous as bison, lumbered to a halt, and were firmly battened down. The passengers ventured hesitantly out of their compartments and growing bolder, began to wander about the decks, abandoning their train without a thought for the usual warning cry, 'Bitte einsteigen!' The children, Boris and I among them of course, felt like heroes. Freed from the usual remonstrations ('What d'you think you're doing? Where on earth are you off to?') we crawled under the carriages and over the rails, to emerge on the far side, bask in the sun, and breathe the fresh, free sea-air we loved so much. All our normal preconceptions about earth-bound trains and sea-borne ships were contradicted and confused—a disorientating sensation I experienced only once again, in 1912, when my train, running along a narrow dam, seemed to swim the straits between the Italian mainland and the islands of the Venetian Republic.

The silence was startling, the peace absolute. Somewhere in the ship, engines were turning and the decks shuddered beneath our feet. Nervous reflections palpitated on the Pullmans' dusty sides; on the dazzling deck beside the train, sunlight thrown by the carriage windows lay in a chain of crooked squares and didn't move. Land was lost in the heat-haze behind us; before us no land could be seen. Briefly, we seemed alone on an open sea, with only the shrill, circling gulls linking us to the invisible shores.

Someone suddenly sighted land. There were no delighted cries from the crow's-nest, though; no wild rejoicings on board, only a sense of disappointment that everything should end so soon. We drew in to the island; chalky cliffs reared above the sound, and soon our ferry slipped into the tight little harbour.

A small engine dragged our carriages ashore, to join the island railway's single track: for the length of the journey, the dull measured tolling of a bell sounded, just as though we perpetually circled a forest belfry calling belated worshippers to service. The number of our fellow passengers dwindled with every halt, till at last we reached the resort of Goehren auf Rügen, our own stop at the extreme end of the line.

Who cares now if the face of a certain old man happens to be embedded in this boy's mind?—a hale old fellow, descending the single main street every Friday evening, announcing something in a tranquil voice. He rang his own small handbell, advertising a ball in the local *Kursaal*. His provincial, north-German pronunciation of the French 'réunion' robbed the proclamation of all its grandeur.

There he is, a pointless phantom, telling you nothing, stranded in a child's memory for eighty years, while the resort's lay-out, the where-abouts of the post-office, the pharmacy, the shops where I was regularly sent on errands for cheese, bread, and exquisite freshly-smoked fish, still redolent of woodsmoke and the sea, the paved street we went down daily to the beach—all these have gone beyond recall!

Goehren auf Rügen lay on a sharp promontory at the northern end of the island. Everyone spent their days on the wide, sandy beach to the right of the promontory. Rough but not dangerous waves broke on the other side, which was steep, wild, and rocky. The village street led down to the beach. An unpaved, dusty track went down to the rocky side, where there were no villas, just the backs of the fishermen's huts and sheds, enclosed by wattle fencing. Raising the dust together, Boris and I used to run down this path to the sea, deserted except for the fishermen, and revel for hours in the forbidden pleasures of naked bathing. The respectable beach, with its gaudy parasols and woven basket-work shelters for each family, its primly dressed bathers and decorously supervised children, held no attractions for us. How could it compare with the wild, deserted cliffs where our best hours were spent in independence and liberty?

At first we were the only Russians there. Boris and I made a close-knit clan of two, till Engel arrived with his family, probably at my parents' recommendation. Apart from his officially recognized musical gifts, Engel was exceptionally good with children and was always surrounded by childish laughter. I can remember many games he initiated, or joined in with, like a teenager forgetting his superior years. For instance . . .

Every boy in the resort admired a beautiful model yacht with super-fine trimmings that was displayed in a shop on the main street. It was a proper scale model—prized by the shop-owner as much as the rest of us and priced understandably high. Even the richest children who gaped at the window, unable to tear themselves away, couldn't afford it. In our pension, Boris and I tried repeatedly to cobble a poor imitation together, till Engel sensibly advised us to buy a cheaper model and trim it up as closely as we could to the original. Naturally, the beauty of our dreams didn't materialize, but the three of us often launched our second-rater in trembling agitation, to watch her capsize. 'Never mind!' Engel consoled us; 'it happens to the best of them, even in real life . . .' All the same, he was so pained by her lamentable unseaworthiness, I sometimes felt he was in even more need of consolation than we. Heroically outfacing her reverses, we carried her home in childish pomp on outstretched hands, like a gift bestowed by the gods. Forgetful of her shortcomings, we stepped out proudly in a ceremonial march, under the envious eyes of the passing children. But one cool early evening she sank like a stone, and even Engel couldn't help us retrieve her.

Maybe the life of this second-class resort *was* monotonous. My parents didn't repine. As always and everywhere, my father lived his artist's life, drawing on the balcony, in the garden, on the beach, at home, whether the resort was boring or not. My mother played a great deal on the villa-pension's piano, and, like him, took no part in the social life of the place. The arrival of the Engel parents and their two daughters changed our lives a good deal. My sisters had already made friends with these girls in Moscow, and here they spent all their time together, mainly on the beach. With Engel's arrival, Boris naturally lost himself in music and his relationship with his master, a man who was also, by nature, deeply sympathetic to him. Our shared lives began to diverge once more, though I often witnessed their lessons together on the beach, interspersed with swimming and sunbathing. In the silence, unnoticed, I could watch their discussions and my brother's reactions to criticism —although there was nothing of the teacher about Engel; rather, it was a matter of chats between bathes, and sudden, relaxed silences of deep thought.

Only my brother's later repudiation of music can explain why he never referred to these months on Goehren beach, in his *Safe Conduct* and *An Essay in Autobiography*. Then, ignorant of the future, he lived for music, and his lessons with Engel were a daily, joyful Golgotha. For he suffered, genuinely and physically, when he failed to achieve the goals he set himself, and which, maybe, even his teacher didn't expect of him.

From their often heated arguments I could see that my brother demanded too much of himself. Yet serious, even professional disagreements would often break out between them. In a characteristic tone of gentle surprise, not even reproach, as though speaking of a third person in a different instance, Engel would express his own—merely personal, mind—uncertainty about how this other person might set about solving such a problem. From these tangential beginnings he passed to direct instructions, anatomizing what my brother, and no third person, had done, frankly and critically demanding: 'How could he? . . . Was it possible such solutions wouldn't even occur to him? . . . Such modulations? . . . Such transitions? . . .' and a run of musical phrases would follow. Reddening and stuttering, my brother would nod, agreeing that of course . . . that was just what . . . he was trying to . . . don't you see, if you do it like this . . . and he too would turn from words to music, humming what he meant. Here something quite strange would happen. Evidently my brother, humming what he thought was a continuation of Engel's last remark, would develop the theme in such a new and idiosyncratic way that Engel himself would fall silent, surprised and uncomprehending. Delighted, he would then jump up, waving his hands and choking, a habit of his in such moments, barely able to squeeze out the repeated 'Oh Borya! well Borya! . . .' And when their first excitement faded, manuscript paper would be brought out and both of them, no longer master and pupil but two musicians together, would scribble away, interrupting each other, humming and whistling like a pair of drunks.

I didn't intrude much in these musical idylls, pining instead for the final flourish when the three of us could plunge into the waiting sea and lark about once more. It was honestly impossible to be bored with Engel around. He was two people at once—a musician and composer, devoted absolutely to his work, and a marvellous adventurer engrossed in play. Involving the other children in communal games, he would carry us and the grown-ups off on great expeditions round the island, visiting the neighbouring resorts and hunting out tiny, unknown fishing hamlets. Five years later we met by the Baltic, and I found him still as energetic, companionable and young as he had been in those unforgettable days on Rügen Island. How often our two families walked together in the quiet pine woods round Goehren, crossing the single railway track, breathing the warm, resinous air, shivered by a rare breeze off the sea. In the open glades lay great grey-blue carpets of succulent bilberries. Far above our heads a solitary hawk would scream, and a bird's shadow swim through the branches. And when the silence of the woods was broken by a bell, we knew now that it was no belfry calling worshippers to service, but the local train dispersing cows that grazed along the line.

Towards the end of the summer, the island's stormy season began. After a particularly violent thunderstorm, the storms confined themselves to the sea. Bathing was forbidden. All the paths down to the beach displayed menacing black-and-white signs, lettered in red, which announced that swimming was *'Polizeilich streng verboten!'** True enough, not a single honest German could be seen in the waves, and the beach was left deserted, swamped by heavy tides, flotsam, and pelts of foam. Our balcony gave us a wonderful view of the wild side of the promontory and its long ranks of white horses. From our vantage point they hardly seemed to move, drawn up in tense formation, so that the sea looked striped and still.

* 'Strictly forbidden, by police orders.'

When the storms were not accompanied by incessant rain, my brother and I used to run down to our bay and shelter from the wind in one of our favourite haunts, a cave well above high-water mark, where we could watch the sea below. The bay where we had placidly swum between the rocks and cliffs, pretending to be survivors of a shipwreck, or aborigines, was unrecognizable now: the water seethed and howled, dashing against the rocks, pouring off in torrents, flying up the opposing cliffs, tossing wooden planks in the air like toothpicks. We couldn't tear ourselves away, attributing significances stolen from our reading to this spectacle of grandiose force, till sheer cold drove us home. On such days the whole resort seemed to die. Everything stewed. The beach was rank with smashed crabs, jelly-fish, and pounded seaweed, cast up and rotting on the sand. That medicinal stench of salt and iodine! I recognized it as soon as I drew breath in Yalta and Odessa, on the Adriatic and the Baltic—an invigorating, curative storm-offering, that is everywhere the same!

We should have taken the hint from those days of increasingly stormy weather; they were a warning. The Engels took the point sooner than we did, and left. A dull two or three weeks passed without them. Forbidding, black-and-white *Polizeilich verboten* signs hardly ever left their posts—and that part of the holidays began when you lose all *joie de vivre* and merely serve out your time, marking off the days till at last the grown-ups say, 'Well, children, oughtn't we to think of going tomorrow?'

That moment came, and our long ingratitude was duly rewarded. We got into our drab train, its four brown Pullman carriages filled with preoccupied families homeward bound. Bell pointlessly ringing, since no cows grazed in the forests so late in the year, the engine drearily trailed us down to the southern port. It shunted us back on a cold ferry, drenched in rain and spray. We slumped in our compartment, without a thought of crawling under carriages and over damascene decks. Slowing down to the sweet jangle of the telegraph directing port and starboard tack, our boat draws into Stralsund harbour. With melancholy clarity, it dawns on us that in a second, and forever, the carriages will touch dry land. Rügen Island will turn into a memory and nothing more.

Only a memory now, for myself and my two sisters. The others died long ago. My brother was the last to go . . .

CHAPTER 16

MUSIC AND MOTHER'S
CONCERTS AGAIN

AT the end of November 1906 we came home again.

Our time abroad had left its mark on each of us. We were all shaken out of our habitual life in the School of Art. Here a distinction should be made. It was not 'our life in Moscow', or 'our life in Russia', but, specifically, our life in the School of Art—for the Art School had a profound influence over our parents' lives, and consequently over us as well. Our sense of liberation during the Berlin sojourn demonstrated the potential flexibility of our previous Moscow life, which we had imagined to be so unalterable. The matriarchal, indivisible unity of the family, it transpired, was neither necessary nor permanent. Our temporary dispersal in Berlin had done none of us any harm. It was a revelation which had the greatest beneficial effect on my mother. When two of the four children broke away and set up on their own, a portion of her vitality was liberated for music again. She was encouraged in this by a Scandinavian violinist also lodging at Fräulein Gebhardie's, who talked her into their playing together. They began with small classic pieces for the violin, but, recognizing each other's capabilities, they soon graduated to a repertoire of violin and piano sonatas. Their playing attracted general attention, first among Fräulein Gebhardie's other guests, and then within the Conservatoire attended by the violinist. Music gradually began to restore my mother's original lively spirits—a vitality which had faded away when I was six or seven and old enough to notice such things.

In Rügen these beginnings were consolidated by Engel's arrival, and on our return to Moscow we all tried to support my mother in her artistic rebirth, not without a certain selfishness on our part. In an atmosphere of delighted spiritual renaissance, music settled back with my mother into a rejuvenated flat, and its full voice began to sound in piano solos, violin and cello trios and sonatas, and, occasionally, my mother's favourite quintets by Schubert and Schumann.

For my part, after the Berlin break, my school work went from bad to worse. I had missed a year and it was very difficult to catch up. Moreover, my independence in Germany now made school life intolerable. The more I neglected my lessons, the worse it got. School began to terrify me, and, seeing no way out, I stopped working altogether, dropping to a position of permanent disgrace at the bottom of the class. The general disapprobation spread from school to home, affecting even my brother's attitude to me, which hurt most of all. And yet I felt no shame in my fall, but gloried in it.

A heavy year passed by—my last in the lower school, since I was to go into the big school when I joined the fifth form in 1907. In the fourth form, perhaps even more after our trip abroad, I felt my real life was at home. In my own eyes I only became a proper person on my daily return from school, a saving happiness which was especially vivid when my mother's playing reached my ears as I climbed the dark stairs to our flat.

Coming home at dusk one day, I found some music on the half-opened piano. Usually my mother played from memory. Evidently she had been sight-reading something new.

It was the score of a violin sonata by Grieg, whom I had known before only as a composer of songs and piano pieces. My mother answered my questions rather vaguely. Yes, this morning she had played with a violinist (I forgot his name immediately), who had come to ask her whether she would do a concert with him. Yes, he wanted to play several violin sonatas and brought this score as a sample. She liked the way he played. He promised to look after all the arrangements, publicity, permissions, and so on. This was decisive, and she agreed.

From that day they began rehearsing their repertoire, beginning with sonatas by Grieg, Mozart, and Beethoven.

Men like Grzhimali, Brandukov, and von Glenn, whom I may have mentioned earlier, were musicians of the highest order, although I could hardly have recognized this at the time. Now equally gifted newcomers began to appear, whose talents I was old enough to appreciate. I was most impressed by Anna Lyubóshitz, who played superbly, and was the first woman cellist I had ever seen. Mikhail Press, and his brother the cellist Josef Press, often came from Berlin. And then there was the new violinist, Alexander Mogilevsky, who enchanted everyone, especially my mother, by his light, sonorous touch, with none of that false squeezing out of sound you get with a bad player. Running to fat, he looked like the incarnation of Dickensian benevolence and *bonhomie*, especially in his pleasantly pouting lips and appealing hands. Alas, later experience convinced me that he was a sharp, even cruel man; yet as a musician he was amazing. His full tone seemed evoked by will alone and a barely perceptible bow-sweep. I never once heard him commit the slightest error of taste in all the many times I heard him play—at our home and his, in concerts, and nearly every day in the summer of 1908, when our families lived at different ends of the same park in Raiki.

After long preparation, my mother's public appearances with Mogilevsky, and sometimes Zisserman, began in the season of 1907–8. These were probably my parents' happiest years. The influence of the Berlin trip was perceptible in new habits and a new freedom which affected every aspect of their lives. They were now regularly at home to visitors—occasions known then by the somewhat pompous, un-Russian name of *jours fixes*. Guests came together by chance, without formal invitation, so there was usually an interesting cross-section of the so-called cultural élite: most often musicians, less often writers, and for some reason, artists almost never. The evenings were always unpretentious, informal, and lively; often one of the guests would play, and if it was a violinist, cellist, or a singer, my mother would accompany them.

Boris avoided these occasions, even when Scriabin, his idol at that time, was present. I suppose it was understandable enough—he didn't want to get drawn into conversation, which would have been inevitable for him. Nothing of that sort hung over me. I wasn't an object of interest to anyone; nobody paid the slightest attention to me, and in my unthreatened security I could listen and learn from the general conversation. I loved the atmosphere of those evenings—the bright lights and festively laid table; the gay gowns and black evening dress; the heightened mood and dispersed murmur of voices, the chink of cutlery and china; the sudden silences. I was struck by the novelty of much that I heard, and many years later fragments would surface again, to be confirmed or confounded by the altered times. Describing them now, I suddenly remembered one incident in all its freshness. It was slight enough but must have made an impression on me at the time.

A conversation about the architecture of Palladio had started up between L. N. Brailovsky (a professor in the School of Art), my father, and, oddly enough, Scriabin himself. They were discussing Palladio's theories of proportion, and the interrelationship of all measurements. It surprised me at the time that a musician should not only talk but argue in such specific detail about architectural questions. In the heat of discussion, Brailovsky started stuttering, with an impassioned pathos typical of him, that in the drawings, forms, and character of Palladian balusters he could clearly see the prototype of a woman's arm. My father teasingly egged him on, and began to expatiate on the deeper connections between art and nature, or something of that sort . . . The name of an architect which meant nothing to me at the time—some Zholtovsky or other—kept coming up in support of Brailovsky's position. Who could have thought then, that in ten or twelve years' time I would myself meet the academician Zholtovsky in the School of Art, where I was a student, and that he should play a decisive role in my own architectural career? I can't remember him ever talking about women's arms and Palladian balusters, but he certainly used to discourse on colour and growth in vegetable nature, and the links between natural forms and architecture.

After dinner we would all go into the drawing-room. Then the musical part of the evening would begin, and everything became at once magical and homely. How simply and unceremoniously those celebrated musicians began to play! The guests never dispersed before two in the morning, and after the last had left my parents would linger a little longer at the empty table, reliving the evening's high spots as the plates were cleared away. Oh, how alive, how new and interesting it all was for me! A schoolboy no longer, I used to feel that I had suddenly matured. But in the morning there were unprepared lessons, the hot moments when I was plucked from my desk to stand before the blackboard, where I fished invented and unconvincing proofs from a vacant brain, till the master dismissed me with the inevitable, resigned sigh, 'All right, sit down!'

From childhood I had dreams of playing like my mother. In the end she agreed to try me, scarcely believing in my powers. At first things went smoothly and she was satisfied. But as soon as we moved on to harder exercises in a quicker tempo, a strange pain started up in my right hand. At first my mother attributed it to a childish lack of stamina, till my continued groans drew her attention to an unusual movement in the tendons governing my fingers. She realized that my complaints had a real cause, and consulted a doctor, a friend of the family. On examination he discovered that there was a defect requiring surgery if I was ever to play the piano seriously. My mother was too uncertain of my musical gifts to agree. So it all finished—to my intense disappointment, and to my relief, since the real pain of practising came to an end. Yet in my childish fantasy I still thought of myself as a pianist capable of the hardest things. If certain passages were played differently from my own conception of them, I felt hurt and angry with the performer, mentally setting his error to rights. In all seriousness I believed that I understood the composer's inmost intentions better than anyone else. This inexplicable sense has not faded with age, and to my shame it sometimes catches me unawares even now.

In the fourth form at school my childish passion to become a practising musician reawakened. Remembering the defect that had made the piano impossible, I was set on learning some instrument which did not depend on dexterity in the right hand. Mogilevsky's playing was a passion with me, and I was particularly struck by the apparent ease of technique required for the violin—which is, in reality, a difficult and even temperamental instrument to master.

I was carried away by dreams of becoming a brilliant, famous violinist. I managed to persuade my mother to ask Mogilevsky whether he had a student at the Conservatoire who might take me on. He responded with professorial caution, raising one objection after another, quite rightly: one's hands, fingers, and even ears were not as easily trained as in early childhood; the demands of school shouldn't be forgotten; the malfunction in my right hand would raise problems, and so on, and so forth. The more impediments he set in my path, the more stubbornly I put them aside. Unexpectedly, he gave in, and took us altogether by surprise when he offered to teach me himself. Then, lamentably quickly, everything came out into the open. What had seemed so easy was impossible. My ears couldn't hear, my fingers wouldn't move, my hands slid rebelliously sideways. The idealistic immaturity of my ambitions was betrayed. And yet I was determined to win through. I skimped my homework, kidding myself that I could make it up later. I worked at my fingering in front of the mirror, on a mute violin, as Mogilevsky had told me, in order to spare my hearers. Two or three years passed, and still I had mastered the merest rudiments, and them only partially.

I used to arrive at my lessons, all self-control lost on the stairs, trembling in miserable anticipation of the shrieks and insults to come and flinching bitterly at the sympathetic glances of Mogilevsky's wife as she opened the door. But how much more humiliating it was to emerge from his study, red-faced and sweating after all those 'chicken claws' and 'donkeys' ears', to walk past the pretty student from the Conservatoire, confidently waiting her turn in the corridor! How often I made some small advance at home, only to lose it utterly under Mogilevsky's eye! Seeing how hopeless it was, I did the only thing left to me, and gave up the violin for ever.

Meanwhile, my mother and I attended Moscow's many concerts together.

The Conservatoire and the Moscow Philharmonia divided nearly all the city's musical occasions between them. There were, of course, smaller concerts given elsewhere but they hardly affected the established equilibrium shared by these two, each of which had characteristic programmes and players. All the Russian classics, and most of the Russian instrumentalists, the musical élite under the Slavophile influence of Stasov at the end of the nineteenth century, gravitated towards their Alma Mater, partly for old time's sake: with some appositeness, therefore, the more conservative music was played in the Conservatoire, attracting its own kind of public. In the Philharmonia the newer, more original music of the West was played by Western musicians. Both centres shared the same high standards. Occasionally some cross-over took place—Scriabin and Stravinsky being performed in the Conservatoire, and Glinka, say, in the Philharmonia. Yet their respective characteristics of old and new, East and West, remained more or less constant. They were so well established that when the *tertium quid* of Koussevitsky's concert seasons started up, they were held in the halls of the Philharmonia, for the simple reason that Koussevitsky drew his conductors and performers mainly from the West.

Concerts were modestly attended in those days, and even when stars like Josef Hofmann or Eugene Ysaÿe arrived, no crowds milled round the box office as they do now. Both the Conservatoire and the Philharmonia had two halls, one Great and one Small, the former for symphonic, choral, and mixed concerts, the latter for vocal, chamber, and solo music. These halls have survived to the present day, though much changed, and I understand that no concerts are now held in the Philharmonia's small auditorium.

The price of tickets depended on each seat's proximity to the performers, as it does today. The first six or ten most expensive rows were made up of wide, comfortable armchairs—real armchairs, with solid backs and armrests. Both these, and the seats of the cheaper rows behind, were of Viennese origin, in the light, elegant style of the Brothers Tonet, their seats and backs of golden, woven cane, their bentwood frames polished a pleasant, deep red-brown. An auditorium filled with this beautiful furniture looked at once festive and domestic. It was in great demand, and every household of the middle-class intelligentsia had its own set of Viennese bentwood chairs.

At the beginning of the concert the seating was ranged in respectable, free-standing rows. But since the same people attended nearly every concert (even without the modern season-tickets), and knew each other well by sight, the arrangement was regularly disturbed by the audience's imperative need to share its pleasures. Auditors, and their chairs beneath them, shifted, straggled, and clustered. By the end of the evening the seating had turned into a map charting the music's magnetic fields of attraction and repulsion. Not a row survived, and the whole place looked like home.

I can't remember exactly when measures were taken against this spirit of public independence. Perhaps it was about 1914 (by which time the audiences had, admittedly, also increased in size) that the back legs of the Viennese chairs were lashed to a long wooden plank passed beneath their seats. But even so the rows had a bad habit of sliding off their sternly marked positions. Consequently, in the Twenties, immobile wooden constructions of mean dimensions and uncomfortable form appeared in the stalls of the Conservatoire's Great Hall. Those flapback wooden 'places', hardly seats, didn't intrude in the freer, simpler, aristocratic Great Hall of the Philharmonia, where the real chairs and armchairs survived; I remember them still in Koussevitsky's time. The democratic spirit of the Conservatoire was made of sterner stuff. It was evident in its attitude to its public, and was intensified by the musicians' oval portraits on the walls, looking down with grave disapproval on the least public disorder below.

The Small Hall of the Philharmonia was particularly welcoming. Its walls were painted an attractive shade of red, the windows and door-frames a warm, marbled ivory. There was no stage, only a small podium, reached by an informal three-stepped ladder on the green-room side. The acoustics here, as in the Philharmonia's Great Hall, were very fine, setting the performers at their ease. In the Twenties it was redecorated and turned into a buffet serving the Great Hall—hardly a good idea, and the misappropriation of this fine concert room was soon rescinded.

*

My mother began rehearsals in earnest at the end of 1906. Apart from her work with Mogilevsky, she agreed to play Tchaikovsky's Trio in A minor with her old partner, Grzhimali, and the cellist Anna Lyubóshitz. The Trio was not yet the concert favourite it later became, and I got to know it well from my mother's practising, so that I was later able to make out exactly which differences of opinion interrupted the trio's joint rehearsals. Sometimes the temperamental Grzhimali would boil over in elderly irritation, raising his voice to defend his own interpretation, then suddenly subside. The music would roll on again, pacifying both players and myself, the distressed eavesdropper in the next-door room. But such outbursts were relatively rare, and in general the trio was harmoniously matched. While they went through their habitual five or six rehearsals together, the inevitable, secondary practicalities were entrusted to one of the younger players, or some young helper from the Conservatoire. The date had to be agreed on, the hall booked, permissions sought from the authorities, posters distributed and notices put in the papers. My mother had her own arrangements to make: she had to choose a piano, arrange for its transport to the concert hall, and book a tuner. She always played on a Bechstein from Zimmerman's on the Kuznetsky Bridge, and we used to arrive in the concert hall on an unfashionably wide-beamed sleigh, which had room for me to hold my mother's piano stool on my knees. She used that stool all her life, cherishing it carefully, and feeling ill at ease on any other. It invariably accompanied her to all her concerts, and it is curious that she left it behind when we went abroad.

I loved going to my mother's final morning rehearsals, particularly when she was playing in the intimate, exquisite Small Hall of the Philharmonia, her usual venue (although she did appear in the Small Hall of the Conservatoire as well). By day, the obliquely sunlit hall seemed to shrink, and with the morning emptiness its excellent acoustics failed. The walls gave back an echo; resonant steps would sound in a distant corridor, ushering in the rare morning auditor—usually one of the many attendants, who were critical but delicate listeners, discreetly whispering among themselves, even when the players paused to argue a point. Those rifts in the music, the exchange of quiet remarks, the louder 'Let's start at letter D', or 'at such and such a bar', and all the below-stairs preparations of the concert appealed to me particularly.

On the night everything changed. There was the ceremonious moment as the chandeliers were lit, the gradual hush, disturbed by rustling programmes, till everything fell silent. The artistes' door opened, and my mother emerged, catching up the train of her white dress, head bowed, Mogilevsky behind her in his black frock-coat, violin tucked under his arm. My mother would run lightly up the steps on to the podium, and with a bow sit down at the piano. Then everything except the music vanished for her. She used to say that she only felt calm when she sat at her instrument and anxiety gave way to heightened concentration.

She sat simply and calmly. The usual remarks about audience contact meant nothing for her. Her main object, she used to say, was contact with her instrument and the composer, her sole concern the elucidation of a common language between them. Apparently impassive, she burnt internally. All her visible movements were simple, laconic, controlled. She made no play with her hands, but her hands played everything as it should be played. Even in the hardest, most emphatic passages, they did not fly up from the keyboard as though plucking themselves free—the school of Leschetizky, she used to say, taught you the muscular control for a strong touch without aerobatics and thumping.

She allowed herself one liberty: in the longer pauses she dried her fingers on her handkerchief, and drew it lightly across the keys. She always had that hanky, like her piano stool, at all her concerts.

At the end of the evening she was as simple as at the start, rising and leaning gently against the piano, acknowledging the applause with a slight inclination of the head. She did not beam and bow. She did not milk applause, but gave an encore if she felt the public (and not she!) deserved it. She was always serious and gentle, rating simplicity and sincerity above all things. Then the public was more temperate than today, and the youngsters only went wild at the concerts of Hofmann, Jan Kubelik, and Ziloti, on his few visits to Moscow. They never broke the rules of decorum, making a vulgar display of ecstasy and temperament by rhythmic clapping, stamping, and the general hullabaloo so common nowadays.

Concerts began at nine in the evening and ended around midnight. Our homecomings were particularly happy. A table waited for us, set with lighted candles, tea and snacks. After the strain we relaxed in quietness, and friends from the audience called on us. Such evenings were not long drawn out: everyone knew how tired the performers must be, and yet they rarely dispersed before two in the morning.

With their departure, and sleep, my mother's sufferings began. The cardiac weakness emerging in her first childhood period of public performance had gradually established itself, and she suffered from heart attacks of ever-increasing strength and frequency. After the concerts ended, she had to pay for everything: the flowers, the success, the applause; the joy of creation; the daring of disturbed equilibrium; her loss of self and the forgotten world. Oh, how she envied others, who could give a series of concerts without penalty! When she remembered her childhood, the tours of twenty concerts or more, two and three at a time in a single town, how conscious she was of her own present weakness! How she missed her deserved triumph, as the students carried her, a child of nine, shoulder high across the cheering hall! And yet even her rare performances gave her new freshness and strength, spoilt though they were by anxiety, muddled fears, worries about neglected duties and, above all, a terrified sense of adverse fate.

No one talked about it at home. I was old enough now to register such conversations, had they taken place, but the subject wasn't touched on. Its only external sign, after each concert ended, was the recurrence of increasingly severe heart trouble, filling us all with foreboding.

The doctors couldn't understand her illness. The diagnoses were various, and therefore untrustworthy. Seeing how the attacks multiplied, they advised her to give up public performances altogether, since the exertion, giving her and us so much joy, was evidently too great a strain. She continued to give concerts at home to an audience of five or six, among them men like Scriabin and Rachmaninov, and much later, Verhaeren, Klyuchevsky, and Prince Kropotkin, as they sat for her husband. It is not for me to comment on how she played. My mother was a modest person. Neither she, nor we, collected cuttings of her many Moscow press reviews.

The cycles of concerts given by Koussevitsky began in 1910, or maybe a little later. He was a fine double-bass player. When he performed solo, people used to say, 'Here comes Koussevitsky with his wardrobe!' He used to get a wonderful tone out of that wardrobe. Actually it was a slightly diminished version of the true counter-bass, standing on a longer spike than usual. Koussevitsky used to visit Germany to study the art of conducting with Nikisch, and directed only a small number of concerts himself. His concert cycles were deservedly popular in Moscow; they had their own marked style and sustained high standards.

On the first anniversary of Tolstoy's death, the Tolstoy Museum approached him with the request that he should organize a memorial concert. Koussevitsky agreed, and the occasion took place on 10 November 1911, in the Great Hall of the Conservatoire. It was an evening of funereal solemnity. Every chandelier in the hall was lit—a unique occurrence, intensifying the atmosphere of formal splendour. Two particular favourites of Tolstoy's made up the musical part of the programme, Tchaikovsky's Trio in A minor, and Beethoven's Fifth Symphony. The Trio was played by my mother, Krein on the violin, and Zisserman on the cello. It ended the first, literary part of the evening; the symphony closed the second. Koussevitsky conducted.

The public can hardly have understood why the piano part of Tchaikovsky's Trio, 'In memory of a great artist', should have sounded so extraordinarily majestic and strong. Who could have known? Yet everyone realized that the music was transformed. The hall died; not a programme rustled, not a whisper was heard.

In the green-room a table was laid with cognac and wine, bowls of fruit, cake, and sandwiches. The light of the chandeliers and sconces glanced on the glasses and polished fittings. I was waiting there, knowing how my mother felt, while my father and sisters sat in the auditorium. In my pocket I had various emergency phials of medicine. A few people, attendants among them, sat silently on the couches and chairs. We were all listening to the music; the supreme severity of the evening drained backstage to us. And yet, for all its intense familiarity, I couldn't recognize what I heard. My mother had never played it like that before: it was as though someone else had discovered in it a new sense of pure grief and loss.

Suddenly I noticed Koussevitsky, standing by the half-opened door to the auditorium. With his black frock-coat, dark hair and sanguine complexion, he made a fine silhouette against the brightly lit stage, its pale, polished boards, and the organ-pipes stacked behind it. He stood without moving, head slightly bowed, following the music with a conductor's concentration. Quite evidently it gripped him. I was not surprised when he started, and drew the back of his hand across his eyes, as if something had struck him. With reason.

My mother's second, short period of public performances, from 1907 to 1911, ended that night. Probably she agreed to play this funereal trio because she had decided to close her musical career. In it she made an unspoken farewell to her audience and expressed the personal grief of a final parting.

CHAPTER 17

THE NEW BOY

ON our return from Germany I found a new boy in my class at school, who had, they said, been transferred from the Koutaisi School in the Caucasus. He struck me as being rather like a hunk of rock—tall, alien, retiring, with a constant, good-natured moroseness of expression. I had too much work to do catching up on my missed year to worry about new boys, but even so it was difficult not to notice him. He quickly gained the distinction of being made outside right in our school football team. After a year, no closer to any of us, he moved up a class. In August of the next year, 1907, we met again in the school hall after our holidays. Somehow, I discovered a newly awakened interest in this fourteen-year-old, Vladimir Mayakovsky.

I feel rather embarrassed at starting my reminiscences about him. Many people who have heard that I spent two years at school with him ask me eagerly about his early years, clearly hoping for some premature sign of genius in the making. I wish I could oblige! But honestly, neither I, nor anyone else in the fifth form, detected any future greatness in him. Even his devotion to the Revolution, and his practical involvement in it at this time, were so scrupulously concealed from us that we guessed nothing. His prime interest utterly escaped us.

I can only write about what I saw with my own eyes. Two incidents are enough. They struck me, then, as unexpected; thinking about my original impressions now, I still find them significant. Oddly enough, they do not coincide with the epithets the future found to character-ize him. They are, indeed, diametrically opposed to his traditional image.

In class we called each other by our surnames or well-established nicknames. Mayakovsky became known as One-Eyed Polyphemus (we were reading the *Odyssey* at the time). The name suited his sombre size, his strength and aloofness, and it stuck. There was nothing offensive about it, and he answered to it quite equably. One day he and I happened to find ourselves in the emptied classroom during break. Our mutual mistrust had already started to fade, and since it seemed silly to stay in different corners, we sat down at the same desk. After a few indifferent remarks, Mayakovsky started shyly describing his Caucasian past to me. In particular, he dwelt on his dead father, whom he had obviously loved very much. Glancing round us like a conspirator to make sure no one had come into the room, he unbuttoned his jacket, and quickly pulled a small black watch from his inside pocket. It was hung on a kind of plaited horsehair chain which was very fashionable at the time. 'Look,' he whispered, 'my father made this chain for me. With his own hands, as a keepsake!' With that he passed it over for me to admire. 'Well?' you might ask, 'Typical schoolboy boasting.' And yet the loving look he gave me with his melancholy, dark eyes, the tone in which he spoke of his father, betrayed a strange tenderness. The chain was pretty enough, but something else showed through. In the usually unsociable renegade I momentarily glimpsed an affection he had painstakingly concealed, an almost girlish sensitivity.

Struck by this unexpected transformation, I drew him out, wanting the intimacy to continue. He answered hesitantly and became thoughtful. Perhaps he wasn't sure how far he could confide in me. Then, rightly deciding he could trust me, he started to go into details, just as the bell rang and the other boys burst into the classroom, banging desks and shouting. The usual school atmosphere took over.

It is strange how quickly and absolutely a person can change! After the five-minute break, the gloomy One-Eyed Polyphemus sat at his desk as usual, and no one noticed any difference in him. Mayakovsky evidently realized his secrets were safe with me, and stopped avoiding me. Even so, a ghost of his watchful moroseness persisted when we were alone and relaxed together.

I don't want to make extravagant claims. We never became close friends, neither then, nor later, when we met again. He stayed true to his nickname; at school he needed none of us, and later this early reserve remained an invariable trait.

Yet there was some kind of ease between us. Often when we found ourselves together we started talking about more serious things, usually on his initiative. Mayakovsky had spent nearly all his childhood in the wilds of the Caucasian mountains, and had much more to tell than a town-dweller like myself. I loved listening to his deep, mellow voice, his laconic descriptions of the mountains and his closely-knit family, their poverty and *joie de vivre*. All this made up the man he kept hidden from us. And then a second incident confirmed my impressions.

It was lunch-break. Mayakovsky and I were on our way to the gymnasium, which turned, at that hour, into a buffet. Three large baskets, filled with every kind of delicacy from Savostyanov's, the shop on the Povarskaya not far from our school, were put on long benches. Under the ushers' watchful eyes, boys of all ages sedately circled the hall, stopping by the baskets to buy something for a few copecks, and eating it as they walked on. But before Mayakovsky and I reached the hall we came across a sadly familiar scene of bullying in a shadowy corner of the deserted corridor. I knew such things from early and bitter personal experience. Here something quite unexpected happened. At the top of his deep bass voice Mayakovsky ordered this victimization to stop at once. The bully ignored him, and Mayakovsky immediately attacked him with such cold-blooded decisiveness that the coward bolted, while Mayakovsky, still enraged, shouted after him that that was the way Polyphemus would deal with any big-headed bullies who dared try out their strength on the little ones. This apparently unimportant incident struck me particularly forcibly, because nobody, in the whole of my school career, had ever reacted to bullying like that. Once again Mayakovsky came alight, hot with his sense of justice, courage, and sympathy. Undoubtedly, too, there was a great deal of hidden kindheartedness in him. Such qualities became significant in the setting of our usual school indifference. To me, they were a final confirmation of his secret nature.*

Our shared school life came to an end as unexpectedly as it had begun. In March of the same school year Mayakovsky left the fifth form.

---

* Compare Boris Pasternak's first meeting with Mayakovsky:

'Now, at the café, I found that I liked the author no less than I had liked his verse. Before me sat a handsome, sombre youth with a boxer's fists, the deep voice of an Archdeacon and an inexhaustible, deadly wit—something between one of Alexander Grin's mythical heroes and a Spanish toreador.

He was handsome, witty, talented—perhaps even superlatively talented, but you knew at once that these were not the most important things about him; the important thing was his iron mastery over himself, the rules or principles of honour, the sense of duty which prevented him from being any different, any less handsome, talented or witty than he was.

His resolute expression and the mane of hair which stood on end as he ruffled it with all five fingers, immediately reminded me of some young terrorist conspirator out of a Dostoyevsky novel, some minor Dostoyevsky character from the provinces.'

Boris Pasternak, *An Essay in Autobiography*, pp. 94–5.

Without warning, he vanished from our world, and I, for one, can't remember the moment of his departure, or any of the emotions one would connect with such a parting. Maybe the explanation lies in his lack of interest in us; more probably, in his evident wish to go unnoticed, like a conspirator. For whatever reason, he left in spring, when all our attention was on exams and the end of the school year. Afterwards, we dispersed for the summer holidays, and on our return in the autumn new anxieties absorbed us, overshadowing his absence. The only news to reach us was that one Mayakovsky, a former pupil of the Moscow Fifth School (and so identifiably our schoolmate) was connected with the revolutionary underground and had been arrested and imprisoned for something or other. What happened to him after that wasn't known. Gradually we forgot the whole thing. So it might have ended: there was a schoolboy, and he vanished. But fate is more whimsical and incomprehensible than that.

When I was in the eighth form in 1910, and particularly when I became a student at the University in 1911, Moscow was full of gossip about a gang of hooligan rebels strolling about the Kuznetsky Bridge with provocatively made-up faces and extravagant clothes. They consisted of an identifiable group of young men, one of whom was particularly conspicuous—a tall good-looker with a monocle and top hat, in a garish yellow and black shirt and sporting an ivory-headed cane. Apparently they used to recite as they walked, offending passers-by with their mocking remarks and generally impudent behaviour. The handsome one in the yellow blouse was referred to as 'some Mayakovsky or other', with such disapproval that it didn't even occur to me that he might be my old classmate. Yet the more I heard the name, the more familiar associations were awakened. Yes, of course—but wait a bit! Mayakovsky? There certainly had been one at school. Could this possibly be him? The outsider I remembered might have been anything, even an active member of the revolutionary underground (as indeed he was, had we but known it). But *Polyphemus* in that idiotic yellow blouse? With a monocle? I couldn't believe it. It must have been a coincidence, just as the newspapers had once reported a story about a peasant woman convicted for embezzlement, whose name happened to be Pasternak. She had nothing to do with our family, and yet she drew down a lot of light-hearted teasing on us.

*

I finished school in the spring of 1911, and entered the Mathematical Faculty of Moscow University. God knows why I chose that faculty! Most probably through sheer folly, for even at school it was obvious that maths and I hardly got on together. We tolerated each other till 1913, when I realized I couldn't bear it any longer. I had long been drawn to architecture, and after the necessary exams I won a place in the department of Architecture in the Art School. As I was climbing its wide stair to go and enrol myself, who but the old Polyphemus should come out. He recognized me with instant delight, and we fell into each other's arms.

The meeting was completely unexpected. Had I arrived a few moments later, or he left a fraction earlier, our paths might never have crossed, and the identity of the yellow-bloused revolutionary would have remained an enigma. Our chance encounter may seem as improbable as a contrived coincidence in fiction. But in fact when such meetings really happen they seem quite natural and unremarkable. It's only in literature that they seem false. My meeting with Mayakovsky is no fantasy; it was only an insignificant intermediate episode between our school past and our future. We were both taken by surprise and didn't talk long. But even after a few sentences I noticed that he had a new, and, for me, rather surprising way of talking—punning, quibbling, going out of his way to mock whoever he was with. Astonished and rather repelled by this manner, which I had never noticed before, I refused to take offence, and instead fell in with his style, capping his taunts with my own. Mayakovsky noticed, laughed gaily, and our conversation grew simpler and less constrained. Yet this affectation of buffoonery, even over the most serious subjects, persisted at our later, increasingly infrequent meetings.

No revulsion kept us apart. Nothing much drew us together. Whenever we met, we kept up a mutually pleasant conversation, embellished though it might have been by the now familiar Mayakovskian tomfoolery. But in spite of his usual friendliness, he sometimes slipped into inexplicable attempts to humiliate me, even to provoke a quarrel between us. Such aberrations were short-lived, perhaps, but unpleasant for all that. I found them quite incomprehensible. For instance, I once bumped into Mayakovsky at the private view of some exhibition. It was a bright, colourful occasion—gay canvases, sunny weather, lots of people, a generally elated atmosphere. Mayakovsky and I were chatting together as we walked about the exhibition halls. As we reached a big crowd of people, the universally recognized Mayakovsky suddenly laughed louder than usual, turned to me with an abrupt lunge, and looked mockingly straight into my eyes. It was obvious that he was deliberately counting on some effect. In his deep bass voice, which had become something of an affectation, and with an unkind grin, he said, deliberately loudly, for all to hear: 'Pasternak, your father is a talented painter! But it would have been better for him to play the cello!'

If he expected an angry outburst in reply, he must have been disappointed. Adopting his tone, with an exaggeratedly anxious expression, I replied, 'D'you really think so? Thank you for warning me—I'll tell him to try!' Slightly taken aback, he laughed more naturally, and we went on as though nothing had happened.

In more or less the same way I once got a note in his hand, which the School porter brought to our flat on the Volkhonka. It was an invitation to some celebration at the Art School, which I kept for a long time as a precious relic, till it was lost in one of our moves. Mayakovsky had written: 'In the soup of our gaiety only you are missing, O Pasternak!'* In my reply, I wrote: 'Mayakovsky, you're right—soup without parsnip is insipid. I'm coming!'

Mayakovsky was on good form and it was a gay evening. At our little table there were a few people I knew well, all pretty tipsy, since Mayakovsky, as usual, had made everyone else drink more than himself. We laughed, punned, and gossiped. Mayakovsky read some fragments of his own work, but mostly improvised imitations of Severyanin, a fellow poet. We dispersed in the early hours of the morning.

Mayakovsky shot himself in 1930. Together with the other mourners, my wife and I passed through the hall of that house on the Povarskaya where he was laid out in his coffin. Then, sitting on a bench in the garden outside, we heard Lunacharsky deliver his impassioned funeral oration. Remembering those words today, I see that much of what he said coincides with my own conclusions, formed while I was still a schoolboy. The lyricism Lunacharsky identified as the basis of Mayakovsky's poetry is inseparable from the character of the man. And it is clear to me that his lyricism was part of that gentle tenderness of soul which survived, even in the later Mayakovsky, the yellow-bloused bully-boy and brawling standard-bearer of the Revolution. A paradox,

---

* In Russian 'Pasternak' means parsnip.

perhaps? Tenderness of soul and aggressive rudeness? It is not for us to explain such mysteries. I can only be grateful to the fates which allowed me to see gifts that Mayakovsky tried so hard to conceal. Such precious glints of personality, though revealed for a moment only, cannot simply vanish. They are the heart of the individual, the secret fund on which he will draw for a lifetime.

CHAPTER 18

THE METAMORPHOSES OF
ISADORA DUNCAN

IN 1908 Isadora Duncan, an artiste then unknown to the Russian public, gave her first season in the Moscow Art Theatre. By chance, I saw the first matinée. I was a schoolboy of fifteen.

At that time it was customary for a performer to distribute complimentary tickets among press critics, influential figures, and friends. Naturally enough, the staff of the School of Art received several tickets addressed to 'any such' of its teachers as 'wish to attend a morning of ancient dance given by Isadora Duncan'. Everyone was intrigued by the absence of the all-clarifying word, 'ballerina', from the invitation. My father, no lover of ballet, didn't enter into the number of 'any such', till he was unexpectedly won over by Serov and Korovin and went along with them as the only three representatives of the Art School. My mother and Boris were both busy that day, so a spare ticket my father picked up fell to me. I was attracted by the mere fact that I would be going out with famous painters like Serov and Korovin, instead of the usual family party; the ticket itself remained an unknown quantity.

Serov often visited us informally; we used to play with his children. The relationship between us was familiar and ordinary, and yet we had to be on our best behaviour towards Serov, who was renowned for his difficult temperament. Although he was, at bottom, a kindly man, everyone was afraid of his melancholy humour (Serov called it his dreary side) and his penchant for malicious sarcasm often hurt his friends. When Korovin vanished altogether, probably backstage, and Serov took a seat on the other side of my father, I settled back to enjoy the matinée in peace.

My response to what I saw is best clarified by some back-tracking. My father had always fostered a cult of ancient art in our family; Kuzma, the watchman, used to come groaning under tomes ordered from the School library, imposing 'folios' and *'ouvrages'*, whose alien names alone were sufficiently awe-inspiring. In these folios we children first met the pictures on which my mother based her bedtime stories of various gods and their adventures, though all that we could see was a number of ordinary people, all of whom seemed to have lost their clothes. I often heard my mother pronounce the incomprehensible word, *nebo-zhiteli*, 'sky-dwellers', which I untangled according to my own childish logic. We had been emphatically forbidden to swear (*bozhitsia*); Mamma told us stories of heroes beyond reproach, and gods too, come to that, who obviously had no need to swear. Hence their name, not-swearers (*ne bozhiteli*). My reasoning completely satisfied me, and everything fell into place. They only became sky-dwellers much later, when I realized where their home, Olympus, was. From Mamma's stories I also learnt that there were not only gods, and mortals, but some kind of half-god—a hard idea to wrap my mind around! Still, I got used to that, and even to the fact that, unlike us, they had to walk about naked. How cold they must have felt in winter! Poor things, I pitied them, till I was told that it was always hot on Olympus, like our holidays sunbathing by the Black Sea. I soon acquired my parents' love of those beautiful, ideal bodies, and took their nakedness for granted.

Probably the same cult led to Boris's and my education in a school where Latin and Greek were compulsory and our childhood predisposition to the classics was fortified and ordered. The sculptures and vase-paintings familiar from father's folios were supplemented by classic texts, illustrations of ruined acropoles and tombs, theatres and stadia, and their far from accurate reconstructions. So classical culture entered my consciousness of its own accord, with little effort or merit on my part. So, too, I had some sense of the beauties of classic art and the naked human body. In all ignorance of the spectacle I was about to see, I entered the theatre, prepared from childhood for this matinée of 'ancient dance'.

When the famous grey curtain with its seagull motif trembled, undulated, and drew back, the usual recess was missing. The canvas backdrop had been brought forward almost as far as the footlights, turning the stage from an arena with the perspective of a market-square to a narrow, two-dimensional corridor running alongside the lights. Only an insignificant doorway leading backstage remained on the audience's left. Suddenly a motionless figure appeared in the space that had been empty a second before. She stood in a light white tunic, short hair unbound, snub-nosed, sweet-faced, modestly smiling. Her entrance had been so inconspicuous that at first no one noticed her.

After the first few moments of confused uncertainty, a staggering likeness struck me. Not only I, but the whole hall, was confounded by the supreme artistry with which this woman, standing so unassumingly by the door, was first petrified to marble, then melted into life, filling the stone of classic sculpture with the warmth of the living form. 'My God!' I nearly shouted out in my rapture; 'My God! But these are the folios of my childhood!'

So the matinée began, to continue in an atmosphere of growing incredulity: the real gave way to palpable unreality; non-existent things flickered into incontrovertible facts. We, the wide-eyed audience, saw the fabled metamorphoses of Ovid transferred from fiction to stage, and the miracle of transubstantiation performed before us. Lightly, simply, without a conjuror's cheap tricks, Isadora Duncan went through her transformations on a brightly lit stage to the silence of an astounded audience. And the history of the ancients was set free.

Just as the prince's kiss in *Sleeping Beauty* restores an entire court to its interrupted life—the cook slaps the scullery boy, the horse's ear twitches and the fly buzzes off—so Isadora Duncan dispelled the sleep of centuries and the classic statues' suspended gestures were completed. What is movement, after all, but the unending chain of action flowing into action, so easily caught in the thousand shots of cinema film? In effect the ancient sculptor simply clipped his chosen frame off the film-strip and fixed it in stone, where the sequence lay trapped till Isadora Duncan set it free, and the film rolled on to its end.

Here, for instance, stands the motionless form of Artemis the huntress, known to us all, alas, from a Roman copy, the Greek original having long been lost. With astonishment we watch as Isadora Duncan continues the theme of her original, and the statue warms into life. In long, beautiful leaps her Artemis pursues a stag, excited by the hazards of the hunt; her light bounds and wide strides have nothing to do with the formal dance rhythms we know, and yet they have a musical sense of their own. On the restricted stage before us, we see the hunt unfold through boundless woods and glades. Everything that is not there can still be seen. Artemis casts her heavy spear; although the dancer's hand is empty, we know from the fling of the arm and the torso's turn that it is thrown, and powerfully too. We can even hear its light whistle through the air, and in her wild delight we see that the stag has fallen. Feet drumming, she whirls and springs, her light dress whisked behind her with a fluttering we know from bas-relief and vase. Can we not hear her triumph over the silenced plains and the bay of distant hounds savaging their quarry?

But a veritable uproar is rising from the hall, stamping, clapping, crying, flinging roses, hundreds of roses on to the stage where she stands, a solitary figure in her white tunic.

Now, she's an Amazon fleeing her Greek attacker. Wounded in the breast, her hand flung behind her head in pain, teeth gritted, she rests a moment, as Polycleitus once saw her. The moment passes. Isadora Duncan, no Amazon now, drops her hand and settles her tunic.

On the frieze of the Wingless Victory, Nike herself, the head, legs, and arms were lopped away long ago. And yet in every fold of drapery pouring down the body's contours, movement is conveyed. Suddenly head, legs, and arms reappeared, the body straightened, the sandal was tied, the foot dropped, and with a godlike slowness the figure moved to the sacrifice, although no visible victim waited on our stage. We watched the battle-scenes of Halicarnassus and Pergamum; we heard the pipes in the flautist's empty hands. The light patter of her naked feet conveyed the confused thunder of the maenads and their giggling tussle with the satyrs. With only one hand Isadora Duncan suggested the Bacchantes' derisive fingers, tickling a stupefied Silenus, non-existent yet convulsed.

Recently a former student of mine asked me whether I remembered any detail from her performance that would interest a fifteen-year-old. For instance, did her bare feet get dirty running about the dusty stage? In all honesty I can swear that, even as a schoolboy, I never noticed such a thing. I did see that her exertions made her sweat freely, despite the lightness of her costume: she drew the back of her hand across her forehead to shake off the sweat that got into her eyes—a gesture often used by our yardsman chopping wood.

Maybe her feet were dirty! Maybe her tunic did stick to her moist body, effectively laying it bare. So what? It was no different from classic sculptures, where the fighting, labouring, dancing figures perspired and their draperies clung. Isadora Duncan invented nothing, she simply reproduced what once had been, improvising on the natural, domestic, and familiar themes depicted by the ancients. My classical training allowed me to be genuinely pleased by my encounter with a friend of long-standing—a Hellene woman in her thigh-length gymnast's tunic of light, loose, semi-transparent stuff (called the *chitoniskos*, to distinguish it from the full-length tunic, or *chiton*). Yet bare feet and naked legs shocked the Muscovites, with their expectations of the ballerina's conventional bodice, tutu, tights, and pumps. Her display of free, freethinking dress was a direct challenge to the established balletic traditions. In some rarely reproduced pictures of the Pompeian frescos I have seen Greek women with black bands about their breasts, undoubtedly the early prototype of the brassières to come, but they were the exception. The women of those times knew little and cared less for such support; and with dedicated seriousness Isadora Duncan took on herself the customs of the past, regardless of opprobrium. Probably the very ignorance of half the audience prompted their irritated catcalls. For them Isadora Duncan's artistry was less important than her 'immodest behaviour', her 'naked irresponsibility', as they called it.

It really is strange that I should have forgotten so many tangential details about that performance. I can't have paid any attention to the properties, the costumes, even the musical accompaniment. Many people have asked me what exactly she wore—and I can only say what I have already said. I was so delighted by that figure in ordinary Hellenic dress, taken, as it were, direct from the clothes-press, that I failed to register the accessories, or even whether she changed costumes from act to act. The same was true of the music. Undoubtedly there was music, but in my pleasure I heard nothing, probably because no dissonance shocked my ear, and what I heard passed me by. I ignored it, as the natural accompaniment to what I saw. Presumably it was played out of sight, in the wings; probably it was light pieces of Gluck, Rameau, Grétry, maybe even Scarlatti, though he would have been too individual for an occasion when the music needed only to be lyric, muted, and neutral.

Every now and then I glanced at my father and Serov, to confirm my own response. There was no doubt that they were carried away by what they saw. Usually my father sketched everything in the notebook permanently sticking out of his pocket, regardless of where he might be—on the tram, at a concert, in the theatre . . . Here, he was so eager not to miss anything on stage, he didn't once grab for his notebook and pencil. No sketch of Isadora Duncan was made at this performance.

And Serov?

Serov was such a stern critic in all questions of art, that it was natural to turn to him as the absolute arbiter, whose opinion became accepted fact. In everything about him now, the way he sat, the way he watched the stage, I could feel his serious concentration, and his pleasure. Always gloomy, unsociable, lowering, this Serov was unrecognizable. A gentle, distracted smile softened the corners of his usually tense mouth. It was obvious that he was satisfied, happy, somehow pacified internally, as though liberated from a permanent, heavy load.

Occasionally I heard him make some curt, Serovian remark, to which my father nodded without a word. They were evidently gripped by a phenomenon that they both, as artists, admired and understood.

Isadora Duncan at the time of her first visit to Russia. Moscow, 1908.

amily group on the dacha veranda. From left to right: Leonid, Rosa, Josephine, Lydia, Bertha Koffmann (Rosa's mother) and Alexander. Molodi, 1914.

Rosa at the piano, Lydia and Josephine listening. Drawing by Leonid
Pasternak. Moscow, 1917.

Boris at the piano. Vsevolodo-Vilva, in the Urals, 1916.

Alexander. Moscow, *c.*1917.

Lydia. Sketch by Alexander. Moscow, 1916.

The opening of the Museum of Fine Art (now known as the Pushkin Museum), with the arriv
of the imperial party. Photograph by Alexander. Moscow, 1913.

CHAPTER 19

BRAVO, UTOCHKIN!

'With a deafening crack the long, clumsy box lifted
over the fence and flew low over the playing field,
swaying slightly. The cab horses backed and
reared . . .'

WITH these words Konstantin Paustovsky begins one chapter of an
unfinished short story called 'Bravo, Utochkin!', published post-
humously for the first time in the thirty-third number of the *Literary
Gazette*, today, 14 August 1968.

I enjoy Paustovsky's prose and have dipped into his reminiscences
with pleasure; his present inaccuracy irritates me. 'The flight struck us
as something simple and safe,' he goes on; 'Utochkin skimmed over the
ground, almost brushing the heads of his spectators.' And yet for us, his
first witnesses, the occasion was a visible miracle. With gross improb-
ability, a lumbering contraption swam through the air. What held it up?
Why didn't it crash instantly to the ground? That was the extraordinary
thing Paustovsky failed to get across! Here, for once, his habitually
ironic mode is ill applied, and our overwhelming sense of the inconceivable is dissipated by his casual, slighting tone. Soon after the event
Paustovsky described I had the good fortune to see Utochkin's flight at
the Khodinskoye Field in Moscow. It would please me if I could honour
Utochkin's memory by correcting Paustovsky's errors.

Strangely enough, I knew Utochkin by name very well. My first cousin*
had been a master technician from his earliest schooldays, a maker and
breaker of the first order, habitually smashing as many household
gadgets as he mended, pocketing all the useful cogs, screws, and springs
for himself in the process. He was such a poor student of everything
except physics and maths that he was barely tolerated at school, and only

* Alexander Freidenberg.

scraped through. But he did brilliantly in the exacting exams for the Petersburg Technical Institute, where his inventive genius immediately became apparent.

As a child he was a keen cyclist, outdistancing all rivals as he spun round St Petersburg. Later he switched crazes and tacked a chance-found motor on to his bike. No one could keep up with him then! Improving his moped, he eventually constructed the first motor bike in Russia. Spouting foul black smoke, with a terrific scraping of cogs and the syncopated percussion of pistons, he roared about town like a lunatic, incensing the passers-by. After he left the Institute he became a racing motor-cyclist under the professional name of Mikhailov, won many prizes, and made a reputation for himself.

His family, like ours, used to spend its summers by the Black Sea, near Odessa. He was the eldest; then came his sister Olga, and a very gifted second son, Evgeny, who died of peritonitis at an early age. We used to spend happy times on the beach together. He was fifteen at the time, if not more, and was already inseparable from his frenetically catarrhal motor bike.

Maybe it was in Odessa that he got to know the tiny workshops where paraffin lamps and fires, mincing machines and punctured bicycles were mended. Maybe it was here he met his fellow enthusiast, the young Utochkin. Certainly I began hearing the name so often from this time that I could hardly forget it. At first Utochkin, like Mikhailov and many others, was set on terrestrial speeds, but he soon abandoned them all, rejecting the earth for the enigmas of the ether. He became an aeronaut, as they were known at the time. When I heard by chance that the latest miracle of invention, the free flight of a man through space, was to be shown in Moscow, I was well prepared. It was no surprise that this wonder would be accomplished by Utochkin himself.

The date and time of the flight on the Khodinskoye Field were finally announced. My cousin Mikhailov came down from Petersburg specially for the occasion. Although he had told me a lot about Utochkin's flights I was sceptical, knowing his love of exaggeration. I had already learnt from him that there would be no flapping of wings: as far as I could gather, everything was based on the theory of the sail, as in a boat: strong, fast air currents meeting the flying machine would raise it from the ground. I waited impatiently and planned to record the event with my old-fashioned camera. The photographs came out, but the glass plates got smashed and lost in our grand tidying sessions and the moves from flat to flat. I didn't care at the time; now I regret their loss. And yet, when I shut my eyes, I can see it all again—a sight inconceivable to us then, and yet irrefutable.

I agreed to go with two school friends. The morning for the flight was ideal, light and sunny, with a delicate breeze. It was early spring; single clouds trailed across a clear sky. We arrived in good time, but for once our hopes of wriggling in without a ticket were quite impracticable. Both entrances were guarded by unprecedented, double ranks of policemen and officers in their charcoal greatcoats. Crowds milled about the gates. Without a word we ran together down the high wooden fence, hoping to find a gap or at least a hole we could peer through. We raced the length of the field to its curved end, without success—and there, at last, came across a great hill of slag or coal, evidently the outlying part of some factory or railway siding. Not thinking what a heap of hot slag might do to us, we scrambled up the slope, and found ourselves in a blissfully cool breeze, cold, shining anthracite under our feet, the impassable fence below, and the whole hippodrome laid out before us. The three of us settled back comfortably, and since only a couple of factory hands joined us later, there was room and to spare.

In the distance gloomed the hump of the grandstand, the field beside it thick with black dots clustering and dispersing in front of the stand, and coagulating round something—a something which would have been absolutely incomprehensible if it hadn't been described and sketched so often by my cousin. Staring hard, I began to make out the flying machine—its interlaced rods and canvas awnings like our traditional dacha blinds ('Marquises', they were called), except that they lacked a scalloped edge. However, the black swarm around it prevented me seeing where Utochkin would actually take up his position, and to what his seat was attached.

The faint sound of a bell reached us, like the warning chime when a train is due to pull out from the station. We saw some white puffs of smoke, heard the snap of a revolver, and the whole ant heap fell apart, allowing us to see the flying machine for the first time. It looked like nothing so much as an unfinished pagoda. Consumed by distance, a fine open-work tracery of bamboo struts and crossbars gleamed hazily against the field, like a half-built, unboarded shed, or the reed awnings over a threshing floor, their thin lines diminished to the delicate strokes of a Japanese engraving. In fact, the whole thing reminded me of the kites we used to buy from the Japanese toy shop on the Kuznetsky Bridge to fly at our dacha, alongside the home-made kites Russian children used to make, and still make, on their holidays. They used to fly so well, those Japanese kites of ours, that their waxed strings often broke in our hands. Their bright, yolk-and-rose canvases and white wooden frames were just like the shape I could make out in front of the grandstand.

The motor began to set the structure in motion. Little dandelion-puffs of smoke darted irregularly into the air. After a pause, a matching pattern of irregular detonations drifted down the field to us. Utochkin's asthmatic engine was choking and catching its breath just like my cousin's motor bike. Evidently there was some technical problem. Bursts of smoke pop-popped, dispersed, subsided altogether. Our faith in the possibility of success began to wane. I felt hurt for Utochkin, dreading his imminent loss of face. Excitement had blunted the discomforts of our uncertain perch, but now there was an edgy awareness of sharp, sliding anthracite. And we began to feel hungry. High in the sky, the hot sun gloated.

But something new was going on over there. Cries reached us, a confused squelching we took for applause. We noticed a change in the position of Utochkin's machine. Rolls of indubitable applause began to grow and spread over the field. They were joined by the even patter of an engine. The black clusters dotted along the fence began to move towards us, like the outriders escorting a procession. Our anxiety was intense: we still could see nothing, and caught a sense of excitement we couldn't understand, since everything we saw was happening at ground level. We drummed our heels against the coal-hill, our hearts thumping, willing Utochkin into the air. Meanwhile his machine drew nearer, following a straight path, still obstinately grounded. It stopped again briefly; then, well within our field of vision, struggled to take off with all the grace and lightness of an old hen. After an ungainly hop and a skip, it subsided back on to the dear old earth, to roll on towards us.

Utochkin adjusted something. Once again the machine edged forward, visibly accelerated—and worked at last! The earth's grip was snapped. With a last skip, the contraption twitched free of gravity. It swam towards us like a boat, and we clearly saw the heavy thing hold itself up in the air without a sign of dropping. Breathless with nervous pleasure, we watched in silence. Laboriously it came towards us, as though overcoming some reluctance, quietly shuddering and swaying on the air, as melon-rinds rock in a sluggish harbour.

Confidently, Utochkin steered his machine along the race-track below, following a course that would lead him past us, round the base of the field, and back to his starting-point. Clearly, he was going to give us a closer view than his observers on the grandstand. The visibility was excellent. The flight was so stately, I could check on every detail my cousin had already described.

Utochkin's flying machine was like an unfinished raft, to which the aviator had added his seat and a motor with blades like a ship's propeller. There were two tiers of canvas awnings. Everything was open to the air, for maximum lightness and minimum resistance to oncoming air-currents. The aviator's seat was simple. I think it was just the usual Viennese bentwood chair (without arm rests). Utochkin wore a finely checked, fashionable grey suit, bright yellow, square-toed American boots, and a straw boater. His feet were placed on some kind of pedals; to either side of his chair, levers could be seen, where his hands rested. His whole attitude resembled that of a pianist at his instrument. But nothing was as extraordinary as the contraption itself. What struck us most was its serene suspension, the complete incompleteness of the raft, which swam, creaking, at a level height.

It was a miracle. Everything was primitive beyond belief. The open-ness of the construction made any kind of subterfuge impossible. Yet my cousin's motor bike, racketing round town at incredible speeds, didn't slip free of the earth, didn't fly off into the blue! Wide-eyed, we watched as the miracle went on and on. In broad daylight we saw Utochkin fly past us and draw away, although the grandiose 'virage' we later read about in the papers was, of course, a fiction: the curve was so gradual that the machine paddled past without even listing, leaving us in a valedictory stench of petrol.

'Seeing him, the cab horses broke free and galloped off in a swirl of dust, to the thunder of wheels and yells of the cabbies. The box flew heavily above us.' It is odd, offensive even, that a good writer like Paustovsky should have had such an extraordinary view of Utochkin's flight. 'The box'! He simply can't leave that word alone. It would have been strange to see a box flying; it's even stranger to have seen a box where there was none—nor, indeed, anything remotely like a box with walled sides. Utochkin's flying machine had no sides. Paustovsky may be right that

Utochkin flew close to the ground. But it was still five metres up. Not that the precise altitude matters; however low, if the engine had faltered for a moment Utochkin and his contraption would have been smashed to pieces. To say, as Paustovsky does, that 'the flights struck us as something simple and safe', is to understate our sense of shock. When my friends and I clambered down the coal heap, we were silent and trembling, not even exchanging glances. One of the two factory hands who had joined us repeated to himself, 'No good can come of it; you'll see, no good can come of it! . . .' We came home like travellers from a distant world. For one hour we had stepped into the future, and should not now indulgently concede the grudging congratulations Paustovsky offers.

CHAPTER 20

'SIGNS OF A NEW IMMATURITY'

IN the spring of 1911 I took my final school examination. For a whole week the city had been inconceivably stuffy. During one of the orals, it grew melodramatically dark. A whirlwind burst through the open windows, licking the papers off the table and beating them up into a cheerful spiral like a flurry of pigeons. In an instant, all the prim inaccessibility of the ceremonially frock-coated examiners, seated in state like the judges in Tolstoy's *Resurrection*, was wiped away. Some jumped up to clap papers on to the table, others scrambled to collect them from the floor, while we schoolboys added to the confusion by noisily slamming the windows.

The unexpected spring thunderstorm broke directly above the school. To the unremitting rumble of thunder and disorderly splatter of lightning the stuffed ciphers on the other side of the green baize table were momentarily transformed into mortals like ourselves, startled by a storm. Ozone cleared the air.

Maybe that transitory disruption of the necessary, ritual proprieties sticks in my mind because I was standing before the examiners, question paper in hand, at the crucial moment. I had already started my answer when the thunder broke everything up. It was as though the shield of Zeus was dropped over me, and in the unsuspected guise of thunder I was enfolded by an Olympian charm against all future suffering.

There now, it's over!

For the last time I went out of the school doors, a boy no longer, uncertain whether I should be glad or regretful. Who knew whether I would miss my lost childhood, and the buildings where I might have left the eight best years of my life? In those days many things happened that seemed to stand for the start of a new existence, full of uncertainty.

For the last six months we had been postponing our move from the expanding Art School to another flat belonging to the School in an entirely unfamiliar part of town. Now that I had finished my exams, the time came for us to go. My mother was to keep Boris as an aide, while the rest of us were to spend the summer in the south, sparing my father all the bother of the move. We had rented a good dacha by the sea near Odessa, and I, an acknowledged grown-up at last, was to stay with my father and look after my sisters.

The bags were packed, the tickets bought. As soon as I had handed in my papers to the University I left Moscow a newly fledged student, although I sensed no particular changes in myself.

There was nothing new for me in that holiday by the sea. Boris and I had explored it all long ago—the house, the shore, the Bodarevsky dacha to the left, the high cliff above the beach to the right. For our sisters, who had only seen the flat, northern Baltic, the Black Sea was a novelty. They had never known such rocks and cliffs, the eternally renewed salvoes of assaulting waves, the vigorous smack of water on shining rock, the flak and leap of white waves and their trickling slide through seaweed and stone. Even in good storms on the grey Baltic, though the white-crested waves gathered in the distance to attack the shore, they rambled out across the sand, weakly dispersing in a scrawl of flotsam, foam, and rotting bladderwrack, before crawling back with a quiet whisper into the sea.

I knew it all too well. For me, this time, the novelty lay in my unfamiliar cockatoo appearance, my embarrassingly gaudy, blue-green corduroy student's trousers, secured, officer-style, by a strap under the foot, and my theatrical collar, which replaced the modest old school shirt with its black belt and badge.

The month passed quickly. Boris and my mother arrived, and everything slipped back into its Muscovite order. Almost immediately the summer spoiled. Storms and high winds rose and fogs descended; invisible on the cliff, the lighthouse siren wailed rhythmically through blank cloud. We began to chafe at the grandeur of elemental powers, monotonously repeated from day to day. Lazing on sunny sands was unthinkable; there was no more swimming, no more *dolce far niente* for which our father could reprove us. Even the fish we used to catch were no more—and we used to get fine ones, using a length of twine dropped from a finger and scraps of meat for bait. On such stormy days they swam far out to sea, while we lounged disconsolately about our rented rooms. Everyone secretly longed to get home to the new flat and the new quarter. What would it be like? What of that Cathedral of Christ the Saviour they said could be seen from our windows?

My brother shut himself up in his room on the second floor of the dacha, 'composing something'. Was it music? The piano stood on the ground floor. We would have heard him if he played. But it sounded very little, alas; even my mother rarely went near it.

The secret of his seclusion emerged after his abrupt departure for Moscow. He left unobtrusively, indifferently—as though slipping out to post a letter. When he was gone, my mother asked me to go upstairs and tidy his room.

A strange sight met me. It was like a room abandoned for flight, or one waiting for the occupant to return in just a minute, to sit down and take up his pen again. What sentence had he abandoned on that half-written page? No one, not even I, bothered to look. But here I should stop and explain.

About the time my brother changed from law to philology, we began to notice that he was drifting away from home. The reason for this mild but genuine rupture might have been something he wanted to hide— something which we didn't need to know. His behaviour offended us; we were first hurt, then angry. There were unnecessary scenes. It became obvious that the situation couldn't be remedied. Most baffling was his obvious love of the family, especially his mother, which intensified rather than diminished with the break. As he often told me in self-justification, the withdrawal caused him a lot of pain.

How easy it is now to explain so much of what was obscure to us! Today's commonplace seemed unnatural then; it betrayed a streak of soulless egotism in him, a cold-heartedness, especially towards my mother, which angered my father most of all. If only we could have guessed at the crucial change taking place in my brother's creative life! But who knew of it then?

How strange it is that my memory should fail to retain any trace of the very events I most need to confirm! Painstakingly and in vain, I grope about the past. Surely, it was somewhere here? Yes, my brother left school in 1908 . . . At that time I was in the fifth form at school. We moved to the Volkhonka in 1911. What filled those last three years on the Myasnitskaya? Is it possible that nothing attracted my attention, even obliquely, to my brother? We went on sharing the room first allotted to us in 1901, just as our sisters shared theirs. Our lives and interests fell to either side of our large general table, beneath the adjustable electric lamp with a green iron shade, suspended by pulleys and a counterweight from the ceiling. Most often, though, my brother slid off to the drawing-room to practise. His piano-playing still continued to sound. What changed in him, then? What struck me? Nothing! Many years later, after all, my brother admitted in *Safe Conduct* that he 'carefully concealed from his friends' (and his family, I might add) 'signs of a new immaturity'. How well that is put! Yes, yes, he hid them so impeccably that even I, sitting at the same table with him, noticed nothing at all.

I was wrong to say that I found a muddle upstairs: it was order of a kind, my brother's order. In my hasty tidying I reduced it to chaos.

Little piles of paper lay anywhere to hand: on the tables, on shelves and window-sills and on the floor. Many of the sheets were pale-blue order forms from the library, densely overwritten on their blank reverse. Recognizing these, I gave up my first intention of burning the lot, and decided to preserve what I assumed to be university notes. I was a little puzzled by the peculiar, columnar form of what he had written, but, not having time to stop and read, I shuffled the papers together according to size, effectively undoing everything he had done. Those packets were brought back to Moscow. When I showed them to Boris, I got no thanks. He had no use for them, he said; I could do whatever I liked with them. So the papers stuck with me, to ripen in the dark of an old trunk for over fifty years. Sorting through a mass of old lumber recently, I found them and passed them on to his son's editorial care. The old manuscripts were in my brother's familiar hand—a hand he had perfected while still at school, a sharp, even, minute script characteristic of the time, with such a dry incisiveness of line it seemed cut with steel, the traditional copperplate. All his exercise books and university notes were in the same hand; it could also be seen in his musical notation, which was just as fluent, sharp, and dry. At that time he preferred black ink (fading in time to pale brown), or occasionally green, but never the typographer's purple, which he abhorred. He used only one kind of steel pen, the 'Eureka', light, nickel-plated, and of the hardest variety. The papers I discovered bore all these marks.

People often ask me now when exactly Boris started writing poetry. They may expect a neat and accurate response, but alas, alas! how can I reply, when Boris himself hid the answer so scrupulously? Even in *Safe Conduct* no dates are given.

The passage describing his meeting with Scriabin, in which his fate as a musician and composer was decided, ends with the words, 'the next day I went and did' as Scriabin advised, tranferring from law to the philosophical section of the philological faculty. This took place in 1909. But at that time we saw no signs of possible poetic composition. In a passage whose contents refer to the beginning of 1910 comes the admission that 'music, which I still only postponed abandoning, began to intertwine with literature'. Here the words 'I still only postponed abandoning' are important. My brother only gave up music for philosophy, not literature. That, after all, was why he went to Marburg in the summer of 1912. 'Music . . . began to intertwine with literature.' Note that he says 'literature', not 'poetry'. The literature he refers to could be the prose he enjoyed reading—Andrey Bely, then Stendhal (through the influence of his friend, Konstantin Loks), or Conrad and Joyce (thanks to his other friend, Sergey Bobrov). The relevant passages of *Safe Conduct* have no references to my brother's poems or to poetry. Even in the reminiscences of the Serdarda group of 1910–11 he speaks of himself as being welcomed 'in my old right as a musician'.

And yet, having written so much, I find myself pausing to think again. Suddenly it becomes clear to me that we should look for the beginnings of my brother's poetic life at the time when he broke away from home altogether. When we arrived at the new flat on the Volkhonka, in which a life for my brother had been provided for, he chose to take rooms on his own in nearby side streets, Gagarinsky, Lebyazhy, Lenivka, Savelovsky, Ostozhenka . . . We mistakenly attributed this solitary life, so baffling and hurtful to us, to quite different causes. In fact, such freedom must have been his best guarantee of success in the poetry he hid from us so carefully. I should add that all the new names in his life began to sound from this time, and that Durylin, Kostya Loks, and Bobrov, who hadn't even existed on the Myasnitskaya, began to appear with him in our new flat. It seems clear to me now that in this sense 1911 was the decisive year in which Boris's artistic life was broken and reformed.

His earlier casual and occasional 'first attempts' (the 'poetic experiments' of *Safe Conduct*) cannot be called the true beginnings of his poetic activity. It should be remembered that at school my brother drew respectably, when the whim took him; perhaps it was much the same with music and philosophy, which turned out to be merely transitional periods in his life. With poetry it was another matter. Referring to 1912 in *Safe Conduct*, my brother said that 'I took up poetry thoroughly. Day and night, whenever, I wrote . . .' That word 'whenever' is introduced to show that the preoccupation with poetry was not a *continual* necessity.

'Continual' is only used about his poetry later, when he describes the summer of 1913 we spent at Molodi. 'Here I set up my working corner . . . I was (already) writing poetry not as a rare exception, but often and continually, as people write . . . music'; that is, as a composer follows a work regime, or as professional musicians practise daily.

Thus, the very first 'signs of a new immaturity' were discovered by me in August 1911, when I found a mass of papers in my brother's room, and, in ignorance of what they contained, I tidied them in piles according to size.

CHAPTER 21

THE VIEW FROM OUR WINDOWS

WE returned to Moscow in the autumn of 1911, to take up our quarters in my father's rent-free flat. It stood in what had once been almost a baronial estate belonging to Prince Golytsin, now under the control of the School of Art.

One side of this estate, a four-storeyed building, opened on to the Maly Znamensky Street, whose other side was bounded by the wall of the Museum of Fine Art, known today as the Pushkin Museum. At that time it hadn't yet been opened to the public. A two-storeyed block joined on to the main building, running along a side-street that bent round to the Volkhonka. Our seven-roomed flat was on the second floor of this building.

Here I spent over twenty years. I would have liked to use the pluperfect tense in the description that follows, not because we settled there sixty-five years ago, but because neither the two-storeyed building, nor anything we found on our arrival, nor any material part of our experiences there, survive today. Nor can I retrieve them, any more than my childhoood can be returned to me.

The nine windows of our living quarters looked over the Volkhonka and across a deep, broad panorama that lost itself in the distance beyond the river, set with low single and two-storeyed houses of the old-fashioned sort. Of course, we were lucky. At that point between Maly Znamensky Street and the Prechistensky Gates (now the entrance to the Kropotkin Metro station), the Volkhonka was only built up along one side. In the nineteenth century the further side had been cleared for a cathedral celebrating our victory over the French, which was originally intended for Sparrow Hills, but finally located here on Chertolye Hill. The cathedral was under construction for forty years; its colossal size required a large adjacent works area. All the intervening buildings were demolished, even the Alexeyev Monastery; none rose to take their place, and so a wonderful view was opened out, almost of its own accord, on to the far side of the river.

The square around the Cathedral of Christ the Saviour was enormous, occupying a vast right-angled terrain bounded by the river below and the Volkhonka above, and drawn in at either side by the two streets linking the Volkhonka to the embankment: to the left, All Saints' Way, which no longer exists; to the right, the Lesnoy, now known as Soymonov Street. The cathedral rose in the middle of the square. From our windows you could see only the section of the square lying between All Saints' Way and the cathedral's eastern wall. For most of the day it lay in shadow, while the cathedral was silhouetted against the sun.

It is curious that we all, unanimously, came to look on our part of the square as the stage of a great open-air theatre, an impression stamped so ineradicably on us that I cannot shake it off even now. The feeling was partly fostered by the area's orientation, plumb opposite the east-west alignment ritually followed by the cathedral. When we gazed out, such a mystic orientation was imperceptible and unimportant, since the cathedral had little significance for us: it lingered perpetually in the wings, heard only in the off-stage sound of bells powerfully chiming, now sullen, now soaring, and in the candlelit procession around its perimeter every Eastertime. More compelling by far was the expansive panorama, the narrow Volkhonka below being invisible from our windows, and the marvellous backdrop beyond the river constantly enticing our eyes.

Granted, our theatre had no curtain, no circular stage; no more had the open-air theatres of the past. Instead we had our stage front, the Volkhonka no one bothered about, an ample centre stage of the cathedral square, and for the wings (which intensify the sense of depth and distance) the buildings set sideways on to the down-dropping All Saints' Way. In the foreground, on the corner of the Volkhonka, stood an ugly single-storeyed house, Edmund Bauer's flower-shop; rarely did its doors open and shut on the chance customer. Behind it, four storeys high and undistinguished, stood the Golovteyev mansion; a few gaps further down lay the last wing, the exquisite bell-tower of the Blessed Virgin on the corner of All Saints' Way and the embankment. It was exceptionally beautiful, pink and white, perfectly proportioned, with a fine dome and cross. Church and bell-tower stood on the plot of the former All Saints' bank, to which I will return. The right-hand wing of our stage was, of course, the cathedral's huge eastern wall.

And beyond the river? The backdrop? My God, what a backdrop! Designed, you must admit, by a divinely inspired hand, laid out on a single plane, the clear relief of the foreground shading imperceptibly to immeasurable distances and the shifting cyclorama of sky and clouds. The first row of houses on the far embankment could be seen quite clearly, with its rare carriages and single, hurrying pedestrians crossing the back of our stage. There was the palace of the Deacon with church and bell-tower beside it, and another building we nicknamed—who knows why?—the house of Malyuta Skuratov,* its two storeys stretching along the waterfront, punctured by a central arch. With binoculars, on a good day, you could see through the archway into the courtyard behind, a patch of brightness in those dark walls. Architecturally as undistinguished as these, and as memorable, especially on frosty days, were the four tall, reddish-brown factory chimneys of the tram station, each proudly trailing a heavy, dark scarf of smoke low to the ground. That was the end of our stage. Behind lay the one-dimensional backdrop, a colourful impasto of variegated roofs, pierced here and there by belfries, domes, and towers. Above all those cupolas and crosses, now glinting gold in the evening sun, now obliquely lit by neighbouring houses, or obscured on misty days, swam the sound of bells—even, distant bells, softened by space, bringing the silent stones to life.

So much for the backdrop and the wings. As for our stage, it was divided into several sections, each with its proper function.

From medieval times the Volkhonka had run along the crest of Chertolye Hill, which rises in some places as much as three metres above the river, and which had long served as the city's western defensive rampart. Times changed, however, and Moscow changed with them. When they cleared the hill's western side for the Cathedral of Christ the Saviour, the hill's hump was also levelled off for a new, ceremonial city square, which was to be named after the cathedral. The natural slopes dropping down to the river, and Lesnoy Street running to the embankment, were faced with blocks of heavy grey granite, as were the river banks. The Volkhonka ran along the nearside edge of the square; All Saints' Way followed a gentle incline downwards until it reached the Golovteyev mansion, where it suddenly burrowed into the shoulder of the hill and dropped abruptly down to the embankment. On

---

* An 'oprichnik', or member of the special administrative élite established in Russia by Ivan the Terrible.

the road's eastern left-hand side, the pavement passing the Golovteyev house continued on the horizontal, bending round the bell-tower on the corner, till it came to rest at a point well above the road running along the embankment. Here the pavement was bounded by a well-designed, massive iron railing. On the right-hand side of All Saints' Way, beside the square, the pavement followed the slope all the way down from the Volkhonka to the river, and thus formed the base to a high wall buttressing the square. A wide granite stairway led from the pavement to the square above. So, from our flat, the whole street lay as if on display, falling directly away from our windows, accentuating the steepness of the descent, suddenly nuzzling into the cliff rising from the river bank, while to right and left the walls' dark silhouettes stood sharp against the airy brightness of the waterfront beyond the hill. This light window gave a striking sense of distance let into the primary plane.

Finally, something should be said of those parts of the cathedral square we could see. The disposition was trite: the huge cathedral cube stood at the centre, with four public gardens at the four corners, each ringed by flowerbeds and low granite parapets. Quite possibly this quincunx arrangement had a religious significance. Naturally we could only see the two gardens on the eastern side of the square. The nearer of the two huddled up to the Volkhonka, almost beneath our windows, or so it seemed to us. The further lay at the top of the stairway rising up from All Saints' Way. The gardens were large and almost perfectly circular. All the rest of the cathedral square was paved: it was an idle, dead area where pigeons bustled unperturbed and the rare yawning nanny perambulated her charge. Only on the eastern side of the square, between 'our' two gardens, did the area come to life—thanks not to nannies or pigeons, but to an unplanned, nameless road branching off All Saints' Way to round the nearer of the two gardens and cut across to the Volkhonka. Especially in winter nearly all the carts and sledges following the embankment from the west used to take this short cut to the Volkhonka, and its milder slope was thronged, day and night, with heavily laden sledges and drays. This long line of caravans, stretching up the hill and round the cathedral, became an inseparable element in our view of the square, the living pulse in the scene. And, just as the background of a Gobelin tapestry stays the same, whatever the details stitched to its surface, so this panorama remained an immutable backcloth to all the vicissitudes of our and the city's life to come.

*

Sailors draping the monument of Tsar Alexander III, before
its ceremonial unveiling. Sketch by Leonid Pasternak.
Moscow, 1913.

Cathedral Square, with plinth minus imperial statue, after the Revolution, *c.*1919.

The Cathedral of Christ the Saviour, with the Church of the Blessed Virgin and the Golovteyev mansion to the right. The Pasternaks' flat lies in the background between them. The empty imperial plinth can be seen to the right of the Cathedral's right-hand entrance.

Alexander (far right) and colleagues, by the door of the Karpov Institute, marked in the author's hand 'my door'. Moscow, c.1924.

Alexander. Drawing by Leonid Pasternak. Berlin, 1924.

[B... by Leonid Pasternak. Berlin, 1923.]

What of the *mise-en-scène* and the actors on our stage?

The morning after our arrival—a cheerful, sunny autumn day—we ran to the windows to see our new world. We were struck at once by the unusual breadth of the panorama, and by an intrusive, inexplicable something, irritating as a splinter, stuck in the middle of the further square. It was like a giant crate propped up by scaffolding and only partially subdued by its grandiose surroundings. We soon learned that it was a workmen's shelter, where they were hurriedly casting a bronze monument of Alexander III, the Tsar's father, to commemorate the Romanovs' tercentenary. In all lights, in rain, snow, and blizzard, the crate magisterially drew to itself the artist's unwilling eye. Drizzle softened everything but its uniformity. Its solid cube and scaffolding were most memorable in misty weather, when it stood out against the blurred backdrop of the houses beyond the river. For two winters it stood in the square, and appeared repeatedly in my father's sketches.

One unremarked day the cube disappeared, to be replaced by a lumpy pyramid of uncertain surfaces, ending in a shapeless, floppy top-knot. Another aeon passed. Swathed in tarpaulin, the statue darkened in snow and rain, bleached as it dried, and gathered dirt and dust, until at last we grew used to this giant, five-ton sack of potatoes with its pine-cone top, where the stained sacking swathing the monarch's head had been tightly tied, above and just beneath the chin.

As my father's sketches record, one sultry day the old tarpaulin was removed and, in an exercise of unexpected confusion and tragic consequences, the naked Tsar was chastely wrapped in white canvas for the formal unveiling. Just as a group of sailors high on a step-ladder were battening down the last corner of clean canvas, a wave of fresh air lifted it loose; it billowed out, flipping ladder and men off the imperial shoulders. The crowds scattered; the ladder disintegrated as it fell. One of the sailors was killed; other injured men were carried off by the first-aid carriage waiting nearby.

No question, our Tsar was unlucky with his memorials to his father. In St Petersburg the bronze cast by Prince Trubetskoy started pouring out of its mould, nearly destroying both monument and creator. Moscow brought no better luck. Nevertheless, one blazing noon soon after this mishap, the statue was ceremonially unveiled, the rituals finally accomplished, and several people treated for sunstroke.

From early morning regiments had been marching down the Volkhonka in unsuitably hot uniforms, each more elaborate than the last.

The cavalry was marvellous. Someone, seeing them coming, shouted, 'Look, the Lohengrins are here!' and I managed to get a snap of them through the double window we had to keep shut on police orders. They passed in swift formation—bronze armour, buckskin breeches, tight hessian boots, bright broadswords and bronze eagle-crested helmets —blisteringly hot, no doubt, and sweating so profusely you had to feel sorry for them. The actual unveiling was too far away for us to see it properly: the square was hidden by the dark mass of court officials allowed to attend, while the celebrities in their grandstands had the pleasure of sitting directly beneath the midday sun. We could only identify the arrival of the Imperial family by the ranks of soldiers snapping to attention, just as the convulsive gesticulations of officers signified other moments of invisible pomp.

It was much more interesting to watch the opening of the Museum of Fine Art from the windows of our neighbours' flat on another occasion. Through double windows, once again shut by order, we could see the entrance gates, the open garden, and the museum's wide entrance stair. Again I managed to take a number of snaps: of the Tsar and Tsaritsa ascending the museum steps, this time, and of the later relaxation of the chamberlains and other high officials when the imperial party had gone inside. Marina Tsvetayeva has a marvellous description of what she saw in the museum halls, where the youthful *joie de vivre* of the classic statuary seemed to her in vivid contrast with the crumbling decrepitude of the court. We, meanwhile, could watch the air of cool dignity outside melt with heat and inanition, till scarlet and gold, ermine and silver scattered and re-formed about the garden, and courtiers and coachmen chatted at ease in the shade together. Such were the scenes I snapped on my Kodak! But let me return to that unveiling . . .

After all the fuss was over, the canvas furled and the barricades withdrawn, the crowds moved in to see what sort of a statue they'd got. Its Petersburg brother was a proper work of art, a good representational likeness with a strong symbolic point. Trubetskoy made it an emblem of the unshakeable solidity of the autocracy; his ponderous cart-horse stood solidly on all four legs under the equally massive Tsar, with the requisite stability there for all to see. There was no such artistic concept in the Moscow offering: in full naturalistic detail, the Tsar sat as a Tsar should sit when he has nothing to think about except the symbolization of his illimitable power. So sat the Pharaohs, but at least they were stylized. Our dummy sat straightbacked in his armchair, hands on knees, encumbered with sceptre and orb, dressed in the semi-ceremonial officer's uniform of his regiment. He appears in the same trappings in Serov's portrait, but there at least we see a real person. This was nothing more than a mannequin. Even the royal robes and crown didn't help. He sat gaping at the distant Kremlin, for such were the orders from above (giving rise to a satiric couplet at the Tsar's expense).* At the plinth's four corners four eagles did what they could to save the situation, and with lowered eyes the people admired them, avoiding the potentate elevated above.

The monument, like the cube and the pyramid before it, served as a hub for the strolling nannies and children playing in the park. But bronze is not immortal stuff, as Horace knew. In 1911 we found the wooden cube with its scaffolding. In 1913 we witnessed its unveiling. For five years the statue of the monarch lingered, a temporary actor on our stage. In 1918 he vanished for ever, and no one now remembers what he looked like, where he stood, or what he stood for.

In 1912 vague rumours began circulating about the possibility of a war in Europe. Soon these inoffensive murmurs grew into categoric prophecies, warnings of impending catastrophe based on 'reliable information'. After my sisters' examinations in the late spring of 1914 we left for our summer holidays, returning to part of a manor house in the Molodi estate, on the Kursk highway, for the second year running. The year before, the place's peaceful neglect had appealed to us; it seemed more than a mere sixty versts from Moscow. They said that the house had served as a lodge for Catherine II's journeys south to the Crimea: certainly the generous proportions of the house and the estate might well have answered such a purpose. The halls, rather than rooms, of the manor's main first floor, their high ceilings, finely sustained proportions and exceptional number, were well in excess of even baronial pretensions. The layout of the park, with its converging avenues, now much overgrown, also suggested royal origins. Here we passed a month in peace, till whispers from the town began to reach us. Soon every visit to the baker's or the station brought ominous letters and newspapers, disturbing the lime-park's tranquil, honey-scented air, till war at last burst into our lives.

One morning doomsday broke. The sun rose as it was meant to do,

---

* Things have come to a pretty fine pass
When the Tsar presents the church with his arse.

laying out its habitual rays of light and shade in their allotted places; the clouds passed as they always did across the clean blue sky; the trees didn't collapse in a dead faint—and yet the day dawned alien and strange, with a crazy, purposeless scurry in the village below. Empty carts raced backwards and forwards along the highway. Old crones were shrieking and lashing out futilely at the horses. In the dust people ran about shouting for no evident reason. Mounted mobilization had begun. War—who knew what war might be? But mobilization was in full swing, and that was another matter.

So the 1914 war began for our village, and every other village on Russian soil. Who could forget that stifling August the fourteenth, with its frightening, incomprehensible panic? By evening everything was noisier, but clearer at least. Peasants, reeling drunk or half sober, thronged the highway; obviously under-aged adolescents marched in ranks to a harmonica, tipsily singing in imitation of the recruits they'd seen in the pictures, ignorant of real war. The Japanese campaigns had dragged on somewhere out there; this, the German war, was virtually next door, and hurt like a pain just here, in your side.

There was little difference when we got back home. For the Muscovites, war began with religious processions, prayers, and portraits of the Tsar swaying between tricoloured flags gaudy in the sun. The monument still sat in its easy-chair staring at the Kremlin. The pigeons went on circling its head, imperturbably whitening the Imperial shoulders and crown. Nannies and governesses walked about the square. The four magnificent eagles were lightly poised, as though just about to flap off their detestable perch. Beaks viciously gaping, they waited for their time to come . . .

Days passed; months and years.* The war ebbed and flowed. Oval portraits of the dead regularly appeared in the Sunday supplements to *The Russian Word*. And at the same time another feeling grew.

A degree of goodwill still muffled indignation. But everyone had had their fill of this sweet chirruping, instead of the bitter, raucous clamour overcharging the stifled air. 'Bread and circuses', the old Roman cry, was simplified into 'Bread, bread!'—and instead of bread, we had to stand in queues, swallowing back our bile at the foul trash they handed out to us. General Khabalov, of course, never tasted bread like ours. The last days of the Russian Pompeii were epitomized by different kinds of bread.

* A quotation from Pasternak's poem, 'High Illness'. See pp. 194–5.

On the stage beneath our windows we watched the latest mysteries, tricked out with chasubles and hymnals, trembling flags, the glint of gold and sounding chords of massive choirs. Borne smoothly in a throng of banners and icons rode the gently rocking portraits of our all-merciful father the Tsar, staring before him with unseeing eyes.

So all things march on to their destined end. Newspapers came out with ever grosser blotches of 'caviare', the black obliterations of the censors nothing could erase. In the Duma the speeches grew hotter. History could not be shaken off its dogged course, and even the old, tried measures failed. The machine juddered and ran awry. Who could have thought that the brazen eagles would clap their broad wings for the first and last time, and with a loud scream sweep up into the sky, abandoning forever their five years' perch?*

As a witness of that time, I would epitomize it as one of *meetings*, impromptu, yet well-disciplined. Many such melted and re-formed of their own accord on the stage beneath our windows, tempestuous, frightening, impassioned, and (a new departure) often dominated by the grey greatcoats of the army. Just one made a lasting impression on us.

Soldiers, a uniformed mass with rifles slung across their shoulders, were marching in ragged ranks down the Volkhonka from the centre of town. At the same time a dark, many-coloured crowd of ordinary demonstrators, coming west along the embankment, turned up the foot of the hill, unaware of the army ahead. They began to climb All Saints' Way, faces turned towards us.

Our windows were still closed against the winter. As in the silent cinema, when the pianist stops playing to draw breath, we saw everything, and heard nothing. At an inaudible command, the soldiers fanned out in formation to turn the corner down the hill, rifles at the ready. Seeing each other for the first time, the leaders of each crowd stopped abruptly, while those in the rear pressed on in ignorance, inertia driving them forward. Neither side could turn back. Everything stilled, as a cat freezes, swaying imperceptibly from side to side, flanks trembling as it collects strength to leap and kill.

That tense confrontation lasted a few seconds, an eternity. Breath-

---

* This metaphor veils a large historical lacuna. It was not the author's intention to write history; nor was he in a position to do so. Omitted here is Yusupov's assassination of Rasputin in December 1916; the Duma's formation of the provisional government, and the abdication of the Tsar in 1917. The occasion described below took place on 27 February 1917, OS, as recorded in a poem by the author's sister.

less, afraid to move, as though our least rustle would set off the explosion, we watched what would happen. Would the soldiers fire on a defenceless crowd? What could they do?

Suddenly both crowds flung themselves forward—*on*, and obviously not *at* each other. Soldiers and workers no longer, people in different dress rushed together, embracing and linking arms, shaking hands, slapping backs; red flags appeared everywhere. There, on All Saints' Way below, we saw armed soldiers, rifles in hand, red banners flying, in unique and complete accord with the workers and intellectuals they were trained to subdue. The way was crowded with dawdling, peacefully talking and smoking groups. Long after, still chatting, they dispersed. The street cleared. The trampled snow could be seen again, not stained with blood, not littered with the unnatural poses of the dead. Shaken by what we had seen, we came away from the window to talk about it late into the night. We had witnessed fraternization, that great abstraction: man driven towards fellow man, even those that yesterday were enemies. It was all so close to us, so grandiose and so glorious, that I am not the only one who still remembers it.

CHAPTER 22

THE MUSIC OF THE TEACUPS

WHEN I turn to past events which have a meaning for me, and those members of my family who are still alive, I am often struck by the number of direct poetic references my brother made to our past. And although I have no gifts or inclinations for literary commentary, I would like to describe one such moment from our family life, which found its second birth in my brother's poem, 'High Illness'.

In *An Essay in Autobiography* Boris explains how he writes, taking, as a random couple of examples, two poems, 'Venice' and 'The Station'. 'I needed to get Venice the city into one poem', he says, 'and the station of Brest into the other.' In the first he was prompted by the city as he had seen it by night: 'the city's reflection swam and multiplied in circles and figures of eight, swelling like a rusk dipped in tea'. In the other, he set out to epitomize 'that valedictory horizon, beyond which the trains disappeared, and which contained a whole history of relationships, incidents, partings and meetings stretching before and after'.

In effect this is a practical realization of my brother's earlier concept of art in *Safe Conduct*, where he says (and I would like to stress this) that 'art did not invent the metaphor of its own accord, but found it in nature and reverently reproduced it'. To this I would like to add my own observation, that my brother never invented anything he wrote about, either in his verse or in his prose. He did not 'compose', he merely reproduced the thing seen, reverently transferring its essence in his packed, concise metaphors. Without hesitation I could add that my brother painted the portraits of what he had seen, just as Van Gogh said he drew a portrait of his chair, and Delacroix, I think it was, made a likeness of his horse.

Yet in this portraiture of life my brother ran the risk that later generations, for whom his originals were lost, would miss the accuracy of what he had described. Even now, many of the commonplaces of his life have vanished, and without explanation his literal metaphors would be incomprehensible. To take, for instance, two poems of different periods, 'February' and 'The Waves'. In the first, vivid phrases like 'the thundering slush' or 'through the ringing of church bells, the wheels' clack', marvellously capture the city in spring in a quite unphotographic way. In the other, images of the waves—'the tide bakes them like waffles' or 'herding into twisted cornets'—are brilliantly suggestive metaphors which draw not on the sea, but on a familiar aspect of past Moscow life. How vividly evocative they are for those of us that remember! But if the originals are gone, how can they be visualized by our successors? Long ago the city lost its cobbles and the oozing slush that drowned spring streets and swallowed up galoshes; there are no more traps and carts drumming across the cobbles on iron wheels, after the silent winter sleighs. The mild spring evening air no longer swims with the sweet, full chime of the city's forty times forty churches, and waffles are no longer sold, as they were in our childhood, on every boulevard and each street square. Before our eyes the familiar vendors baked waffles for a few coppers on wheeled braziers. Wonderfully smelling, thin, fresh waffles, which were twisted, still hot, into cornets and crammed with cream—the very image of waves, heaving hump-backed and white-crested as they reach the shore, to topple, curl and close like the wave of Hokusai!

Our flat on the Volkhonka was unusually shaped for its size. In effect, it was an unpretentious, miniature model of a palace suite. Our small rooms lined the street façade, communicating by a series of double doors set opposite each other on the street and window side. Standing in the drawing-room, you could look down a perspective of opened doors to a diminished figure framed in the doorway of the seventh and final room—an imposing, beautiful arrangement quite as unnecessary as any other dated luxury. Our family was a large one; we lived two to a room in three out of the seven; between them and the drawing-room lay my father's modest studio, where he worked for the next seven years.

I spent my time at the University here. I was in the third year of my training as an architect in the School of Art when the 1914–18 War began. The war progressed with 'fluctuating successes'—that is, pretty badly, all in all, and as it got increasingly out of hand the idiotic, unstable politics of the time grew all the more apparent. Life became difficult materially, and—worse still—morally, till the inevitable release came with the bloodless revolution of February 1917. Yet, though it was bloodless enough, it could achieve very little. Nor did it last long. By

October, together with the much vaunted and gleeful victories of red-ribboned sailors, soldiers, students, and citizens of the new republic, signs of future dislocation and collapse came sneaking into our lives, with a pretence of diffidence, and yet shamelessly and rudely none the less. Day by day life grew harder. There were shortages of fuel, then of bread; paraffin was impossible to find. The country starved and froze.

The high expectations of the past dwindled; all one could hope for was to stop the cracks that had already appeared. With extraordinary speed our preconceptions of the necessities of life were abandoned. Values dropped and money (which itself became devalued) was desperately needed. Many of our possessions were sold for absurdly little. Life simplified. Who needed receptions, servants and etiquette, or an elaborate dinner service with umpteen plates and a clutter of cutlery at each setting, when a single plate would do?

The Dutch ovens, which had previously been stoked once and even twice a day in frosty weather, stood cold. Only recently my wife and I took a walk past the site of our old flat on the Volkhonka, when a Tartar voice called out to us. We stopped. An old man we didn't recognize came up—but his speech was familiar enough, with its unfinished sentences and mimicking drawl. It was Galliulin, our cheerful young stoker and yardhand of the past. He knew about my brother's death, and the sufferings of his last years. He spoke warmly of him, of our life on the Volkhonka; he told us about his own family, his daughter who was training as a teacher, his son who was 'a great fellow'. That chance encounter reminded me of so many things . . .

Alive before my eyes, Boris kneels by the stove in felt boots and a borrowed padded jacket, neatly and economically laying the fire with birch blocks so that it should burn out evenly, with golden heat and light-blue flames still running across the embers. We all enjoyed making up the fire, but no one could equal my brother's artistry. He would have put a trained stoker to shame. It was done with the beautiful, ingenious swiftness characteristic of all his work. If a single chock was left smouldering after the rest had died, he would rescue it for another time, running with it smoking in his tongs, to douse it under the kitchen tap, or plunge it in a bucket of water whispering with steam.

But even with such economies the stocks of wood dwindled. Fuel had to be carefully selected and conserved. In that crazy time your feelings were sharpened by hunger, tension, and cold, and life seemed more richly saturated than it had been in the past. Boris was writing 'Kremlin in storm', 'The patient's pullover', 'It could be . . .'—the whole poetic cycle of 'Illness', in fact. How well he conveys the atmosphere of those times! Wood ran out at last; the frosts bit hard. At night Boris and I used to climb into the attics to saw off rafter-ends, since it seemed safe enough, and we came away with good, dry firewood. Our roof survived, to fall only when the house was demolished in 1960, though I remember many buildings at that time whose roofs had collapsed under the weight of snow, their rafters ignorantly pillaged. But then, men had to live, and warmth was vital.

Even with our rafters for fuel it grew colder. The beautiful enfilade of rooms became a nuisance; life shrank in on itself. Denial after denial drove each Moscow family back to a primitive existence, huddled in the lair of a single, barely heated room within the inimical chill of the surrounding flat.

My father went on working in his studio, where we first installed a little tiled stove, its chimney trained into the flue of the abandoned Dutch oven. His swollen fingers froze in their gloves; he held his palette with difficulty. His oils thickened with the cold, their fat caterpillars could barely be smeared across the canvas. The drawing-room next door accumulated cold like a country cellar, and on the tuner's advice the piano was abandoned there, to settle with the surrounding atmosphere. As a mammoth frozen in the ice melts to yield fresh meat and pelt, so the Bechstein stoically accepted the cold, coming to itself with the spring, its exquisite voice intact. No one disturbed its anabiosis; all winter it lay unvisited in its icy cellar, while we, like it, waited for warmth, sunlight, and a return to life. When it seemed there was no strength left and the end was imminent, the longed-for, always unexpected awakening came. How wonderful it was then to open the sealed doors with impunity, to fling up the windows on to the fresh, sweet street air! On one of the first warm days of spring, just such a day of universal door-openings, I remember going into the drawing-room with Boris to see how the old Bechstein had weathered the winter. The doors parted reluctantly on cold hinges. We caught a whiff of damp, musty air, a breath of mould. On the piano's dusty, black-lacquered lid, a teacup stood, forgotten the autumn before, in its dusty saucer. In the half-drained cup lay a transparent disc of smooth yellow ice. An ordinary sight, perhaps? But that ice, that death in the cup, resting on the piano, the silent source of life, overwhelmed me, like the sign of some insuperable fate.

Recently, I took up again my brother's poem, 'High Illness', which I had always loved, and stumbled on the phrase, 'we were music in the ice', and again, 'we were the music of the teacups'. How could I fail to recognize the cellar chill of the drawing-room, the cup on the Bechstein? I was riddled with memories. But Boris was dead; there was no one I could ask if that was the ice-filled cup. I began reading again, carefully reconstructing . . . Yes, yes, of course, the poem is a portrait of our life on the Volkhonka in 1918, that terrible, typhoid year! The ice, the music, the windows, the slippery back stairs—everything rose out of the past, as bright and clear as pictures on a gently unrolling scroll.

'The slush-slobbered back stairs'!* How many absurdly tragic pictures hang about that back entrance! Our pipes had burst; there was no water in the flat, and up that steep, sharply twisting stair we lugged water, logs, and food. The buckets tipped and spilled, water froze on the increasingly hazardous stairs. That year our stove was out of action as well, and food was ferried up and down to the caretaker's cooker above. Once, to our intense distress, Boris, or one of my sisters, slipped with a pan of precious slops, and our soup for the day trickled and froze in icy rivulets down the stairs. It may seem funny: it was tragic then.

I am no literary commentator. I have nothing to prove, nothing to distort. Where did that image of the forgotten teacup, the Bechstein sunk in winter chill, come from? A chance coincidence, perhaps. Or one of the many details from our life at that time, which passed, transformed, into my brother's poetry, and which I can only point out to his future readers.

* Another quotation from 'High Illness'. Together with '1905' and 'Lieutenant Schmidt', these three long poems give a series of impressionistic glimpses of the revolutionary period. Many of their oblique and metaphoric details are clarified in this prose account, just as its historical lacunae are filled in by the poems.

CHAPTER 23

A LAST MEETING

In those heavy revolutionary years my mother virtually gave up the piano. In 1921 both my parents and sisters left for Germany, with the help of Lunacharsky, the Minister of Culture at the time. My mother was to take a cure; my father hoped to have an eye operation which was not possible in Russia. They set out in the certainty that they would live abroad for a while, and then return home as they had often done before. My brother and I were left alone together for the first time in our lives.

Other acquaintances were already billeted in our flat, which had become a communal Moscow flat of the type familiar now. Everyone had his own room; the utility quarters were shared. I settled in the old drawing-room, my brother in the studio. Two years passed quickly, and in 1923 Boris, now a recognized writer, was given permission to visit Berlin with his wife. On his return in the same year he told me so much about the trips to Marburg, the Harz, Weimar, the meetings, the new paintings my father had done, my mother's improved health and renewed playing, ending each story with 'but it's so easy, go and see it all for yourself!', that in the end I began to take his suggestions seriously.

At that time I was finishing my first architectural project, the Karpov Chemical Institute. All the interesting work was my responsibility: I had to design the smallest details, down to the window-frames and door handles, because everything was unavailable then, and either had to be made specially, or approximations borrowed from the exceptionally high-quality sleeping-cars of the International Railway. The construction of the Institute was a rarity at that time, when little was built and much destroyed. For this reason it attracted the attention of the Supreme National Economic Council, and even some members of the Soviet People's Commissariat. The opening was a very grand affair; government representatives and other notables arrived, and I, still a beginner, was congratulated, my work praised.

I wouldn't have gone into all this, if it hadn't been that this commission was to play an important part in getting me abroad. In January that